SH... DICTIO... POWER AND STRUGGLE

LANGUAGE OF CIVIL RESISTANCE IN CONFLICTS

Gene Sharp
Senior Scholar
Albert Einstein Institution

with the assistance of
April Carter and Bruce Jenkins

and a Foreword by
Professor Sir Adam Roberts
President of the British Academy

OXFORD
UNIVERSITY PRESS

OXFORD
UNIVERSITY PRESS

Oxford University Press, Inc., publishes works that further
Oxford University's objective of excellence
in research, scholarship, and education.

Oxford   New York
Auckland   Cape Town   Dar es Salaam   Hong Kong   Karachi
Kuala Lumpur   Madrid   Melbourne   Mexico City   Nairobi
New Delhi   Shanghai   Taipei   Toronto

With offices in
Argentina   Austria   Brazil   Chile   Czech Republic   France   Greece
Guatemala   Hungary   Italy   Japan   Poland   Portugal   Singapore
South Korea   Switzerland   Thailand   Turkey   Ukraine   Vietnam

Copyright © 2012 by Oxford University Press

Published by Oxford University Press, Inc.
198 Madison Avenue, New York, New York 10016
www.oup.com

Library of Congress Cataloging-in-Publication Data

Sharp, Gene.
Sharp's dictionary of power and struggle : language of civil resistance in
conflicts / Gene Sharp ; with the assistance of April Carter and Bruce Jenkins
and a foreword by Sir Adam Roberts.
p. cm.
Includes bibliographical references.
ISBN 978-0-19-982989-7 — ISBN 978-0-19-982988-0
1. Nonviolence—Dictionaries. 2. Nonviolence—History—Dictionaries. 3. Power
(Social sciences)—Dictionaries. 4. Government, Resistance to—History—Dictionaries.
I. Title. II. Title: Dictionary of power and struggle.
HM1281.S525 2011
303.6'103—dc23
2011023581

1   3   5   7   9   8   6   4   2

Printed in the United States of America
on acid-free paper

Dedicated to all those who have struggled bravely
whose names have been lost to history

★

CONTENTS

FOREWORD

This dictionary has a clear central purpose: to bring some degree of clarity to academic and public discussion of nonviolent action. Ahimsa, boycott, civil disobedience, direct action—all these and over eight hundred other terms are defined in simple and straightforward language. A particular strength of the dictionary is that it reflects the author's interest in many forms of social struggle, and in the whole problem of controlling political power in its many dimensions. Thus the range of terms that are defined is notably wide. In short, this is a dictionary not only for those with a specific interest in civil resistance, but also for students and practitioners of political struggle more generally.

There are basically two types of dictionaries. The first type is descriptive, setting out current usage in all its glorious and contradictory complexity—as Dr. Samuel Johnson did in his famous *Dictionary of the English Language*, published in London in 1755. The second type is more explicitly didactic, setting out proper usage that should be followed—as, famously, the Académie Française has attempted in successive versions of its *Dictionnaire de l'Académie française*, first published in Paris in 1694.

In its own special area, the present dictionary leans in the direction of the second type. Dr. Sharp does not shrink from expressing his views trenchantly. Thus, after offering two acceptable meanings of the term "nonviolence," he goes on to say that the term "has also been used with diverse and even contradictory meanings," and he gives an example of one confusing meaning that the reader is urged to avoid. Hurrah! That is one strength that a specialist dictionary can have: that it is written by one person who really knows his subject and is not afraid to expound a clear and strong viewpoint on it.

I must declare an interest. At Oxford, back in my student days in the early 1960s, I first met Gene Sharp when attending an evening meeting of a student society. He was doing a doctorate, while I was still studying, rather spasmodically, for a first degree. At this first meeting he gave me a list of books I should read, and generally impressed me with his seriousness. This was more than ten years before he completed his groundbreaking book *The Politics of Nonviolent Action*, published in 1973, but the idea was already there in his head. He was, and remains, someone with a distinctive and important point of view on how "people power" can play a significant part in tackling some of the great problems of politics: dictatorship, discrimination, and foreign occupation. He helped to develop my nascent interest in these fields. In the intervening years our paths have sometimes diverged, but the debt I owe him is lasting and I am happy to acknowledge it here.

Dr. Johnson famously mocked his own labors in producing his great work: *Lexicographer*: "a writer of dictionaries; a harmless drudge that busies himself in tracing the original, and detailing the signification of words." Certainly the preparation of a dictionary requires hard work over a long period; Sharp's work, like all good dictionaries, has been decades in the making. However, producing dictionaries is no mere harmless drudgery. Whether descriptive or prescriptive, dictionaries have a crucial role in helping to advance a common language, and to bring at least a degree of order to a cacophony of voices. In its particular field, *Sharp's Dictionary of Power and Struggle* is an important contribution. This long-awaited compilation of definitions may or may not receive from readers the deadly compliment of being labeled "definitive." However, there is no doubt in my mind that it will have the rather more important and attractive role of serving as a landmark.

Sir Adam Roberts
Oxford, April 2009

AUTHOR'S PREFACE

★

This dictionary arises from a decades-long endeavor to develop greater conceptual clarity for a vastly important phenomenon of social, economic, and political conflict: nonviolent action. Terminological confusion has long accompanied this aspect of domestic and international conflict. This dictionary is intended to contribute to clarification.

Nonviolent means of waging conflicts often occur in the context of social or political systems that can wage violent repression. The nature of those systems and the option of violent struggle also need to be understood and taken into full account by analysts of conflicts. Terms related to those phenomena are therefore also included here, as are other tangential phenomena.

The text of this volume contains two accounts prepared by other authors: "Serbia, 1996–2000" by Joshua Paulson and "The Tunisian Uprising and Protests, December 2010–January 2011" by Jamila Raqib. The Serbia account was originally published in my *Waging Nonviolent Struggle* (Porter Sargent Publishers, 2005). These accounts help to show the relevance of much of the subject matter of the dictionary.

The Serbian struggle was the model often in mind in the several "color revolutions" that have followed it, especially in Ukraine and Georgia. It also demonstrates how the dynamics of nonviolent struggle could so weaken an established autocrat that his power dissolves, step by step, almost exactly as outlined in the "Power and Realism" essay. The events in Tunisia demonstrate that some preconceptions about limitations of this type of action are at least subject to reassessment. This was the first of several cases of nonviolent uprisings in the Arab world. This case shows that small beginnings can have major consequences.

I hope that these pages will contribute to better understandings and more satisfactory outcomes of future conflicts.

Gene Sharp
Boston, March 2011

INTRODUCTION

"An abstract term is like a box with a false bottom,
you may put in it what ideas you please,
and take them out again without being observed."[1]
—Alexis de Tocqueville

Every field of study and thought requires clear concepts, terms, and understood meanings. Without them, description, analysis, communication, and the transfer of knowledge are impaired, if not impossible. As Alexis de Tocqueville observed, the dangers of misunderstanding are especially acute in dealing with more abstract notions. When the focus is on phenomena about which strong opinions and beliefs often surpass understanding, confusion will reign.

The present dictionary arises from a decades-long endeavor to introduce greater conceptual clarity to the phenomenon of nonviolent conflict—that is, the waging of conflict, usually with one side using social, economic, psychological, and political methods. Terminological confusion has long accompanied this aspect of domestic and international conflict. It is my hope that this technical dictionary will provide increased clarity to scholars, activists, students, policy makers, and general readers, so that they can better understand nonviolent alternatives to both passivity and violent conflict.

THE PHENOMENON OF NONVIOLENT ACTION

The field of nonviolent action encompasses a myriad of methods of protest, noncooperation, and intervention, all without physical violence.

Such activities have occurred everywhere throughout human history, in highly diverse cultures, situations, and conditions.

Human freedoms and civil liberties have often been won by such means, often in the face of violent repression. Workers have gained great power. Dictatorships have been dissolved, foreign invaders challenged, and power structures changed through nonviolent struggles.

Nonviolent struggles have played exceedingly important, but insufficiently recognized, roles in many historic and contemporary struggles. Sometimes these roles have been parts of a movement that included popular violence, and sometimes nonviolent conflict was applied as the primary mode of resistance.

Cases of nonviolent action include the three noncooperation campaigns (1765–1775) of the American Revolution,[2] international woman suffrage movements, labor movements applying strikes and economic boycotts, the destruction of the tsarist system of Imperial Russia, and the undermining of the dictators of El Salvador and Guatemala in 1944. Even the Nazis and their puppets were not exempt, as in Norway, Denmark, and elsewhere, and at times in Germany itself. These means were also important in the U.S. civil rights movement, especially in the 1950s and 1960s; in Chile in the 1980s; in the ousting of presidents in the Philippines in 1986 and 1991; and in the liberation of Poland, East Germany, Czechoslovakia, Estonia, Latvia, and Lithuania in the late 1980s and early 1990s. Later, they were decisive in the struggle for democracy in Serbia—especially in 2000—in Georgia in 2003, Ukraine in 2004, Lebanon in 2005, Kyrgyzstan in 2005, and Nepal in 2006.[3] In 2011 remarkable movements against autocratic rulers occurred in Tunisia, Egypt, Yemen, and elsewhere.

Nonviolent action is to be understood as the waging of conflict by methods of protest, noncooperation, and intervention without physical violence. Nonviolent action is identified by what people do, not by what they believe. This type of conflict includes (a) acts of omission—that is, the participants refuse to perform acts which they usually perform, are expected by custom to perform, or are required by law to perform; (b) acts of commission—that is, the participants perform acts which they usually do not perform, are not expected by custom to perform, or are forbidden by law or regulation from performing; or (c) a combination of both.

A discovery of our collective heritage of nonviolent struggles has been under way for some years.[4] Introductions to nonviolent action and analyses of its potential are available elsewhere,[5] and this dictionary is not a substitute for them. The objective here is only to help to meet the present conceptual and terminological needs of this and tangential fields.

TERMINOLOGICAL CONFUSION

Accurate perceptions of nonviolent conflicts have in the past been seriously impeded by conceptual, terminological, and definitional problems. At times, terms to describe important processes and events have been lacking altogether. In much of the older literature on "nonviolence," the language is often highly ambiguous, contradictory, and even moralistic—all quite unsuited for description and analysis of conflicts. The term "nonviolence," for example, has been used to mean nonviolent direct action, love of all humanity, passivity and surrender, noninjury to all living beings in thought and action, absence of all violence, or militant struggle without violence.

"Violence" has sometimes meant killing or physically injuring people, ill will, hostility of any kind, any harm whatsoever to people (whether directly inflicted or derivative of social conditions), destruction of property, all injustices, or illegitimate use of violence. "Power" has been identified as physical violence, any domination over other people, a positive need, a quality of self-direction all people should possess, or a general evil to be renounced. These diverse meanings illustrate the past confusion which has impeded thought and communication in this general field of conflict.

This ambiguity, bias, and at times even the nonexistence of concepts and terms have made it extraordinarily difficult to describe and to think about specific events and movements, much less the general field of nonviolent conflict. Conceptual and terminological confusion has also rendered attempts at objective evaluation of the potential of this technique extraordinarily difficult or impossible.

THE DICTIONARY

The general field of this dictionary is conflict and struggle, including social, economic, political, domestic, and international conflict and struggle. The focus is primarily, but far from exclusively, on those forms of action that are waged by people in such conflicts without use of physical violence. Many of the entries are descriptive and analytical terms related to nonviolent action, as well as concepts that are fundamental to that phenomenon. Many terms refer to specific methods of action, such as types of economic boycotts. Other terms included here refer to the ways in which the technique of nonviolent action "works," when it does, against repressive opponents, the technique's dynamics of operation, and its mechanisms of change.

However, it would distort reality and impede clear thought to focus in this dictionary solely on nonviolent action. Such struggles often occur within the context of contrasting phenomena, including dictatorships, aggression, oppression, and injustices. Violent types of action, including military means, have been carried out alongside—or in place of—nonviolent struggle. Peaceful means of conflict resolution, short of any type of struggle, are also included here.

Nonviolent struggle is often met with repression and other countermeasures. Alternative military and other violent means of waging conflict also need to be clarified. Ideologies, political systems, and movements of the past and present that have attempted to wage—or to crush—nonviolent struggle are relevant and are included here. So are other directly related and tangential phenomena.

Necessarily, then, this dictionary encompasses terms describing phenomena that are quite different from nonviolent action: political violence, dictatorship, repression, structures of control and domination, and alternative means of dealing with conflicts. Concepts related to the nature of politics—authority, power, sanctions, sovereignty, and the like—are relevant as well, as are various sociological terms, such as social control, social conflict, social movements, and social change. Terms related to personal nonviolence based on moral or religious principles are also here; so are terms from additional ways of dealing with conflicts, such as conflict resolution.

The language of strategy and tactics, and of the clashing of forces of various types, is essential to the understanding of the means by which people conduct conflicts and wage struggles, both nonviolently and violently. Words that assist understanding of these needs are offered in this technical dictionary.

It should be noted that, except in a few cases, proper names of people, places, and events that have been significant in the history of nonviolent struggles are not included here.[6]

A NOTE ON USAGE

This dictionary is intended to provide clear concepts, terms, and definitions that do not contain built-in moral or political judgments. The definitions offered here are intended to be precise and accurate. In various instances it has been necessary to formulate new concepts, to propose new terms, or to recommend new definitions.

The definitions offered in this dictionary are only those that are deemed relevant for the included subject matter. Naturally, many of these words have additional meanings in other contexts, which will be found in any good large dictionary of the English language.

Where two words are used as a single term—such as "nonviolent action"—the meaning is *not* simply the combination of the common usage of each word (i.e., all action which is not violent). Instead, the combined term is given a much more specific meaning. Wherever possible this meaning is refined from earlier informed usage.

A serious attempt has been made to formulate the definitions as accurately and objectively as possible, so that they communicate the nature of the phenomena to which they refer. If this effort has been successful, these definitions may be accepted by persons with diverse motivations, beliefs, and opinions. The aim has been to develop a recommended terminology for the defined phenomena that may be used by anyone.

Not all of the concepts and definitions offered in this dictionary will necessarily gain immediate acceptance. If a definition seems strange or even jarring, it may very well be because conventional wisdom has blocked development of a more precise and accurate presentation of meaning. Discourses about political power and conflict, for example, are often rife with inaccurate assumptions: violence equals power, military equals defense, dictatorships are omnipotent, and others. Given the long history of nonviolent conflicts, many common assumptions about conflict, struggle, power, defense, politics, rebellion, and other matters require sober reanalysis. Reconceptualization of the meanings of some terms has been needed.

MOVING FORWARD

In general, the field of nonviolent conflict has often been neglected. Because of this, it is not surprising that the terms and concepts needed to understand and think about nonviolent action have often been unclear, if they existed at all. Some scholars are now seeking to correct the long academic neglect of this important phenomenon.

Some earlier studies regarding certain methods of nonviolent action (e.g., labor strikes and economic boycotts) have advanced our understanding and influenced general usage. Varying degrees of precision have also been brought to definitions of other methods of this technique, such as "noncooperation" and "civil disobedience," used in movements associated with Mohandas K. Gandhi.

There is now growing awareness of the broad spectrum of nonviolent ways of conducting conflicts. Current interest in nonviolent action derives from various motivations: policy potential, research aims, action questions, ethical concerns, and usefulness for social change. Interest exists in the potential of nonviolent action as an alternative to violence and war, if the alternative proves to be at least equally effective. This policy interest includes the potential of this technique for bringing down dictatorships and for providing national defense against coups d'état and foreign aggression. The policy of civilian-based defense of prepared noncooperation and defiance is designed to deter and defend against these contingencies.

Several studies examining the potential of a defense policy incorporating, or based primarily upon, preparations for nonviolent resistance were published during the Cold War, and a number of European governments commissioned research on such resistance. Terms such as "civilian defense," "nonviolent defense," and "social defense" were coined to discuss this approach.[7] The term preferred here is "civilian-based defense."[8]

The resolution of the most serious conceptual and terminological problems for the general field of nonviolent conflict is an important precondition for exploring the potential relevance of this field for policy, scholarship, conflict, ethical concerns, and social change. This technical dictionary is an attempt to help to resolve those problems and to contribute to an accurate understanding and serious evaluation of the phenomenon of nonviolent forms of conflict.

TERMS MERITING FRESH ATTENTION

There are three groups of terms that require new attention in this dictionary.

Standard usage of some words has built-in assumptions and biases that are based on a belief in the necessity of violence and military means of combat. Sometimes these assumptions are quite explicit. Other times they are implicit. This is not to say that such judgments should not be made, nor that common views are necessarily in error. Rather, such determinations about the necessity of violence and military means should be made separately from definitions. Those determinations should be made on their own merits, and should not be built into words that already have a clear meaning without a built-in judgment about the presumed necessity of violent or military means. Some words in this dictionary have therefore been reconceptualized in order to remove built-in biases.

For example, "political power" is widely assumed to require some type of violence—whether applied, implied, or threatened—as a means of last resort. Similarly, "force" often has strong connotations of violence and military capacity, although it encompasses far broader meaning. When "force" is used to mean "military might," it often serves a political purpose to make such action sound more acceptable, as the words "violence" and "military" are avoided.

In common usage it is assumed that "defense" and "military means" are basically identical. The United States War Department was renamed the Department of Defense in 1949. As military means may also be used to attack, destroy, retaliate, and even repress a State's own population, they can hardly be equated with "defense." Furthermore, military means may at times not be able to defend in the sense of protecting against attacks.

"Defense" and "military" differ, both conceptually and in practice. "Defense" denotes the objective, or at times refers to the means that can produce that protection. Military action has been widely used to achieve that objective. However, it may or may not be able to do so. Clear meanings of the word "defense" are not always insisted on, even by those most responsible for providing defense. For example, the U.S. *Department of Defense Dictionary of Military and Associated Terms* issued by the Joint Chiefs of Staff does not contain a definition of "defense" or "national defense."[9]

It must be remembered that defense, understood as preserving and protecting, has actually at times been attempted and provided by nonmilitary means. This occurred, for example, in resistance movements against foreign military occupation (as with the German Ruhr in 1923 and in Czechoslovakia from 1968 to 1969), internal collaborators (as during the Nazi occupation of Norway in the 1940s), and attempted coups d'état (for instance, Germany in 1920).

Whether or not military means can at any given time *defend* (strictly defined), or whether nonmilitary means can do so, are important questions. They require independent analyses. An answer should not be simply built into the words and the meanings attached to them, thereby preempting investigation. When subversion of language occurs and is accepted, reasoned independent examination of issues becomes almost impossible.

There are other problems with our language for examining acute conflicts. For example, the phrase "overthrowing a dictatorship" subtly implies that in order to end a dictatorship by internal efforts, opposition forces require a massive violent uprising. In contrast, the alternative phrases of "terminating a dictatorship" or "toppling a dictatorship" would allow consideration of various means to achieve the same end.

However, those phrases are rarely used. The alternative phrases "undermining a dictatorship" or "disintegrating a dictatorship" would clearly allow for the possibility that nonmilitary means might do the job from below.

Therefore, some terminology and definitions need to be reassessed, and in a few instances reconceptualized, in order to allow for the possibility of clear, rational choices of alternative policies. Some of the entries of this technical dictionary have been reconceptualized. That is to say, their definitions offered here convey only the basic concept without also including unexamined assumptions. Examples of these reconceptualized words are "coercion," "defense," "force," and "power." The aim here is to salvage the basic meaning of these words. Reconceptualized words are identified as such.

A second group of terms in this technical dictionary includes those that refer to the nature and operation of conflict without physical violence—that is, nonviolent action. New words or definitions are sometimes needed for these actions or processes because the relevant phenomena have previously not been well-known or understood.

Some of the concepts and phenomena involved in nonviolent action were presented in *The Politics of Nonviolent Action*.[10] Examples include "dynamics of nonviolent action," "mechanisms of change," "technique," "method," and "phased campaign." Some such terms are used here in different contexts than is usual in the vocabulary of most people. Where this occurs, a parenthetical note calls attention to their different use in this dictionary. Some individual methods of nonviolent action, such as types of strikes, however, are not indicated with a parenthetical note, as they have been identified in the literature for several decades.[11]

Mass resistance movements against authoritarian regimes in the late twentieth and early twenty-first century, conducted predominantly without major violence, have brought wider attention to the alternative political reality of nonviolent conflict. Noncooperation and defiance by masses of people have produced undeniable major political results that previously were often thought by some people to be impossible by nonviolent means.

In response to these movements, our language has already become a bit more flexible. For example, in response to electoral fraud in the Philippines in 1986, a mass nonviolent uprising ousted President Ferdinand Marcos. As a result, the term "people power" came into the language. Corrective terminology for such phenomena had taken a step.

Also, in more recent discussions, some completely new terms, such as "contaminant,"[12] have been introduced to communicate recently expanded understandings.

A third group of entries here consists of terms that are associated with resistance against dictatorships, foreign invasions, and coups d'état. These terms are in part related to proposals for national defense by civilian-based defense. Examples are "decollaboration," "executive usurpation," "nonviolent positional war," "political paralysis," and "stalling and obstruction." These and related terms are identified as primarily relating to civilian-based defense.

CLEAR THINKING AND LANGUAGE

Simple repetition of inadequate terms and definitions, or unquestioning acceptance of common usage, perpetuates biases and impedes understanding and thinking. Whatever may be our political perspectives and favored policies, the language we use should assist, not hinder, clear thinking.

Some parts of our language require careful examination and, in some cases, even reconceptualization. New terms and definitions may need to be adopted. Such increased clarity will help us seek realistic solutions to serious problems in a world of excessive violence and oppression.

This technical dictionary is intended to contribute to better understanding of our world as we continue to confront problems of acute conflicts. Recognition of reality, clear thinking, and informed analysis are essential as we face an uncertain future. It is hoped that this technical dictionary will help to meet the need for fresh ways of looking at surrounding phenomena and to better understand the possibilities before us.

NOTES TO THE INTRODUCTION

1. Alexis de Tocqueville, *Democracy in America* (London: Longmans Green, 1889), vol. 2, p. 63.

2. See Walter H. Conser Jr., Ronald M. McCarthy, David J. Toscano, and Gene Sharp, eds., *Resistance, Politics, and the American Struggle for Independence, 1765–1775* (Boulder, Colo.: Lynne Rienner, 1986).

3. For references to cases in English-language sources prior to 1996, see Ronald M. McCarthy and Gene Sharp, *Nonviolent Action: A Research Guide* (New York and London: Garland, 1997). Also, see April Carter, Howard Clark, and Michael Randle, compilers, *People Power and Protest since 1945: A Bibliography of Nonviolent Action* (London: Housmans, 2006).

4. See, for example, Bart de Ligt, *The Conquest of Violence: An Essay on War and Revolution* (London: Routledge, 1937; new edition: London: Pluto, 1989, and Winchester, Mass.: Unwin Hyman, 1989).

5. See, for example, Gene Sharp, *Waging Nonviolent Struggle: 20th Century Practice and 21st Century Potential* (Boston: Porter Sargent, 2005); Peter Ackerman and Jack Duvall, *A Force More Powerful: One Hundred Years of Nonviolent Conflict* (New York: St. Martin's Press, 2000); Peter Ackerman and Christopher Kruegler, *Strategic Nonviolent Conflict: The Dynamics of People Power in the Twentieth Century* (Westport, Conn., and London: Praeger, 1994); Gene Sharp, *The Politics of Nonviolent Action* (Boston: Porter Sargent, 1973); Adam Roberts, ed., *Civilian Resistance as a National Defense* (Harrisburg, Pa.: Stackpole, 1968; U.K. ed., *The Strategy of Civilian Defence.* London: Faber & Faber, 1967; Paperback: Harmondsworth, England, and Baltimore: Penguin, 1969); and Adam Roberts and Timothy Garton Ash, eds., *Civil Resistance and Power Politics: The Experience of Non-violent Action from Gandhi to the Present* (Oxford and New York: Oxford University Press, 2009).

6. Many of these references can be found in Roger S. Powers and William B. Vogele, eds., *Protest, Power, and Change: An Encyclopedia of Nonviolent Action* (New York and London: Garland, 1997).

7. See Roberts, *Civilian Resistance as a National Defense*; Gene Sharp, *Civilian-Based Defense: A Post-Military Weapons System* (Princeton, N.J., and London: Princeton University Press, 1990); and Anders Boserup and Andrew Mack, *War Without Weapons: Nonviolence in National Defence* (London: Frances Pinter, 1974).

8. See the entry for civilian-based defense in the main text of this *Dictionary*.

9. Joint Chiefs of Staff, Joint Publication 1-02, 12 April 2001 (as amended through 26 August 2008).

10. Boston: Porter Sargent, 1973 and later printings.

11. Definitions and examples of almost all methods included here are provided in *The Politics of Nonviolent Action*.

12. "Contaminant" in the context of nonviolent action was introduced by Robert L. Helvey. See his *On Strategic Nonviolent Conflict: Thinking About the Fundamentals* (Boston: Albert Einstein Institution, 2004 and 2007).

AN ESSAY
ON POWER
AND REALISM

★

Our world is filled with conflicts. They often cause us grave problems. However, conflicts themselves are not the real problem. Conflicts are often positive and a given conflict can have meritorious purposes. Problems arise principally from the means by which conflicts are often waged: through violence.

Many political groups and virtually all governments operate on the unexamined assumption that the means of last resort and greatest effectiveness is violence, especially in a military capacity. Violence is certainly necessary to support certain objectives, among them oppression, dictatorship, and mass killings. If we oppose those objectives we need to think about how otherwise to act so that our actions truly weaken the possibility of oppression, dictatorship, or mass killings, and do not unintentionally contribute to their growth.

The choice to use violence is determined by our understanding of the nature of political power. We need to understand better both the power possessed by our opponents and the power available to those who reject their opponents' objectives. Opponents in "no-compromise conflicts" are understood to be able to wield massive power. We know that the power they use for hostile purposes must be counteracted by equal or greater power. If it is not, the opponents' objectives will likely be achieved.

Our opponents' power is often understood to be strong, solid, and long-lasting. If we choose to act against our opponents with violence, it is because we believe that our capacity to wage violent conflict is needed—that is, our opponents' power for hostile purposes cannot be successfully defeated without violence. But in choosing to fight with violence we have agreed to fight with our opponents' best weapons. We think that extreme risks are justified because our opponents' power is likely to triumph unless it is confronted by greater violence. We do not examine whether our understanding of power is accurate.

POLITICAL POWER DEFINED

In our quest for better understanding of what is possible in extreme conflicts, we must start by asking a fundamental question: What is "political power"?

Drawing on the insights of respected political theorists and analysts, we understand that political power is nothing less than the totality of means, influences, and pressures available to determine and implement policies and governance of a society. This especially refers to the institutions of government, the State, and those who oppose them. Such power may be directly applied or may be held as a reserve capacity, as in negotiations. In such cases power is no less present than it is in open conflict.

Power is intrinsic to politics. It is involved, directly or indirectly, in all political action. It may be measured by the ability to control a situation, to control people and institutions, or to mobilize people and institutions for a certain activity. Political power may be used to achieve a goal, to implement or change policies, to induce others to behave as the wielders of power wish, or to oppose—or support—the established system, policies, and relationships. Power is also used to change, destroy, or replace the previous distribution of power, or to accomplish a combination of these objectives.

We are challenged to look afresh at the nature of political power. We know that it can accomplish horrendous objectives. But is there anything about power that could reveal dictatorships to be less than omnipotent and reveal our opponents' massive military power as a serious problem, but not a guarantor of the regime's success in every conflict? Is there something about power that reveals a potential for serving positive goals?

IGNORED EVIDENCE

We have concrete evidence for why we should question the usual understanding of political power. Over twenty years ago, during the remarkable events in Central and Eastern Europe, my neighborhood news vendor came close to such questioning. He commented, "A funny thing is happening. The people *without* guns are winning!"

The successful self-liberation of Poland in a ten-year struggle, despite earlier decades of Nazi and Soviet occupations and the continued presence of Soviet troops, has not shaken our preconceptions of political reality. Similarly, note what happened in the small Baltic nations of Estonia, Latvia, and Lithuania, which also experienced both Nazi and Soviet occupations and had even been annexed into the Soviet Union when it was still intact. That these small nations could regain independence without firing a single shot does not amaze us. Reality is ignored. Similar refutations of our usual view of political reality came from the collapse of other dictatorships in Central and Eastern Europe and Central Asia.

And then there is South Africa, where for many years intelligent, concerned people assumed there would be no liberation from the apartheid regime without a massive, probably racial, war. Almost no one expected that an African imprisoned for almost three decades would soon become president, and that this would signal the end, or at least the beginning of the end, of a deeply ingrained, deeply repressive policy.

There have been other clear refutations of our usual understanding of power in politics. We have ignored or explained them away. Apparently, the assumption of the omnipotence of extreme dictatorships and of massive violence is false. We rarely recognize the importance of occasional evidence that powerful dictatorships and great violence have been defeated through nonviolent means. We have become so indoctrinated to believe in the near omnipotence of extreme dictatorships and massive military might that we cannot see the reality of contradicting events. When supposedly "impossible" political events occur, we find "explanations" to block our seeing reality.

A more accurate understanding of political power may depend on examining afresh the basic nature of such power.

IDENTIFYING SOURCES OF POWER

Political power has sources in the society. According to respected political theorists these are authority (legitimacy), human resources, skills and knowledge, intangible factors, material resources, and sanctions (punishments). Sanctions are usually a key element of political power.[1]

It is highly significant that political power is seen to derive from these six sources. We need to understand these sources and their fragility.

Authority is perceived legitimacy. Authority makes a person or institution accepted voluntarily as superior in some way. Persons or institutions with authority are seen to have the right to command and be obeyed or followed. Authority is clearly a major source of political power.

Human resources refers to the number of persons who obey, cooperate with, and assist the rulers, and their proportion in the population. The extent and forms of their organizations are also relevant.

The *skills and knowledge* of those persons, and how those capacities relate to the needs of the rulers, also are a significant source of political power.

Intangible factors as sources of power include the habits and attitudes of the population towards obedience and submission. These may be affected by the presence or absence of a common faith, ideology, or sense of mission.

Material resources also help to determine the extent of the power of the rulers. These include property, natural resources, finances, communications, transportation, and the economic system.

Finally, the type and extent of *sanctions* (punishments) that rulers have available to enforce obedience by the population and to conduct acute conflicts with other States are important sources of political power. Sanctions prominently include military capacity and police forces for governments and, for nongovernmental groups, selective violence and terrorism. Sanctions also include government-directed economic embargoes and nongovernmental noncooperation.

The existence of political power, and its strength, depend on the continuous availability of these sources.

(For further details on each of these sources of power, see the definitions in the dictionary that follows.)

VULNERABLE SOURCES OF POWER

Many people and institutions make these sources of political power available. This does not mean that all subjects of all rulers prefer the established order. Consent is at times given because of positive approval. However, consent is also often given because people are unwilling to endure the consequences of a refusal of consent. In essence, this type of consent arises from intimidation. Refusal of consent requires self-confidence, strong motivation to resist, and knowledge of how to act in order to refuse.

The amount of power at the disposal of rulers depends on the extent to which the sources of power are provided. The provision of those sources depends on the cooperation, assistance, obedience, and compliance of multiple individuals, populations, and institutions. When that support is given in full measure, the potential power of rulers will be virtually unlimited. The rulers can then do almost whatever they wish. The situation can become akin to tyranny.

Although that support may be provided most of the time, in unusual circumstances support may become restricted or refused. The withholding of cooperation, assistance, and obedience can wield great power. That simple fact explains the unusual events and major political changes in Poland, the Baltics, and elsewhere, as cited earlier.

When the reasons for obedience are weak, rulers may seek to secure reliable obedience and cooperation by applying sanctions or by offering increased rewards for obedience and cooperation. However, sanctions do not guarantee the rulers' success at achieving their goals.

Under certain circumstances, members of the population will become willing to endure the punishments that can follow noncooperation and disobedience, rather than submit passively to rulers whose actions can no longer be tolerated. A change in a population's will, sense of purpose, or intention may lead to withdrawal of its obedience and cooperation.

When important sources of power on which the rulers depend are denied for long enough, the political power of rulers weakens. In extreme situations the power potentially can be dissolved. The precise ways in which the sources of power are thereby restricted or severed varies, as does the extent to which they are removed. Some of the methods of symbolic protest will simply reveal the degree to which the sources of power have already been restricted by earlier noncooperation. Various methods of political and economic noncooperation can directly shrink or sever the supply of important sources of power.

Noncooperation becomes coercive in a conflict when people and institutions withhold or withdraw their obedience and cooperation to a decisive degree, despite penalties.[2] This potential is of the greatest political significance. Whether the end result for resisters of a specific struggle waged by noncooperation is defeat, success, or mixed results, the power capacities of the contending parties will be changed.[3]

LOSS OF THE SOURCES OF POWER

If the rulers' power is being used for purposes that we abhor, the question becomes: How can the availability of the sources of power be shrunk or severed? That would appear to be the most basic, and potentially most effective, means to halt the applications of power for purposes we reject.

The loss of *authority* removes the single most important reason for obedience. The loss of obedience affects not only the general population but at times also the opponents' bureaucracy, military forces, and police. Any loss of the opponents' authority among these bodies will weaken the opponents' power. If the general population no longer feels an obligation to obey, if the noncooperation is powerful, and if the troops and police are no longer reliable in repressing resisters, the rejected rulers may not remain rulers much longer.

Massive civil resistance may make the regime's ability to retain the necessary *human resources* extremely difficult or impossible.

Rulers may need the cooperation of some people more than others, because of the specialized *skills and knowledge* they possess. Therefore, the noncooperation of relatively small numbers of individuals with those capacities may have a disproportionate impact. Refusal of assistance by key subjects may make it difficult for the opponents to develop and carry out policies appropriate to the situation they face. This may lead to the acceptance of policies that prove to be political mistakes or to an inability to implement—or at least a difficulty in implementing— chosen policies.

Intangible factors, such as habits of unquestioning obedience and general acceptance of political beliefs that support reliable obedience, cooperation, and submission, may be weakened or destroyed by a widespread noncooperation movement. This can in turn facilitate additional noncooperation and defiance.

The availability of *material resources* may be restricted by a noncooperation struggle. Material resources include control of the economic system, communications, financial resources, raw materials, and the like. A large percentage of the many methods of noncooperation have direct economic consequences, and others do so indirectly. Large-scale strikes, economic shutdowns, consumers' boycotts, and embargoes can have major political impacts.

The powers that be may attempt to control resisters by legal prohibitions and by actions of police and troops. However, the rulers' ability to apply *sanctions* can also vary, as we have seen. This variation can at times be consciously influenced, most directly by troops or police themselves. Police and troops may carry out orders for repression inefficiently, or more rarely may ignore them completely. Even more rarely, they may actively assist the resistance. For example, in Prague, during resistance to the Warsaw Pact invasion in 1968, police cars transported resistance newspapers throughout the city.

APPLICATION OF THIS POWER ANALYSIS

The application of this power analysis in actual conflicts will never be simple or easy. However, compared to the applications of the doctrine that power comes out of the barrel of a gun, these difficulties are to be much preferred.

The weakening or severance of the supply of the sources of power often requires large numbers of people acting together despite repression. Individual protest and disobedience can be heroic and exemplary, but group noncooperation can wield real power. The resisting institution may be a long-established one—such as the Norwegian teachers' organization in the 1942 struggle against fascist control of schools during the Nazi occupation—or it may be a new institution created during the struggle, such as the workers' councils of the 1956–1957 Hungarian Revolution.

Just as individuals and independent groups and institutions may refuse to cooperate fully, so too the subsidiary units and organizations within the ruling body may at times also become unreliable. No complex organization or institution, including the State, can carry out orders and policies if the individuals, organizations, and unit bodies that compose the overall ruling institution do not enable it to do so.

Being accustomed to widespread obedience and cooperation, rulers do not always anticipate generalized noncompliance and therefore have difficulties handling strong disobedience and noncooperation. The answer to uncontrolled political power, that is, to oppression, therefore may lie in learning how to carry out and maintain withdrawal of obedience and cooperation, and to sustain that withdrawal despite repression. This will not be easy.

A REQUIREMENT FOR FREEDOM

The degree of liberty or tyranny in any government is, in large part, a reflection of the relative determination of the population to be free and their willingness and ability to resist efforts to enslave them. "For the tyrant has the power to inflict only that which we lack the strength to resist," wrote the Indian sociologist Krishnalal Shridharani.[4]

A technique of action capable of accomplishing those controls over the power of rulers, and of mobilizing the power potential of the population, should be one that will give the population a lasting capacity to control any rulers and to defend the population's capacity to rule itself. A type of action with the potential to achieve such controls is "people power"—that is, the technique of nonviolent action.

NOTES TO AN ESSAY ON POWER AND STRUGGLE

1. For detailed analyses of the sources of political power and the insights of political theorists and analysts on which this essay is based, see Gene Sharp, *The Politics of Nonviolent Action* (Boston: Porter Sargent, 1973) Part One, "Power and Struggle," pp. 7–62; Gene Sharp, *Social Power and Political Freedom* (Boston: Porter Sargent, 1980), pp. 21–67.

2. See Sharp, *The Politics of Nonviolent Action*, pp. 744–755.

3. For discussion of these changes see Sharp, *The Politics of Nonviolent Action*, pp. 744–754. For a list of factors influencing the outcome of conflicts waged by nonviolent struggle, see pp. 815–817.

4. Krishnalal Shridharani, *War without Violence: Study of Gandhi's Method and Its Accomplishments* (New York: Harcourt, Brace, 1939), p. 305.

CASE STUDY:
SERBIA,
1996-2000

JOSHUA PAULSON

EARLY DISSENT

Serbian and Yugoslav president Slobodan Milosevic ruled for eleven years, from 1989 to 2000. His tenure was marked by the breakup of Yugoslavia, Serbia's participation in four wars that resulted in more than 210,000 deaths, the creation of nearly three million refugees, and isolation from the international community. After fomenting genocidal "ethnic cleansing" in the former Yugoslav states of Croatia and Bosnia-Herzegovina, as well as in the province of Kosovo, Milosevic was indicted on war crimes charges by the International War Crimes Tribunal at The Hague.

Demonstrations against Milosevic's near-dictatorial rule occurred frequently during the 1990s and were often met with repression. Opposition leaders were arrested, tanks were sometimes called into the streets, and crowds were occasionally fired on by police or army units. Although large anti-government demonstrations swept through the capital, Belgrade, in 1991, Milosevic and his Socialist Party of Serbia managed to hold on to power, largely by promoting popular nationalist policies and the expansionist dream of a "Greater Serbia."

By the second half of the decade, much of the population was dissatisfied with international isolation, the stigma of lost wars, thousands of dead, a ruined economy, average salaries under $70 per month, staggering inflation, and high unemployment. Many blamed Milosevic directly for their problems, but the "established" democratic opposition had difficulties uniting around an anti-Milosevic platform. The divided opposition allowed Milosevic to maintain a stranglehold on local and state government even as he and his party lost popularity.

MUNICIPAL ELECTIONS AND STUDENT PROTESTS

On November 17, 1996, municipal elections across Serbia proved to be a turning point. A loose opposition coalition of five small parties known as Zajedno ("Together") won for the first time in forty cities, including Belgrade, Nis, and Cacak. Milosevic, however, had packed local election committees with members of his own party, and they refused to certify opposition victories in those forty cities.

The Zajedno coalition called for marches and street protests to demand recognition of their electoral victories, and within two weeks the daily demonstrations in Belgrade grew from under two thousand participants to more than one hundred thousand. Workers were notably absent in the demonstrations, unlike the protests that swept the rest of Central and Eastern Europe seven years earlier.

Serbian students, meanwhile, called for parallel protests of their own. They demanded recognition of the Zajedno victories, as well as the resignations of top University of Belgrade officials. The removal of Slobodan Milosevic did not yet figure among the student demands.

At first, Milosevic responded by ignoring the protesters altogether. When this did not seem to work, the government took action against the independent media and the opposition press, shutting down Radio B-92 on December 3 and jamming the signal of Radio Index. Some arrests were made. Still, the daily demonstrations continued well into 1997.

On day 55 of the protests, following an all-night standoff between student protesters and police in the frozen Belgrade streets, a delegation of students met with government representatives. The government then announced it had agreed to respect "the will of the citizens" and to reinstate the stolen opposition victories. Zajedno protests came to an end as opposition politicians took office in Belgrade and thirty-nine other municipalities. Student protests continued for another fifty-one days until the rector and the dean of the university finally submitted their resignations.

OTPOR

In 1997, Slobodan Milosevic's term in office as president of Serbia ended and he was constitutionally ineligible to serve another term. To remain in power, he had himself elected president of Yugoslavia and eventually rewrote the constitution to allow himself to be reelected two more times to the new post. A few students, however, were committed to making sure his new term in office would be his last.

On October 10, 1998, a handful of student veterans of the 1996–1997 protests gathered in Belgrade to form a new organization known as Otpor ("Resistance"). Although their earliest organizing focused on opposing new repressive university and media laws, they soon realized that they could "do nothing by opposing only part of the Milosevic system."[1] Their primary objective then shifted toward ridding themselves of Slobodan Milosevic. To that end, they had three key demands: free and fair elections in Serbia, a free university, and guarantees for independent media.

Otpor, like much of the population, had little faith in the established political opposition, which was composed largely of bickering political parties with power-hungry and protagonistic leaders. Many opposition politicians had ties either to the governing regime or to the former Communist state, and few were considered honest or trustworthy. The students therefore decided to shape Otpor into a new type of political organization. It had a horizontal leadership structure, completely decentralized, without any "heads" to be beheaded or co-opted by the regime. Each regional office was virtually autonomous, while being supported in its actions by all the other Otpor chapters. "The idea was, cut off one Otpor head, and another fifteen heads would instantly appear," said one member of the group.[2] Its aim was to spread resistance through the countryside, where Milosevic's support had always been strong.

These students had no confidence in violence because they saw that guerrilla warfare tactics would only play into Milosevic's hands.[3] When Otpor was founded, its members firmly committed the organization to the use of only nonviolent forms of resistance. Otpor strove to use creative yet courageous methods of nonviolent action, rather than violence, in order to achieve its goals. The symbol that the group chose as its trademark was a stylized black-and-white raised fist, consciously drawing on 1930s-era Communist imagery.

On December 17, 1998, Otpor carried out its first nationwide action, a march from Belgrade to Novi Sad. Conscious of the fact that the level of opposition would have to rise dramatically in the provinces for Milosevic to be defeated, the students took back roads along the route, passing through as many small rural communities as possible. Belgrade, where the main Otpor office was based, was already an opposition stronghold, so most of Otpor's organizing was concentrated in other university towns and small communities.

Otpor's campaigns were generally of a symbolic nature, using nonviolent methods of protest and persuasion. They worked first and foremost to eliminate the climate of fear among the population, knowing that "when fear disappears the regime loses a central pillar of its power."[4] One of Otpor's first targets was a new Information Law restricting freedom of expression. They printed and distributed leaflets, held marches and sit-ins, painted anti-Milosevic slogans on walls, and engaged in witty street theater and other creative acts of defiance often intended to ridicule the regime. To a significant degree, as many activists noted, Otpor existed more as a "state of mind" than as an organized group. Srdja Popovic, one of Otpor's founders, put it simply: "Our ambition is to change the political consciousness of the Serbian populace."[5]

Otpor organizers developed the movement's tactics based on a continual analysis of the regime's sources of power. The goal was to alter the balance of power among the Milosevic government, the democratic opposition, and the "third sector" of nongovernmental organizations and "uncommitted" elements of civil society. Otpor identified Milosevic's authority[6] as his most important source of power, and also his most vulnerable. Otpor's actions were thus consciously designed simultaneously to bolster the students' moral authority among the population at large and to weaken the authority of the regime. This effect was accentuated when large-scale arrests and repression began several months after the group's founding congress.

During the first half of 1999, Otpor was relatively inactive because of the seventy-eight-day NATO bombing war against Yugoslavia. During the bombing, almost all anti-Milosevic activities came to a halt.[7] In the summer, with the war over, Otpor reorganized with a new intensity aimed at increasing its presence in the Milosevic heartland of rural Serbia. By December, Otpor had established fifty regional branches in smaller towns across the country. The number had grown to eighty by the time Otpor held its founding congress on February 17, 2000. One thousand representatives from seventy cities across Serbia attended the congress. The resolutions adopted by the congress asked Otpor members to "cooperate with other local democratic forces and with all individuals, independent media, unions and NGOs who are aware of the situation" in Serbia. The group also demanded that "the authorities stop immediately the language of hatred, repression and threats, violence and State terrorism," since "no government is worth even one drop of Serbian blood." Finally, Otpor called on "all citizens of Serbia, sons and daughters as well as their parents, to fight poverty, fear, oppression and desperation and by doing so become a part of the widest front of Otpor and support the idea of free Serbia."[8]

After its founding congress, Otpor grew rapidly. Believing that the easiest and quickest way to remove Milosevic would be to pressure him to call early elections, then win those elections and defend the popular will, the group developed a broad plan of action with three phases. The first phase was to "establish a strong nonviolent movement whose goal is to run a campaign against Milosevic." This was to be carried out primarily through small, often symbolic actions that would be likely to produce positive results. The campaign would be considered successful when Milosevic agreed to new elections. The second phase would be to win those elections, by creating "a big campaign machine, whose only goal is to generate a massive turnout." The idea for this second phase, according to Popovic, was "to get the maximum number of people involved in political life. This we saw as the route to a better future, *beyond* the removal of Slobodan Milosevic." The third, and most ambitious, stage would then be to take advantage of the new political climate to "change the system," educate a new political generation with new values, and turn Serbia, then the "pariah of the Balkans," into a normal European nation.[9]

ASSISTANCE

Otpor, like other opposition organizations, received technical and financial assistance from external sources during this period. Both the U.S.-based National Democratic Institute and the International Republican Institute had for some time been sponsoring pro-democratic activities in Yugoslavia. The National Democratic Institute had focused primarily on support for building opposition political parties and means of improving contacts in the media.

In September 1999, the Center for Civic Initiatives, a Serbian nongovernmental organization, translated and published Gene Sharp's *From Dictatorship to Democracy*. According to the Center, in all about 5,500 copies were distributed. Members of Otpor and the Democratic Party, one of the country's largest opposition parties, were among those who obtained copies.

Between March 31 and April 2, 2000, the International Republican Institute sponsored a workshop on the technique of nonviolent struggle in Budapest for thirty Otpor activists. The workshop primarily focused on the "theory of power, its sources, how those sources of power are expressed in organizations and institutions (pillars of support), how to analyze them to identify strengths and weaknesses, then how to think strategically to neutralize or destroy them."[10] Otpor coordinators believed this workshop, given by Albert Einstein Institution consultant Robert Helvey, a retired U.S. Army colonel, provided them with "invaluable practical training" in helping them to improve their use of nonviolent methods, to which they were already committed.[11] The major influence in Otpor's strategic planning for nonviolent struggle is credited by Popovic to the power analysis in Sharp's *The Politics of Nonviolent Action*, supplied by Helvey during the Budapest workshop.[12]

TRAINING MANUALS

Otpor drafted a training manual for the group's members, titled "Resistance in Your Neighborhood: How to Resolve the Serbian Crisis Peacefully." The manual included adapted and condensed elements of *The Politics of Nonviolent Action*.[13] It emphasized the need to analyze the regime's six sources of power. Attention was then called to the groups and institutions supplying those sources, known as "pillars of support." Once they were identified, it was necessary to systematically undermine and remove those pillars supporting the regime by use of nonviolent struggle methods.

The manual offered a comparative analysis of the strengths and weaknesses both of the regime and of Otpor. It then presented the characteristics of nonviolent struggle and its mechanisms of change. The manual also identified factors in the choice and application of a winning technique, the inevitability of repression, and the need for offering the population low-risk resistance methods. Specific suggestions were made for acts of resistance. The importance of planning was emphasized, and the basics of organization were also presented. On these bases, a mass Otpor campaign would develop.

According to Popovic, "Through two years of our nonviolent struggle, Otpor's human resources team developed six different training programs based on the technique of nonviolent struggle. More than four hundred activists of Otpor were trained in nonviolent methods, through Otpor's 'user manual' for working with activists, based on various 'working with volunteers' manuals, and especially Gene Sharp's *Politics of Nonviolent Struggle* [sic]. More than one thousand activists were basically trained in methods of nonviolent action in forty-two cities of Serbia."[14] These activists, meanwhile, used the Otpor manual to train thousands of other members across Serbia in the year 2000.

Otpor encouraged acts of individual resistance for new activists, such as individual conversations at the workplace or in social situations, the placing of Otpor stickers in prominent places, telephone calls to repressive institutions (such as to the police to complain about a particular arrest or a repressive measure), cheerful distribution of Otpor printed material to neighbors, and the ignoring of government representatives in the local vicinity.

Once individual actions succeeded in creating a handful of committed activists in a particular neighborhood, group actions could then be performed. Although again mostly symbolic in nature, such actions tended to be creative and witty, and sometimes provocative, virtually taunting the regime to take repressive action against the participants. Actions included the promotion of banned music and the publication and distribution of anti-Milosevic materials, conducting street theater productions designed to ridicule the government, and the organization of marches and concerts against the regime and in defense of independent media.

REPRESSION AND RESPONSE

When repression against the movement began in earnest shortly after the Otpor founding congress, it was welcomed by the group, as they found there was a direct correlation between arrests of Otpor members and membership spurts. "In one case," said an Otpor activist, "we got 500 new members in one day." Another Otpor member added, "We fed on the repression of the regime, and in all towns and cities where they arrested our people, the movement accelerated its growth. Immediately afterwards we were approached by new people, sometimes even pensioners, prepared to continue with resistance."[15]

Repression usually took the form of censorship, arrests, or beatings. The repression exposed the nature of the regime, which became more "dictatorial" with each passing day as it shut down independent media and arrested Otpor activists. Because of the raised stakes, each visible Otpor action also had a pronounced effect in helping the populace at large cast off its fear of the regime. After Otpor members were jailed, crowds of demonstrators repeatedly rallied in front of the police stations to demand their release. "We showed them that we could be arrested and then come back to fight again and again," said one activist.[16]

By May 2000, Otpor was present in over one hundred towns across Serbia, and had nearly twenty thousand members. Only about

60 percent were students. Approximately three hundred Otpor activists had been arrested by this time, although most spent a maximum of just a few days in jail. Within two months, more than a thousand other Otpor members would be detained as the government stepped up its repressive campaign against the resistance movement.

On May 16, the government accused Otpor of planting bombs at the offices of Milosevic's Socialist Party of Serbia and of the Yugoslav Left, the political party run by Milosevic's wife. Otpor was also accused of attempting to murder a prominent Milosevic ally, and of assassinating Bosko Perosevic, the Socialist Party governor of the Vojvodina province. On May 17, the government seized control of Studio B, Belgrade's independent television and radio station, and shut down independent Radio B-92 and Radio Index. Over the following two days, police in Belgrade violently dispersed Otpor and student protests, arresting and beating dozens.

Meanwhile, posters appeared around Belgrade accusing Otpor activists of being "Madeleine Youth" (in a reference to U.S. secretary of state Madeleine Albright, the original sponsor of the 1999 NATO bombing war against Yugoslavia). These posters were designed to resemble the Nazi occupation posters of the Hitler Youth organization. Some posters depicted the Otpor trademark fist stuffed with U.S. dollar bills. At the end of the month, authorities closed Belgrade University and banned student gatherings on the campus. Government authorities labeled Otpor an illegal and violent terrorist organization.

During this time, discipline among the opposition activists became increasingly important. Otpor leaders concede that they were "almost forced to go underground." Communication between organizers often was carried out only through coded messages. Otpor training sessions during this time focused on disarming the repressive machine through fear control and by helping activists prepare for arrest. The group also intentionally made its symbolic actions even more "silly and benign," in order to make the "inevitable arrests of activists all the more senseless."[17]

During the late spring and early summer, Otpor continued to grow, and arrests and beatings were on the rise. The group campaigned to unite the various opposition political parties around a single platform focused on winning the local and legislative elections scheduled for later in the year. The 1996 Zajedno coalition had long since collapsed, but several key opposition parties had tentatively signed a unity agreement in January with the goal of free elections. In the spring, however, they continued to bicker over personal and political differences, and it was unclear whether they would manage to enter the fall elections as a unified block. Otpor, which at this point was larger and more popular than any single political party, insisted on opposition unification in nearly all of its public statements.

MILOSEVIC CALLS EARLY ELECTIONS

Increasingly concerned about the possibilities of a unified opposition, Slobodan Milosevic announced on July 27 that he was calling an early presidential election, to be held at the same time as the local and legislative elections on September 24. His term as Yugoslav president was not set to expire until July 2001, but since he had recently changed the constitution, allowing himself to be reelected to two additional four-year terms, he was now banking on the hope that the opposition parties would fail to unite before September. He was wrong.

Otpor managed essentially to shame eighteen opposition parties into forming a coalition known as the Democratic Opposition of Serbia (DOS), and promised them they would deliver at least five hundred thousand votes if the coalition launched a common candidate for federal president. The candidate who emerged, Vojislav Kostunica, was a constitutional lawyer known as "the nonviolent nationalist." He had been a cofounder of the Democratic Party in 1992 before splitting off to form the Democratic Party of Serbia. He was noncharismatic, but was considered honest and shared Otpor's underlying interest in turning Yugoslavia into a "normal" European nation.

Otpor, meanwhile, had a head start on the election campaign. The group's contacts in the government had leaked Milosevic's decision to call early elections nearly two weeks beforehand, so that when the president made the announcement, Otpor already had more than sixty tons of anti-Milosevic electoral propaganda printed and awaiting distribution. By this time, Otpor had acquired extensive experience in mass-marketing techniques and had begun to focus its energies on two campaigns to win the elections for the opposition coalition and Kostunica. The first, *Gotov Je!* ("He's Finished!"), was designed to break the Serbian mindset that Milsosevic was invincible. The campaign was also intended to change a common voting tendency of casting ballots for whoever was already in power. Hundreds of thousands of posters went up across the country with images of Milosevic under the "He's Finished" slogan, effectively declaring that the dictator had already lost. T-shirts were printed and television spots were taken out with the same message.

The second campaign, *Vreme Je!* ("It's Time!"), was a simple get-out-the-vote campaign that was nonpartisan in nature. Otpor figured that the key to defeating Milosevic at the polls was high turnout, and that if at least four million voters cast ballots, Milosevic would be history, even if he attempted to use fraud (which Otpor assumed he would do).

Meanwhile, Otpor's humorous street theater continued to provoke the wrath of the regime. Four Otpor activists and two of their mothers were arrested in Belgrade for distributing badges to passersby labeled "I'm a national hero," in mocking reference to Milosevic's attempts to have himself officially designated a national hero. On September 3 and 4, the offices of Otpor in Belgrade, Novi Sad, and Mladenovac were raided by police. More than ten tons of computers, printed campaign material, posters, T-shirts, and other items were seized in what seemed to be a final attempt at intimidation against Otpor before the elections. In the same week, more than 250 Otpor activists had been arrested nationwide.

Otpor, however, had the last laugh: after its offices were raided, the group publicly announced the time and place for delivery of what it said would be replacement materials. On that date, large trucks arrived at the Otpor office. When the police arrived to confiscate the "subversive" material, they were caught on camera seizing what turned out to be completely empty boxes.

ELECTIONS

The Yugoslav general elections were held on September 24. Turnout was the highest ever, about 80 percent, thanks in part to the Otpor campaign. This was the key to the election victory. Early returns released by the opposition late on the night of September 24 suggested that Kostunica, the DOS coalition's presidential candidate, had won 55 percent of the vote, compared to just 34 percent for Milosevic.[18] The opposition also swept local elections in Belgrade and other important cities.

Over twenty thousand people gathered in Belgrade the following evening for an opposition victory rally and concert in support of Kostunica. Milosevic, however, had yet to concede his defeat. On September 26, the government-controlled Federal Election Commission accepted Milosevic's second-place showing, but denied that Kostunica had achieved the necessary votes to win outright in the first round. The commission reported Kostunica won only 48.22 percent, compared with 40.23 percent for Milosevic, and called for a runoff election to be held between the two on October 8.

Opposition members of the Federal Election Commission claimed fraud and said they had been excluded from the official certification proceedings. Based on returns from 98 percent of the constituencies, the leaders of the opposition coalition continued to insist that Kostunica had won over 50 percent of the vote in the first round, and that a runoff was out of the question. "This is an offer that must be rejected," said Kostunica. "The victory is obvious, and we will defend it by all nonviolent means."[19] Thousands of people in Cacak and Novi Sad protested the official results, and the DOS leaders called for mass demonstrations in Belgrade and other major cities on September 27. The leader of the Serbian Orthodox Church, Patriarch Pavle, even met with Milosevic and urged him to concede. The Patriarch further called on "everyone, including the army and the police, to defend the interests of the people and the state rather than individuals."[20]

On Wednesday, September 27, over two hundred thousand Kostunica supporters gathered in Republic Square in Belgrade. It was the largest opposition demonstration ever recorded in Serbia.

Meanwhile, thirty-five thousand people demonstrated in Novi Sad, twenty-five thousand in Nis, and fifteen thousand in Kragujevac. During the Belgrade rally, Kostunica reached out to the army and police forces: "Our message to the army and the police is that we are one. The army and the police are part of the people; they exist to protect the people, not one man and his family."[21] Thousands of people shouted *Gotov Je!* ("He's finished!"), a key Otpor slogan, and shook baby rattles, apparently in reference to an expression suggesting that Milosevic was "broken like an old baby rattle."

Opposition leaders were worried that a boycott of the runoff election might allow Milosevic to claim a default victory by running unopposed. Realizing that they had only until October 8 to force Milosevic to accept defeat and step down, the leaders of the eighteen opposition parties in the coalition met twice on September 28, and emerged with a three-part campaign scheduled to last ten days. First, they would challenge the official results from the first round of balloting in the courts. Second, they would employ popular pressure on the regime through the use of demonstrations, selective strikes, and civil disobedience. Finally, they would encourage Milosevic's political and military allies to desert him and join the opposition.

FOCUS ON THE PROVINCES

Some sectors of the opposition, including Otpor, did their best to prepare for a post-electoral contingency against fraud. They were sure Milosevic would both lose the election and then try to steal it. The Democratic Opposition of Serbia therefore called for a massive rally in Belgrade on Friday, September 29. Opposition leaders planned to ask the Serbian people to "perform any act of civil disobedience they have at their disposal" or simply to remain in the square until Milosevic accepted defeat. However, so few people turned out that the demonstration was suspended until the evening. One of the protesters, a seventeen-year-old student, said, "We'll stay to protest, but I don't think he'll go that easily. We need total civil disobedience, not this kind of thing today, which is ridiculous. Everyone needs to come out on the street and block the system."[22]

In the provinces, where Otpor had put so much effort into promoting creative resistance, that is exactly what happened. While Belgrade politicians worried about the low turnout for demonstrations in the capital, major national highways were blocked across the country. Much larger demonstrations took place in Cacak, Nis, Novi Sad, Valjevo, and Kraljevo. The once-monolithic State media began to crack, as State television workers in Kragujevac temporarily halted regularly scheduled programming to protest the bias of "official" news. At the Novi Sad television station, 150 workers signed a petition asking for the resignation of the chief editor. Six other editors at the station were fired when they refused to broadcast the State news program and promised equal coverage of opposition activities.

A few strikes also broke out, mainly in opposition strongholds such as Cacak. Students walked out of classes, artists and actors went on strike, and some public and private offices closed. Quietly, 7,500 workers at the Kolubara coal mines forty miles south of Belgrade walked off the job, insisting they would not return to work until Kostunica's electoral victory was recognized. The Kolubara mines produced coal for the Obrenovac power station, which in turn produced nearly half of Serbia's electricity. A prolonged strike at the mines would seriously jeopardize the ability of the country to function normally.

Meanwhile, opposition leaders arrived at a consensus that Monday, October 2, must be "D-Day," the time to step up the pressure on Milosevic using rolling strikes, demonstrations, road blockades, and school boycotts. In many parts of the country, limited blockades and strikes began a day early. One thousand workers at the Kostolac coal mine in eastern Serbia joined their Kolubara comrades and walked off the job.

In Belgrade, newly elected opposition mayor Milan Protic called for a citywide general strike. He said he believed the pressure would have to be systematically increased throughout the coming week, with an escalation of opposition actions and strikes "until Milosevic realizes he is no longer president."[23] Protic's call was echoed by Velimir Ilic, the charismatic and popular opposition mayor of Cacak, who called for a total blockade of his own town. "Our victory is as pure as a diamond. Kostunica is the elected president, and we must persist in our resistance," he told a crowd of ten thousand that had gathered for the seventh consecutive night of demonstrations in Cacak.[24]

At the Kolubara mines, general manager Slobodan Jankovic resigned in support of the striking workers. Later in the day, hundreds of special police entered the mine in an attempt to keep it in operation. They failed, largely because the workers had already removed key parts of important equipment and machinery, precisely in case of a police take-over. "It would take us three days to get working again," said one worker, "but it would take them 15 days."[25]

Meanwhile, cracks grew wider in the State media. More than sixty reporters at *Vecernje Novosti*, a popular tabloid paper that had been put under State control earlier in the year, signed a petition demanding that the paper produce balanced news coverage within twenty-four hours and recognize Kostunica's electoral victory. Eight local Belgrade radio stations said they would stop broadcasting state news. And at Studio B, a television station formerly controlled by the opposition before it was taken over by State authorities in May, workers threatened a strike unless news coverage became balanced.

GENERAL STRIKE

On Monday, October 2, the general strike began. It was the first attempt at a nationwide general strike in Serbia since World War II. The objective was to shut down roads and highways throughout the country, fortify the strikes at Kolubara and other key industries, and close schools and businesses. The aim was "to try and show to Mr. Milosevic that he can no longer command the country."[26]

Although garbage piled up in Belgrade, and students took to the streets, the capital city was relatively unaffected on the first day of the strike. Once again it was in the provinces, formerly the most important base of Milosevic's support, where resistance was strongest. Novi Sad, Cacak, Pancevo, Uzice, and Nis were shut down completely. Highways and railroads were blocked across the country by cars, trucks, and throngs of people. Most schools and businesses were closed.

State-run television stations were stormed by demonstrators in the towns of Prokuplje and Novi Sad. Government workers in Novi Sad joined the strike as well. Industrial workers and railway employees in Ucize also went on strike, and the main highway there was blockaded by hundreds of protesters. Even the Serbian Society of Composers and the Alliance of Composers' Organizations of Yugoslavia asked their respective memberships to stop composing music until Milosevic conceded the election. The government weather bureau said there would be no more forecasts until Milosevic left office.

At the Kolubara mines, striking workers received a visit from Vojislav Kostunica, who told them, "Thank you for what you've started, just hold on and we will finish this struggle together."[27] Opposition leaders announced the strikes would continue through the week, culminating in a mass rally in Belgrade on Thursday, October 5, attended by hundreds of thousands of people from across the country.

Milosevic responded with an appearance on nationwide television to denounce the actions of what he called the "traitorous opposition." He accused the opposition leadership of working for foreign governments and NATO. He added: "The leadership of the democratic opposition, with the money that they have received from abroad, is buying, blackmailing, and scaring citizens . . . and is organizing strikes and violence in order to stop production, work and any activity—to stop life in Serbia."[28]

On the following day, October 3, the Milosevic government threatened a harsh crackdown against the opposition, promising that "special measures" would be taken against strike leaders and organizers. Strikes and highway blockades were declared illegal, and opposition media were banned. In the early morning, the police arrested Dragoljub Stosic, the head of the Belgrade public transport union, and forcibly removed a human blockade of the bus garage. Arrest warrants were issued for eleven leaders of the Kolubara strike, as well as for two opposition politicians who had assisted the Kolubara strikers, on "accusations of sabotage." During these days, the regime drew up a list of forty opponents targeted for assassination. Otpor's Srdja Popovic was number eight.[29] The government also initiated rolling blackouts in opposition-controlled districts, blaming the Kolubara strikers and the opposition for the lack of coal needed to power the electricity generators.

Despite such repression, the resistance continued to spread. In Belgrade, fifty thousand students marched from the city center toward Dedinje, the suburban home of Milosevic, chanting "The police are with us!" Thirty thousand people demonstrated in Novi Sad, ten thousand in Nis, and forty thousand in Kragujevac, where Kostunica made a morale-boosting visit to his supporters. The city of Cacak remained on strike and almost fully barricaded from within. In Majdanpek, workers at the copper mine used their dump trucks and other equipment to block all entryways to the mine with rocks and dirt, then promptly declared themselves to be on strike.

For the first time since the elections, reports surfaced of divisions within the security forces. Press reports spoke of entire special police units who did nothing but stand by and watch as protesters blocked roads. One special police battalion in Belgrade was reported to have turned in its riot equipment, and in at least one instance, local police flatly refused orders to remove roadblocks established by the opposition.

The ongoing strike at the Kolubara mines, meanwhile, had become the focal point of resistance to the regime. The workers themselves were aware of the mines' strategic importance, even though most opposition leaders were slow to come to this realization. As one Kolubara worker put it, "This is the only industry that really works in this country. This is the heart of Serbia, and we have to keep our grip on it."[30] One of the major differences between the opposition demonstrations of 1996 and those of October 2000 was that the former included few, if any, workers. The fact that miners had gone out on strike against the Socialist regime of President Milosevic had an important symbolic effect similar to that produced by the workers of Poland's Solidarity movement when they struck against a workers' State in 1980.

The government was perhaps faster than the opposition in recognizing the threat posed by the Kolubara strike, and General Nebojsa Pavkovic, Yugoslavia's top military commander and Milosevic's chief of staff, was sent to the mines to try to coerce the workers to end the strike. He left empty-handed several hours later. Later, one of the Kolubara workers explained the strikers' determination in simple but stark terms: "We can either stay here four more days or four more years. It's really a very simple choice."[31]

VICTORY AT KOLUBARA

On Wednesday morning, October 4, hundreds of special police armed and outfitted in full riot gear were sent into the Kolubara mines to occupy the facilities, arrest the strike leaders, and beat back demonstrators. The workers refused to leave and used cellular phones to call for help. In nearby Lazarevac, the independent radio announced the police takeover. Within hours, more than twenty thousand people from surrounding towns, and some from as far away as Cacak and Belgrade, arrived at the mines to confront the police.

By early afternoon, more than a thousand civilian demonstrators were backed up on a bridge near the mine entrance, blocked by a police barricade. The police themselves were uneasy about their assigned task and showed no hurry to disperse the demonstrators. Then, slowly, a bulldozer driven by three elderly men approached the police barricade and "almost gently" plowed right through it. The police did not dare intervene as thousands of people surged forward into the mine complex, some of them shouting "Otpor!" One police commander was reported to have commented, "I'm fed up with this. After this, I'm throwing my hat away and going home. The police in Serbia are more democratic than you think."[32]

In the evening, President-elect Kostunica visited the victorious miners and their supporters. By the following morning, the police sent by Milosevic to end the strike had disappeared.

THE PROVINCES COME TO BELGRADE

On the night of October 4, the opposition was presented with a new piece of outrageous news. The Milosevic-dominated constitutional court had heard the appeal by the opposition coalition of the election certification, and theoretically ruled in its favor. But rather than declare Kostunica the winner of the presidential election, the court simply said there had been fraud on September 24, and that the whole presidential election would therefore have to be run over again on a future date to be decided by the federal parliament, itself controlled by Milosevic supporters. For the opposition, the decision was considered worse than the idea of holding a second round of voting on October 8, as it implied that Milosevic would be allowed to stay in power until his legal term expired in July. If the opposition coalition needed a spark to make people angry and give the resistance additional momentum on the eve of its planned mass concentration in Belgrade, this was it.

Thursday, October 5, was the day selected by the opposition for the provinces to come to Belgrade and hold a massive rally against Milosevic. The Democratic Opposition of Serbia had set a deadline of 3:00 P.M. for Milosevic to concede defeat, cancel the arrest warrants issued on October 3, and fire the top management of Radio Television Serbia. According to opposition coalition leader Zoran Djindjic, "Our idea was to assemble a large crowd to sit down in front of the federal parliament and stay there until the election commission turned up with real results."[33] Several massive motorcades of vehicles, sometimes covering all four lanes of superhighways, poured into Belgrade. They often peacefully talked drivers blockading their movement into moving aside, and blocking trucks were pushed to the side of the road. By noon, nearly half a million people from the countryside had swarmed into Belgrade. But to Djindjic's surprise, few shared his idea of sitting and waiting.

Of those who made their way into Belgrade on October 5, a large contingent hailed from the opposition stronghold of Cacak. The mayor, Velimir Ilic, had his own idea of how the day's events should proceed. Ilic personally led a twelve-mile-long column of cars and trucks with more than ten thousand people from Cacak to Belgrade on the morning of October 5. They brought along bulldozers—dubbed "people's tanks"—which helped them break through a half-dozen police barricades on the outskirts of the city. Prior to the journey, Ilic had coordinated his plans with two special police officers from Cacak and two from Belgrade, who in turn encouraged other crucial police elements in the capital to defect. Their plan was to fill Belgrade with demonstrators and seize two key pillars of the Milosevic regime: the federal parliament building and the broadcasting studios of Radio Television Serbia. "We wanted to get rid of Milosevic once and for all," said Ilic, "and we knew we could only achieve that by liberating the parliament and television."[34]

Ilic was not the only opposition leader negotiating defections out of the security forces. Otpor and other opposition leaders had been deepening their contacts with elements of the police, anti-terrorist units, and the army well before the September elections. During the first few days of October, Otpor sent polite letters to army commanders and the police general headquarters, letting them know in advance that "Serbia was coming to Belgrade." The group also sent individual "care packages" of food and newspapers to soldiers and policemen.

The mayor of the southern city of Nis and an important Otpor ally, Zoran Zivkovic, later reported that "we had secret talks with the army and police, the units we knew would be drafted to intervene. And the deal was that they would not disobey, but neither would they execute. If they had said no, other units would have been brought in. So they said yes when Milosevic asked for action—and they did nothing."[35]

By early afternoon, the Cacak delegation had joined hundreds of thousands of other demonstrators outside the federal parliament building, which was protected by special police forces. Many of these police, however, were now secretly working for the opposition. As crowds pressed against the barricades, the Cacak bulldozer pulled up and parked on the steps of the federal parliament. When the police line broke, many of the police either refused their orders to attack the protesters or, in some cases, attacked or restrained those police who had not yet switched sides. Nevertheless, hundreds of rounds of tear gas were quickly fired against the demonstrators, provoking outrage among the impassioned crowds. Thousands of people, some armed with sticks and metal bars, surged forward into the parliament building. After a short clash, the remaining police surrendered and a few rooms in the building were set afire.

One block away, another group of protesters attacked the offices of Radio Television Serbia. The building was under heavier guard than the federal parliament building, and police there fired live ammunition at the crowd, wounding four people. One woman was killed when she was run over by an opposition bulldozer nearby. The street battle outside the television station lasted about an hour. When it was over, the police retreated and protesters burned the building. A police station in Belgrade was also set afire. The downtown police station was stormed, looted, and trashed, but was not burned. Radio Television Serbia broadcasts went off the air, to be replaced in the evening by a slide reading "This is the new Radio Television Serbia broadcasting. . . ."

Later in the afternoon, confronted with thousands of demonstrators outside ready to storm the building, the central police station in Belgrade surrendered to the opposition. The official news agency Tanjug suddenly defected as well, and released a bulletin calling Vojislav Kostunica the "elected president of Yugoslavia." Demonstrators also took back independent radio station B-92 and Studio B Television for the opposition, and both quickly resumed broadcasting. With the State media and many of the security forces now on the side of the opposition, and the army confined to its barracks, Milosevic's strongest pillars of support had crumbled beneath him. In the evening, more than one hundred thousand people gathered outside the still-smoldering federal parliament and Belgrade city hall, chanting the Otpor campaign slogan *Gotov Je! Gotov Je!*

THE DICTATOR FALLS

On the following morning, October 6, Russian foreign minister Igor S. Ivanov met with both Milosevic and Kostunica. Russia had been the only important nation supporting Milosevic's attempts to hold onto power by not recognizing an outright Kostunica victory in the first round of elections. But after the uprising of the previous day, even Russia had now switched sides. Ivanov told Milosevic that if he "gave up power now, the world would not press for his extradition to face war crimes charges in The Hague."[36] After that, events moved rapidly.

The Constitutional Court suddenly and inexplicably reversed its earlier ruling, saying it had approved Kostunica's appeal of the September 24 election results. Rather than invalidate the election, it now ruled Kostunica the winner of the first round with just over 50 percent of the vote. In the evening, Kostunica announced that he had met during the day with Milosevic and army chief of staff Pavkovic, and that both men had congratulated him on his election as president.

Shortly before midnight on October 6, Milosevic addressed the nation on television and announced his immediate resignation as president of Yugoslavia. Attempting to maintain an air of legality around all his actions the past week, he said: "I've just received official information that Vojislav Kostunica won the elections. The decision was made by the body that was authorized to do so under the Constitution, and I consider that it has to be respected."[37]

WE'LL BE WATCHING YOU . . .

On Saturday, October 7, Kostunica was sworn in as Yugoslavia's president before the newly elected Yugoslav parliament. Since the federal parliament building had been partly damaged by fire, the ceremony was held in a Belgrade convention center.

Early the following week, key Milosevic allies in the government, including the prime minister and interior minister, tendered their resignations. The European Union lifted major economic sanctions against Yugoslavia and pledged $2 billion for national reconstruction efforts. Early elections were called for the powerful Serbian parliament in December, which were won by the Democratic Opposition of Serbia coalition with a two-thirds majority.

Meanwhile, Otpor, the student organization whose creativity and courage laid the groundwork for Milosevic's electoral defeat and subsequent collapse, placed at least eighty large, looming billboards around the country, aimed at the new government. Featuring a large bulldozer in Otpor's trademark black-and-white imagery, the message read, "Be careful. . . . We're watching you."

Otpor's short-term goal of removing the dictator had succeeded. Now, with the opposition in power, the more formidable goal of changing the system and turning Serbia into a "normal" European nation was just beginning.

NOTES TO CASE STUDY: SERBIA, 1996–2000

1. Vukasin Petrovic, interview by Steve York.

2. Roger Cohen, "The Hidden Revolution: Who Really Brought Down Milosevic?" *New York Times Magazine*, November 26, 2000, p. 45.

3. Cohen, "The Hidden Revolution," p. 45.

4. Cohen, "The Hidden Revolution," p. 44.

5. http://www.otpor.net.

6. "Authority" here refers to legitimacy, or the right to direct, guide, or be obeyed voluntarily. Authority is a main source of power.

7. Various discussions in Belgrade, reported by Gene Sharp, May 2001.

8. http://www.otpor.net.

9. Srdja Popovic, interview by Steve York.

10. Robert Helvey, correspondence with author, February 22, 2001.

11. Srdja Popovic, "The Theory and Practice of Strategic Nonviolence: An Analytical Overview of the Application of Gene Sharp's Theory of Nonviolent Action in Milosevic's Serbia." Unpublished draft, cited with permission.

12. Srdja Popovic, conversations with Christopher A. Miller and Gene Sharp, Belgrade, May 2001.

13. Gene Sharp, *The Politics of Nonviolent Action* (Boston: Porter Sargent, 1973 and later printings).

14. E-mail, Srdja Popovic to Rosalyn Abraham in the office of Peter Ackerman.

15. From a *Vreme* article, republished on http://www.otpor.net.

16. Vukasin Petrovic, interview by Steve York.

17. Srdja Popovic, "The Theory and Practice of Strategic Nonviolence."

18. Later in the week, the opposition downgraded these figures to 51.34 percent for Kostunica and 36.22 percent for Milosevic, still within the bounds of a first-round victory. Final official results released after the revolution, on October 7, gave Kostunica 50.24 percent of the vote, to 37.15 percent for Milosevic.

19. Steven Erlanger, "Milosevic Seeking a Runoff Election after His Setback," *New York Times*, September 27, 2000.

20. Serbian Orthodox Church statement, cited in Erlanger, "Milosevic Seeking a Runoff Election."

21. Steven Erlanger, "After Yugoslavs Celebrate, Belgrade Orders a Runoff," *New York Times*, September 28, 2000.

22. Steve Erlanger, "Milosevic Foes Stage Protests to Force Him to Concede," *New York Times*, September 30, 2000.

23. *Boston Globe*, October 2, 2000.

24. *Boston Globe*, October 2, 2000.

25. Steven Erlanger, "Striking Serbian Coal Miners Maintain Solidarity," *New York Times*, October 4, 2000.

26. Steve Erlanger, "Serb Police Move Into Key Mine as General Strike Looms," *New York Times*, October 2, 2000.

27. Steve Erlanger, "Milosevic Attacks Opponents on TV," *New York Times*, October 3, 2000.

28. Erlanger, "Milosevic Attacks Opponents on TV."

29. Srdja Popovic, discussion with Christopher A. Miller and Gene Sharp, Belgrade, May 27, 2001.

30. Erlanger, "Striking Serbian Coal Miners Maintain Solidarity."

31. Erlanger, "Striking Serbian Coal Miners Maintain Solidarity."

32. Steve Erlanger, "Serbian Strikers, Joined by 20,000, Face Down Police," *New York Times*, October 5, 2000.

33. Johanna McGeary, "The End of Milosevic," *Time*, October 16, 2000, p. 63.

34. McGeary, "The End of Milosevic," p. 63.

35. Cohen, "The Hidden Revolution," p. 118.

36. Steven Erlanger, "Showdown in Yugoslavia: The Overview; Milosevic Concedes His Defeat; Yugoslavs Celebrate New Era," *New York Times*, October 7, 2000. Six months later, however, Milosevic was extradited to The Hague.

37. Erlanger, "Showdown in Yugoslavia."

We are grateful for corrections and comments by Velimir Curgus Kazimir of the Fund for an Open Society Yugoslavia.

CASE STUDY: THE TUNISIAN UPRISING AND PROTESTS, DECEMBER 2010– JANUARY 2011

JAMILA RAQIB

During President Zine El Abidine Ben Ali's twenty-three years of rule, Tunisia was governed largely as a police state. His presidency ended abruptly in January 2011 after a nearly month-long wave of expanding unrest forced him to leave Tunisia and seek exile in Saudi Arabia. Ben Ali's departure followed a stunning display of people power as Tunisians took to the streets demanding an end to the corruption, economic deprivation, and political oppression that had plagued their country during Ben Ali's rule.

Ben Ali seized power in 1987 by charging that the independence leader Habib Bourguiba was no longer competent to rule. Twenty-three years later, Tunisians had solid grounds for dissatisfaction with his rule. Ben Ali was praised for turning his country into a successful tourist destination,[1] and he was a key ally in the U.S. fight against terrorism.[2] But Ben Ali was often criticized by human rights groups for his systematic political repression against opponents, including Islamists and Communists, and his attacks on civil liberties.

Although the regime was vocal about Tunisia's progress as a model of prosperity and stability, few Tunisians felt the effects of this "progress" in their lives. Economic reforms were seen by many as justification for continued disenfranchisement of the population and for enabling a small number of people in the inner circles of power to amass large fortunes. The wave of unrest that lasted nearly a month was sparked by the self-immolation of a young man in an act of protest over corruption and unemployment.

According to a 2009 Amnesty International report on the country titled "Tunisia's Economic Performance Hides Dire Human Rights Situation," Ben Ali's economic and educational reforms had improved living standards for many Tunisians in recent decades.[3] Governmental initiatives had resulted in substantial progress in alleviating poverty, providing universal primary education for boys and girls, and lowering rates of infant mortality. However, not all areas had benefited from these efforts. The northern and coastal regions, as well as areas that attracted tourists, were heavily favored. The 2009 report states:

[T]he centre, west and south of the country have been left far behind in terms of access to basic infrastructure and social services. As a result, they have higher rates of illiteracy and unemployment. They also lack or have inadequate access to drinking water, sewage and sanitation services, electricity, household equipment and adequate housing.[4]

A cable written on June 23, 2008, by Robert F. Godec, the U.S. ambassador to Tunisia, outlining grave economic conditions, was released on December 7, 2010, by the anti-secrecy organization WikiLeaks, and was banned in Tunisia. However, its contents became widely known. The cable further exacerbated the growing anger among many Tunisians who blamed corruption among the elite for the country's pervasive unemployment and poverty.

Although the petty corruption rankles, it is the excesses of President Ben Ali's family that inspire outrage among Tunisians. With Tunisians facing rising inflation and high unemployment, the conspicuous displays of wealth and persistent rumors of corruption have added fuel to the fire.[5]

The Tunisian government tried to block access to a website carrying the report, but the details were disseminated by Tunisian websites and blogs. This helped to fuel the popular anger and resentment against Ben Ali.[6] Some have called the Tunisian uprising "the first WikiLeaks revolution," referring to the cables' important role in focusing anger on the excesses of the regime, and on the rampant nepotism and corruption.[7]

Tunisia's growing population is composed largely of young people who are both educated and unemployed. The educational system delivered skills and qualifications to its population, but not the means to utilize them, or to provide an income. Tunisia's educational system, often touted as a model for the region, provides for compulsory education until age sixteen, and free college education. However, there is no labor market to absorb graduates, which number around eighty thousand annually.[8] The country's official unemployment rate is 14 percent, concentrated among young people. However, some union leaders put the rate much higher—more than 30 percent in Sidi Bouzid, where the uprising began, 165 miles south of the capital, Tunis.[9]

Economic opportunities were available to few people outside the president's inner circle. Average Tunisians, who overwhelmingly live in poverty, grew to resent the excesses of the president, his family, and the controlling elite.

Political power remained in the hands of a small minority, and the government exerted tight social and political controls. The regime created a facade of democracy, but it aggressively put in place policies designed to restrict opposition activities, and used legal, penal, and economic measures to stifle dissent. Political dissent was viewed as subversion. The regime considered any opposition as a challenge to its rule. Human rights activists and journalists were targeted and faced severe restrictions. State surveillance was pervasive. Some websites were blocked.[10]

During the 2009 presidential election, Ben Ali received 90 percent of the vote, amid charges of repression of political opponents and "constraints on media, assembly, and expression."[11]

The most significant protests in Tunisia before 2010 took place in 2008, in the mining areas of Gafsa, in southwestern Tunisia. Sporadic protests had occurred there over unemployment, rising inflation and cost of living, and the unfair recruitment practices of the Gafsa Phosphate Company, the main regional employer. Security forces in the town of Redeyef responded by using live ammunition to disperse protesters. The Gafsa protests resulted in the arrests and subsequent prison sentences of trade union members. Referring to the 2008 Gafsa protests, a report by the French writer Eric Gobe states that resistance took the forms of:

> ... the classic hunger strike, demonstrations or sit-ins at various public locations. They also organized long-lasting sit-ins by setting up tents at certain strategic sites, in order to stop, or at least slow down, the economic activity in the phosphate extraction areas. Camps were set up in front of the iron-ore washing plants, or along railway tracks, in order to stop the trains carrying the phosphate; at the same time, some high-school students and young unemployed men set out to tear apart hundreds of meters of railway tracks linking M'dhila to Moularès [two towns located in the Gafsa mining region].[12]

The report continues:

> Within Tunisia's authoritarian context, this Revolt of the Mining Basin has shown that significant segments of the Tunisian population were able to voice their protest; at the same time, however, the protest movement, due to the limited support it enjoyed within Tunisian society, was unable to grow, nor was it able to withstand the coercive policy of Ben Ali's regime.

The Tunisian government and its economic partners cited the economic and social developments in the country as justification for repressive policies.[13] Until the events of December 2010 and January 2011, it was thought that the majority of Tunisians accepted restricted political rights and Ben Ali's authoritarian leadership in return for relative stability, and slow but steady economic growth. The administration counted on this acquiescence to contain calls for greater social and political freedom.[14]

SELF-IMMOLATION AND PROTEST

The 2010 protests began with the desperate action of a single man, followed by protests that began small, and grew to draw in tens of thousands of people, eventually culminating in the ouster of President Ben Ali.

In the impoverished central Tunisian town of Sidi Bouzid on December 17, 2010, Mohammed Bouazizi, a twenty-six-year-old street vendor and university graduate, set himself on fire. Bouazizi, who did not have a permit to sell produce out of a small cart that was the sole source of income for him and his family, had his goods confiscated by local officials. After they refused to hear his complaint, Bouazizi doused himself with gasoline and committed self-immolation in an act of protest over unemployment and corruption.

The protests in Sidi Bouzid began with the street vendor's relatives and friends, who gathered outside of the governor's office the day of the self-immolation. Throwing coins at the gate, they yelled "Here is your bribe."[15] Over the next two days, the small group was joined by hundreds of unemployed youth. They were met by lines of police.

The protest turned destructive at times, with protesters smashing shop windows and damaging cars. Police responded with tear gas and beatings.

Within days, in response to the growing protests, and in an effort to contain the unrest, the authorities sealed off Sidi Bouzid. However, news of the self-immolation and the unrest that it sparked, as well as the accompanying police brutality, was spread on the internet by people who posted videos and news on their Facebook pages. A journalist from the news channel Al Jazeera saw one person's posts and began reporting on the story, carrying information on the growing protests to its viewers. Al Jazeera is based in Qatar and has a large Middle Eastern–based audience.[16]

STRENGTHENING PROTESTS AND GOVERNMENT RESPONSE

Sidi Bouzid, where the protests began, is viewed as the epicenter and spiritual home of the protests. The revolution began in the poor and neglected areas of the country. The degree of spontaneity was such that, initially, the country's main opposition parties, the Democratic Progressive Party, the Renewal Movement, and the Democratic Forum for Labor and Liberties, as well as the exiled Renaissance (*Nahda*) Party, were reported to have no significant role in planning or leading the events.

As the demonstrations spread to other towns throughout the Tunisian interior, away from the capital and Tunisia's tourist areas, they began to gain strength. They were very quickly endorsed by opposition groups and labor unions. This endorsement helped the protests to spread to all regions, and eventually to the capital, Tunis.

Labor leaders reported that their members quickly joined the demonstrations, along with students, teachers, lawyers, journalists, human rights activists, trade unionists, and opposition politicians.

Protesters were met with increasingly brutal police action. Two men were shot and later died of their wounds.[17]

During the earlier wave of strikes and demonstrations in the city of Gafsa in southwest Tunisia in 2008, the government had responded quickly with extreme repression in an attempt to prevent the protests from spreading throughout the country. This included killing protesters and strikers and arresting journalists. In the 2010–2011 events, by contrast, government repression strengthened the protests. The violent response of the authorities—which included police opening fire on protesters— further exacerbated anger and set off additional demonstrations.

The population was youthful. In 2005, 21 percent of Tunisians were between the ages of fifteen and twenty-four. High rates of unemployment and poverty fueled the protest. Protesters demanded jobs and better living conditions. They were joined by human rights organizations, journalists, lawyers, and opposition parties, who protested against the brutality of the government's response and its restrictions on press freedoms. Economic and political grievances became linked, drawing in the support of a range of civil society organizations. This resulted in the mobilization of large numbers of people, transcending class and region. One opposition activist, Fares Mabrouk, said:

> People are asking for recovering their dignity. And the interesting part is that in all the slogans we hear in Tunis until today, notice there is no slogan related to religion, there is no slogan related to specific parties or a specific political party or movements. The slogans are all about dignity—the dignity to speak, to express ourselves, and to decide—contribute in the decision on our future.[18]

On December 20, in a move designed to contain the protests, development minister Mohamed Al Nouri Al Juwayni traveled to Sidi Bouzid to announce a new $10 million employment program. However, the move did not come soon enough.[19] Protests continued to spread. Slogans remained secular, and religion did not play any significant role.

On December 22, a protester committed suicide during a demonstration in Sidi Bouzid, throwing himself onto high-voltage cables. On December 24, one protester was shot and killed and one injured by police during demonstrations in the central town of Menzel Bouzaiene. Also on December 24, hundreds of demonstrators, protesting unemployment, gathered in front of the Tunisian labor union headquarters demanding jobs and expressing solidarity with protesters in Sidi Bouzid. Tunisian security forces clashed with protesters in the central towns of al-Ragab and Miknassi. Security forces conducted overnight raids, with large-scale arrests.

On December 25 and 26, large demonstrations were reported in the interior towns of Kairouan, Sfax, Ben Guerdane, and Menzel Bouzaiene. In Menzel Bouzaiene, near Sidi Bouzid, one person was killed and others injured when members of Tunisia's National Guard opened fire on protesters.

On December 25, the protests reached Tunis. A demonstration was held in solidarity with those protesting in Sidi Bouzid. An Interior Ministry spokesperson was quoted by the state-run news agency

TAP that police were driven to use their weapons in order to protect themselves after non-lethal means failed to disperse protesters who were setting police cars and buildings on fire.

A second demonstration in Tunis took place on December 27, in a show of solidarity with those protesting in Sidi Bouzid and poorer regions. It was larger than the protest of December 25. Eyewitnesses reported that security forces outnumbered protesters, who sang the Tunisian national anthem and shouted slogans demanding the right to dignity and employment, freedom of the press, and freedom to protest. Armed with truncheons and clubs, police prevented the protesters from marching. Four people were reportedly severely injured, but were not permitted to be taken to the hospital. The interior minister was reported to have been personally present at the scene of the clashes, which reportedly lasted for at least two hours.

On December 28, Ben Ali appeared on national television and declared that the protests were unacceptable and warned of their negative economic impact. Ben Ali criticized the use of violence in the streets by what he called "a minority of extremists and agitators in the pay of others":

> This is a negative and anti-civil behavior that presents a distorted image of our country and impedes the flow of investors and tourists, which impacts negatively on job creation, while we need them to curb joblessness. Law will be enforced rigorously against these people.[20]

Also on December 28, the newspapers of two opposition parties, *Tareeq al-jadid* and *al-Mawqif*, were banned, and their distribution was blocked because of their coverage of the unrest. On the same day, a rally organized by the Tunisian Federation of Labor Unions in Gafsa province in southern Tunisia's mining region was dispersed by security forces.

Meanwhile, in Tunis, about three hundred lawyers gathered in front of the Court of First Instance. They shouted slogans expressing their support for protesters in Sidi Bouzid, and against the ruling party, the ruling family, and the Ministry of the Interior. They also sang the national anthem. The lawyers gave speeches about the unrest in poorer regions, and demonstrators joined in with their own stories. The event attracted a heavy presence by security forces. Lawyers marched in several other cities as well.[21]

In efforts to respond to the crises, on December 28 the governors of Sidi Bouzid, Jendouba, and Zaghouan provinces, as well as the ministers of communication, trade and handicrafts, and religious affairs, were dismissed as a response to the uprising, although no official reason was given.

Demonstrations on December 29, in the coastal town of Monastir and in Sbikha, west of Monastir, were broken up by security forces, with reports of continued police brutality. After twelve days of protests, Nessma TV, a private news channel, began to cover the unrest, becoming the first major domestic news outlet to do so.

On December 31, lawyers, wearing red badges, gathered in central Tunis. Others assembled in the capital's suburbs, the town of Monastir, and elsewhere in the country, to demand the release of lawyers arrested in earlier demonstrations, and in solidarity with those protesting in Sidi Bouzid. The protesters were met with violence. The Tunisian Human Rights League (LTDH) reported that lawyers across Tunisia were severely beaten, with the most severe repression in the capital. The police also reportedly confiscated cell phones to prevent people from filming the protest and the brutal response of the security forces.[22]

On January 3, 250 protesters, mainly students, marched in the central Tunisian city of Thala. Police responded with tear gas, injuring nine protesters. Protesters set fire to tires and attacked the local office of the ruling party.

Also on January 3, "hacktivists" from a group calling itself Anonymous attacked at least eight official Tunisian websites, including those belonging to the government and the stock exchange. A press release released by the group stated that "ANONYMOUS has heard the cries for freedom from the Tunisian people and has decided to help them win this battle against oppression."[23]

Mohamed Bouazizi, who survived his self-immolation for two and a half weeks, died on January 4. His funeral was held in Sidi Abouzid, and five thousand people walked in the procession through Sidi Bouzid to his nearby village. Police prevented the procession from passing the site of Bouazizi's self-immolation.

Protests now spread to cities throughout the country. On January 6, the Tunisian Bar Association held a nationwide strike in protest over attacks by security forces against its members during a march on December 31 in support of the people of Sidi Abouzid. The association said that 95 percent of Tunisia's eight thousand lawyers took part in the strike, demanding an end to police brutality. The lawyers were supported by students, professionals, and young people.

Protests and the accompanying government repression continued. On January 7, in a crackdown on dissent, authorities arrested a group of bloggers, journalists, and activists, as well as a rap singer. The following day, in Tala, a town near the Algerian border, six protesters were killed and six wounded when police shot protesters who set fire to a government building, after police were unable to disperse the crowd using a water canon. Three were killed in the eastern town of Kasserine.

On January 9, two protesters were shot dead in Miknassi in southern Tunisia. Protests continued in Kasserine and Thala, in western Tunisia, and in the central-western town of Regueb. On January 10, funerals of victims of the previous days' violence resulted in clashes between police and mourners.

In a bid to calm the protests, Ben Ali offered unprecedented concessions. It was announced that he had fired his interior minister, Rafik Belhaj Kacem. Addressing the protesters' anger against high unemployment, Ben Ali promised to create three hundred thousand jobs between 2011 and 2012, and vowed not to run for reelection in 2014.[24]

On January 12, a nighttime curfew was imposed on Tunis and the surrounding suburbs from 8 p.m. until 6 a.m. Protests continued in defiance of the curfew.[25]

On January 13, Ben Ali appeared on television once again. In an effort to calm protests, he admitted errors during his rule, pledging to punish those in his government who had misled him. He condemned the use of live ammunition against demonstrators. He also promised to lower food prices and allow greater press freedom, ordered the release of political prisoners, and announced the creation of a commission to investigate corruption. Addressing the population in local Tunisian dialect for the first time, rather than standard Arabic, he stated that significant changes were needed: "Yes, I have understood you. I have understood all of you: the unemployed, the needy, the politician and those asking for more freedoms."[26]

Despite the concessions offered by Ben Ali, the unrest continued. Members of his family were reported to be fleeing the country.

The government continued its efforts to crack down on use of the internet, and specifically on social networking platforms like Facebook and Twitter that were used to call for continued protests. Participation in the protests was bolstered by these informal online networks, as well as by mobile phones. In addition to drawing in masses of unemployed youth demanding jobs and protesting government corruption, these tools assisted people in circulating reports on the protests and speeches—and in documenting police abuse and the brutality of security forces in dispersing demonstrators. In at least two cases, Twitter was used to identify locations of police snipers who were shooting protesters.

On January 12, an unprecedented number of protesters demonstrated in Tunis. Expressing solidarity with those protesting in poorer areas, they demanded the ouster of Ben Ali.

On January 13, ignoring the dusk-to-dawn curfew, hundreds of Ben Ali loyalists chanted their support for him in Tunis. About a dozen people were reportedly killed in Tunis and surrounding towns in overnight clashes. The same day, French prime minister François Fillon accused Ben Ali of using disproportionate violence against the protesters.[27]

LAST EFFORTS BY BEN ALI

On January 14, a mass demonstration of ten thousand to fifteen thousand people was held in Tunis in front of the Interior Ministry. Police clashed with protesters and used batons and tear gas to disperse them. A chaotic scene followed. Armored military vehicles were sent to the scene of the clashes. State media reported that gatherings of more than three people were banned and that security forces were authorized to use violence against violators.[28]

Ben Ali declared a state of emergency and fired the country's government. He promised fresh legislative elections within six months, and pledged to introduce more freedoms, enact widespread reforms, and investigate the killings of protesters. Formerly blocked or banned websites became accessible. That night, reports surfaced that the army had taken control of Tunisia's main airport and closed the country's airspace.[29]

Later that same day, and after a month of confrontations in which dozens of protesters were killed, Ben Ali fled the country. The following day, Saudi Arabia's state news agency announced that Ben Ali and his family had arrived in Saudi Arabia and would be given sanctuary by the Saudi government. As word of Ben Ali's departure began to spread, chanting was heard from rooftops in Tunis.[30]

It was later reported that General Rachid Ammar, head of the Tunisian military, had refused to fire on protesters, which was a factor that led to Ben Ali's departure. Al-Arabiya, the Arabic news channel, also reported that the president was forced to flee after he was told by the head of his security detail that the presidential palace was about to be stormed by hostile protesters.[31]

Prime Minister Mohammad Ghannouchi, whose government had been fired by Ben Ali only hours earlier, later appeared on state television. He announced that he would be assuming the role of interim president under Chapter 56 of the Tunisian constitution. He also said that the speaker of parliament would preside over a government council. He vowed to abide by the constitution in laying the groundwork for a vote to choose a new government as soon as possible. He promised to consult with all political factions and social groups. Giving no explanation for Ben Ali's removal, Ghannouchi stated that "since the President is temporarily without the capacity to carry out his duties, it has been decided that the prime minister would exercise his functions. I call on Tunisians of all political and regional tendencies to show patriotism and unity."[32]

Ghannouchi's action actually violated the Tunisian constitution, which provides for a succession by the head of parliament, a provision that Ghannouchi sidestepped by describing Ben Ali as "temporarily" unable to serve. That same day, Tunisian Facebook pages previously inscribed with the uprising's slogan, "Ben Ali Out," had been changed to "Ghannouchi Out" to show the name of the interim president.[33]

Within twenty-four hours, Tunisia's Constitutional Council, the country's highest constitutional body, ruled that the rightful interim president was Fouad Mebazaa, the speaker of the parliament.

AFTER BEN ALI

In the days following Ben Ali's departure, looting was reported in Tunis. The military stepped in to control the looting, and to protect civilians from members of Ben Ali's security forces. Various members of Ben Ali's family and Tunisia's former interior minister Rafik Belhaj, seen as responsible for the government's heavy-handed response to the protests, were arrested.

In efforts to prevent further protests, Ghannouchi promised to announce a new coalition government. He announced widespread reforms and promised press freedom. He also pledged to lift the ban on human rights groups working in Tunisia and to release political prisoners.[34]

Many Tunisians, along with exiled opposition leaders, were dissatisfied with the new government, which included members of the old guard in key positions. These included the defense, interior, and foreign ministers. In the days following the announcement of the new "unity" government, protests continued.[35]

Soon after, the minister of training and employment, the minister of prime ministerial affairs, and the newly appointed health minister, along with the junior minister for transportation, resigned in protest over the composition of the new government, saying it heavily favored members of the former ruling party. Other opposition ministers also threatened to resign. The ministers aligned themselves with the protesters who insisted that real democratic change was not possible while so many old-guard politicians continued to hold powerful cabinet posts, despite having renounced their affiliation with the Constitutional Democratic Rally (RCD, the former ruling party).[36]

Demonstrators, including the group's supporters, held a protest in central Tunis, calling for a general strike, constitutional changes, and the release of all imprisoned union leaders. Protests were held in at least seven cities and police responded with tear gas. Supporters of the once-banned Ennahdha Islamist party joined the protest, along with UGTT (the main trade union) members, calling for the RCD to be dissolved. The union, which has half a million members, had an earlier history of political dissent, but more recently had been co-opted by the Ben Ali regime. When the protests in Sidi Bouzid and surrounding towns initially broke out, the union officially simply watched the protests. However, the union quickly broke free of its government ties and its members joined protesters. The union first demanded economic development and Ben Ali's resignation. Later, it called for the dissolution of the former ruling party, becoming the most powerful organization to do so.[37]

In attempts to calm the demonstrators and opposition groups, and distance themselves from Ben Ali, Prime Minister Ghannouchi and Interim President Mebazaa resigned from the RCD, the former ruling party.

On January 18, the opposition leader Moncef Marzouki, of the formerly banned Congress for the Republic Party (CPR), returned to the country after two decades in exile. He urged Tunisians to continue their struggle to prevent the RCD from continuing to dominate Tunisian government positions. "Don't let anyone steal this blessed revolution from you," Marzouki said.[38]

In an interview with French radio, Ghannouchi said that Tunisia has now begun "an era of liberty," and continued, "give us a chance so that we can put in place this ambitious program of reform." He defended the Tunisian cabinet, and stated that ministers with experience were needed during the transition, in advance of elections.

Ghannouchi pledged to free political prisoners and allow greater freedoms, including removing restrictions on the Tunisian League for the Defense of Human Rights. He also announced that the government would establish commissions to study political reform, investigate corruption, and examine human rights abuses during the recent unrest.[39]

January 21 was the first day of a three-day period of national mourning for the dozens of people who were killed during the protests and clashes with security forces, who had used tear gas and live ammunition to disperse crowds. The United Nations High Commissioner for Human Rights estimated that about a hundred people had died in the weeks since the protests began in Tunisia.[40] Protesters gathered in Tunis, demanding the dissolution of the new government or the removal of RCD members from cabinet positions. Responding to these calls, Ghannouchi attempted to calm critics. He announced that he intended to quit after legislative and presidential elections were held.

In the following days, protests in Tunis continued, drawing thousands of people, along with about two thousand police officers who demanded improved working conditions and the establishment of a new police union. Police also demonstrated, declaring that they were not to blame for the deaths that occurred during the protests, but that they were also victims.

Meanwhile, a teachers' union called a strike on January 24, in which an estimated 90 percent of schoolteachers participated. They had defied government measures to return to normalcy by reopening schools after they had been ordered closed by Ben Ali.[41]

Also on January 24, General Rachid Ammar, in his first public appearance since Ben Ali's departure, spoke to more than a thousand protesters. "Our revolution is your revolution," he said, and "the army will protect the revolution." Tunisian media acclaimed General Ammar as a national savior, and the military as largely responsible for maintaining security and preserving the interim government.

On January 20 the Tunisian government recognized formerly banned political parties and extended amnesty to all political prisoners. On January 30, Rachid al-Ghannouchi (no relation to the prime minister), opposition leader of the formerly banned Islamist al-Nahda (Renaissance) party, returned to the country.

The struggle in Tunisia continued for some time, as did concerns about the new interim government. Some protested its closure of a popular privately owned television network on January 23, calling it a violation of the government's promises for greater freedom of expression.

In defiance of a nighttime curfew, hundreds of Tunisians from rural areas set off for the capital on January 22 to join ongoing protests.

They demanded the removal of politicians tied to the former regime. The protesters also aimed to safeguard the objectives of their protests in what they called "the Freedom Caravan." They gathered at the prime minister's office, where they vowed to remain until their demands were met.

On January 26, Tunisia's interim justice minister announced that the new government was seeking the arrest of Ben Ali and his family to face trial for theft and currency offenses. The next day, Kamel Morjane, foreign minister in the earlier government, announced his resignation.

Tunisian police stormed a protest camp on January 28 to disperse demonstrators taking part in a five-day sit-in in front of the prime minister's office, demanding the resignation of the interim government.

A SPREADING PHENOMENON?

The Tunisian uprising sparked a debate among people throughout the world about whether it could prove to be a model to bring about democratic change. Could it provide political means for people with similar grievances to challenge regimes in other countries in the region?

Many people pointed to the fact that the revolution in Tunisia was conducted without help from outside powers, including the distrusted United States. In contrast, the U.S. claimed to deliver democracy to people in Iraq and Afghanistan through military means. Experts say that two factors contributed to the movement's success: a sustained leaderless movement and sustained nonviolent discipline. It was also extremely significant that young people were not the only ones participating in the protests. Civil society groups, which had been thought to be either co-opted by the regime or too afraid to act, joined the youth and took up the cause. The linking of economic issues with demands for human rights and greater democratic freedoms has also been identified as an important factor that helped to mobilize demographically diverse individuals and groups to struggle for a common objective: ouster of the dictator.

In the weeks following the Tunisian events, protests erupted in Egypt, and smaller protests took place in Jordan, Yemen, and neighboring Algeria.

There were seven self-immolations in Algeria alone between January 12 and January 19, and others in Egypt and Mauritania.

Regimes across the Arab world, and beyond, are playing close attention to the events in Tunisia and Egypt. In China, authorities who fear the spread of mass protests and other resistance activity have limited coverage of the events in North Africa and censored references to the protests taking place there.

As the struggles continue, many wonder at their eventual outcome. What is clear is that the Tunisian people, and people in neighboring countries and beyond, have learned the power of the technique of nonviolent action. That new awareness will hold massive significance and relevance for those struggling against oppression and injustice, and for the way in which those conflicts are waged.

NOTES TO CASE STUDY: THE TUNISIAN UPRISING AND PROTESTS, DECEMBER 2010–JANUARY 2011

1. Roula Khalaf and Scheherazade Daneshkhu, "France Regrets Misjudgment over Ben Ali," *Financial Times*, January 18, 2011.

2. "Tunisian–American Cooperation," Embassy of the United States, Tunis, Tunisia. http://tunisia.usembassy.gov/ustunisianrelations.html.

3. "Tunisia's Economic Performance Hides Dire Human Rights Situation," Amnesty International, June 18, 2009.

4. "Tunisia's Economic Performance."

5. Scott Shane, "Cables from American Diplomats Portray U.S. Ambivalence on Tunisia," *New York Times*, January 15, 2011.

6. Lina Ben Mhenni, "Tunisia: Censorship Continues as Wikileaks Cables Make the Rounds," Global Voices, December 7, 2010. http://globalvoicesonline.org/2010/12/07/tunisia-censorship-continues-as-wikileaks-cables-make-the-rounds/.

7. Elizabeth Dickinson, "The First WikiLeaks Revolution," *Foreign Policy*, January 13, 2011.

8. Sherif Khalifa, "The Tunisian Syndrome," *Foreign Policy Journal*, January 21, 2011.

9. Kareem Fahim, "Slap to a Man's Pride Set Off Tumult in Tunisia," *New York Times*, January 21, 2011.

10. "Tunisian Government Should Respect Human Rights," United Nations High Commissioner for Refugees, December 30, 2010.

11. "Tunisia: Elections in an Atmosphere of Repression," *Human Rights Watch*, October 23, 2009.

12. Eric Gobe, "The Gafsa Mining Basin between Riots and a Social Movement: Meaning and Significance of a Protest Movement in Ben Ali's Tunisia," *Sciences de l'Homme et de la Société*, Version 1, January 20, 2011.

13. "Behind Tunisia's 'Economic Miracle': Inequality and Criminalization of Protest," Amnesty International, June 2009.

14. "Q&A: Tunisia Crises," BBC, January 19, 2011. http://www.bbc.co.uk/news/world-africa-12157599.

15. Fahim, "Slap to a Man's Pride."

16. Fahim, "Slap to a Man's Pride."

17. Fahim, "Slap to a Man's Pride."

18. Fares Mabrouk, interview with *Democracy Now*, January 18, 2011.

19. Bilal Randeree, "Protests Continue in Tunisia," Al Jazeera English, January 4, 2010. http://english.aljazeera.net/news/africa/2011/01/201114101752467578.html.

20. President Ben Ali's address to the Tunisian people, December 28, 2010.

21. Lina Ben Mhenni, "Tunisia: Lawyers Assaulted for Their Sidi Bouzid Stand," Global Voices, January 1, 2011. http://globalvoicesonline.org/2011/01/01/tunisia-lawyers-assaulted/.

22. Yasmine Ryan, "Another Tunisian Protester Dies," Al Jazeera English, December 31, 2010. http://english.aljazeera.net/news/africa/2010/12/201012317536678834.html.

23. "An Open Letter to the Government of Tunisia," anonymous press release, January 3, 2011. http://www.anonnews.org/index.php?p=press&a=item&i=133on.

24. Vivienne Walt, "Tension Grips Tunisia's Capital after Leader Flees," *Time*, January 14, 2011.

25. Walt, "Tension Grips Tunisia's Capital."

26. Borzou Daragahi and Sihem Hassaini, "Tunisia President Appeals for Peace, Pledges Reform," *Los Angeles Times*, January 13, 2011.

27. Edward Cody and Joby Warrick, "Unrest Continues in Tunisia as President Ben Ali Flees Country," *Washington Post*, January 15, 2011.

28. David D. Kirkpatrick, "Tunisia Leader Flees and Prime Minister Claims Power," *New York Times*, January 14, 2011.

29. "Emergency Rule Imposed in Tunisia," Al Jazeera English, January 14, 2011. http://english.aljazeera.net/news/africa/2011/01/201111410345507518.html.

30. Ryan Rifai, "Timeline: Tunisia's Uprising," Al Jazeera English, January 23, 2011. http://english.aljazeera.net/indepth/spotlight/tunisia/2011/01/2011141142223827361.html.

31. Alan Cowell, "Rule No. 1 for Dictators: Don't Blink," *New York Times*, January 21, 2011.

32. Cody and Warrick, "Unrest Continues."

33. Kirkpatrick, "Tunisia Leader Flees."

34. "Tunisia PM to Unveil New Government," Al Jazeera English, January 17, 2011. http://english.aljazeera.net/news/africa/2011/01/2011116191514949896.html.

35. Rifai, "Timeline."

36. "Tunisia's New Government in Trouble," Al Jazeera English, January 18, 2011. http://english.aljazeera.net/news/africa/2011/01/2011118194731826312.html.

37. David D. Kirkpatrick, "Protesters Say Ruling Party in Tunisia Must Dissolve," *New York Times*, January 21, 2011.

38. "Tunisian Minister and Ex-dissident Defends Cabinet," BBC News, January 19, 2011. http://www.bbc.co.uk/news/world-africa-12223043.

39. "Three Ministers Quit New Tunisia Government," Associated Press, January 18, 2011.

40. Mark Leon Goldberg, "UN Rights Chief Says at Least 100 People Killed in Tunisia Violence," January 19, 2011. http://www.undispatch.com/un-rights-chief-says-at-least-100-people-killed-in-tunisia-violence.

41. Margaret Coker, "New Strikes Add to the Unrest in Tunisia," *Wall Street Journal*, January 25, 2011.

Lina Ben Mhenni's blog (http://atunisiangirl.blogspot.com) was useful in helping to confirm and supplement information reported by other media sources. Her courage and wisdom in helping to document the events of December 2010 and January 2011 have provided an important service to the historical record of this case account. We are also grateful for corrections and comments by Walid Ben Aissa.

THE DICTIONARY

★

ABSOLUTISM. The doctrine or form of *government in which the *rulers claim unlimited *authority, or in which the actual authority and the effective power of the rulers are extremely wide and are not limited by strong legal or *de facto constraints. The concept of absolutism is historically associated with those European monarchs who claimed the right to rule without any legal or political limitations. Absolutism is present in several forms of *dictatorship and may be contrasted with democratic governance.

See also AUTOCRACY, DESPOTISM, TOTALITARIANISM, and TYRANNY.

ACCOMMODATION (associated with nonviolent action). A *mechanism of change in a conflict using *nonviolent action in which the *opponents resolve, while they still have a choice, to grant at least certain demands of the *nonviolent actionists, although they have not changed their views nor been nonviolently coerced.

Accommodation may result from influences which, if continued, might have led to the opponents' *conversion or *nonviolent coercion or a mixture of both.

ACCOMPANIMENT. The practice, in times of great danger to advocates of *social change and *civil liberties, of individuals from another *country publicly and nonviolently accompanying the endangered advocate. The aim is to increase the likelihood of publicity if *violence is used, and so to deter such violence. Foreigners are also likely to have greater immunity from *attack and are thus able to confer some protection.

Accompaniment has been used in a variety of countries with repressive *regimes, and is usually linked to building an extensive network of wider *resistance or diplomatic contacts. While not an absolute guarantee of safety, the practice has usually protected the endangered persons without the accompaniers themselves suffering violence.

ACTIONIST (associated with nonviolent action). Short for ""*nonviolent actionist," one who is participating in an application of the *technique of *nonviolent action.

See also ACTIVIST.

ACTIVE DEFENSE. An *offensive use of available *civilian-based defense *forces against *opponents who have attacked.

ACTIVE RECONCILIATION. A type of "this-worldly" oriented *principled nonviolence or *pacifism whose adherents favor an attitude of positive goodwill to all, personal *reconciliation with *opponents, and improvement of their own lives. These believers emphasize the potential of transforming their opponents and the positive actions they will use, rather than the *violent actions they will not use.

*Coercion, even by *nonviolent means, is deprecated, and even contention may be discouraged. Active reconcilers may support *nonviolent action, although they generally prefer milder means.

Active reconciliation is not to be confused with the *technique of nonviolent action.

See also NONRESISTANCE.

ACTIVIST. A person who diligently and repeatedly tries to achieve some social, economic, or political objective, especially by participation in *protest, pressure, organizing, or *resistance.

See also ACTIONIST.

ADMINISTRATIVE SYSTEM. See OVERLOADING OF ADMINISTRATIVE SYSTEMS.

ADVANCE. See STRATEGIC ADVANCE and TACTICAL ADVANCE.

ADVERSARY. A group of *opponents in a *conflict.

ADVOCATE. One who espouses a cause in a *conflict.

AFFINITY GROUP (associated with nonviolent action). A small group of protesters or resisters, possibly formed in advance, who foster personal links and stay physically close during a larger *demonstration to provide each other with support and solidarity to strengthen and maintain their morale, discipline, and reliability during the action and the aftermath.

AGENT. A person who acts on behalf of another person, group, or institution, especially a political or governmental body.

AGENT PROVOCATEUR (associated with nonviolent action). A person who deliberately encourages, stimulates, or commits *violent acts during a *nonviolent struggle or other peaceful *opposition activities. The aim is to give the movement a violent image in an attempt to alienate public support, to justify *repression, or to induce the movement to shift fully to violent means (which may precede its demise).

Usually agents provocateurs are in the employ of the *political police. They may also act on behalf of political groups opposed to the nonviolent struggle movement. More rarely, they may also be lone individuals aiming to undercut the action movement for personal or political motives.

At other times, persons or groups may sincerely intend their *violence to advance the cause of the *actionists, but in fact produce similar results to actions of hostile agents provocateurs.

See also COLLABORATION, INFILTRATION, and NONVIOLENT DISCIPLINE.

AGGRESSION. 1. An *attack initiated by *military *forces of one *State on the territory, population, or military forces of another *country.

2. An attack by an individual or group on the persons or material possessions of other individuals or groups. Aggression as a special type of action should be distinguished from psychological disposition toward *hostility and *aggressiveness.

AGGRESSIVE. Characterized by verbal and other symbolic expressions of *hostility, or by acts of *aggression, or by both.

AGGRESSIVENESS. An underlying tendency, drive, or disposition to engage in contention, *conflict, and acts of *aggression on others. This underlying factor or condition may be expressed in mild acts of self-assertion as well as displays of pugnacity. Not to be equated with *violence.

AGITATION. An attempt to change or intensify people's opinions concerning existing social, economic, or political practices, or to stir people to action in an effort to change or support those practices.
　　Hence, "agitator" and "agitate."

AGRICULTURAL STRIKE. See FARM WORKERS' STRIKE and PEASANT STRIKE.

AHIMSA. A Hindi term roughly translated as "nonviolence," referring to noninjury in thought, word, and deed to all forms of life.

AIR RAIDS. See NONVIOLENT AIR RAIDS.

ALIENATION. 1. A psychological condition of perceived estrangement or separation of individuals from *society and its institutions.
　　2. The separation between a person and a part of that person's life, especially a part under the control of others.
　　Socially and politically, alienation is associated with a sense of hopelessness and *powerlessness to influence the course of society and *government policy, and even to control the individual's own life. This may produce personal isolation, inaction, and submissive *conformity to the established order, accompanied by distrust of the

political system and cynicism concerning possible remedies. However, if new factors that are seen as grounds for hope are introduced, alienation may be the prelude to *dissident, messianism, *protest, or revolutionary *social movements.

ALLEGIANCE. Emotional attachment, feelings of loyalty, or legal ties of individuals to a group, institution, movement, *nation, *rulers, or *government and its symbols.

Such bonds are usually associated with *obedience and assistance of individuals and groups to the larger unit. In return for that allegiance rulers may be seen to owe the individuals protection or other service. Allegiance may be perceived as either unlimited or limited, unconditional or conditional, and as permanent or subject to restriction, severance, or transfer. The presence, strength, or absence of allegiance is of great importance to rulers.

See also WITHHOLDING OR WITHDRAWAL OF ALLEGIANCE.

ALLIANCE (associated with civilian-based defense). The joining together of groups, institutions, or *governments for joint action to accomplish some constructive task or for action against a commonly perceived threat. The joint action may involve constructive activities, *military assistance, or aid for *civilian-based defense in the face of *aggression.

See also CIVILIAN-BASED DEFENSE MUTUAL ASSISTANCE PACT and CIVILIAN-BASED DEFENSE TREATY ORGANIZATION.

ALTERNATE DAYS STRIKE. See LIMITED STRIKE.

ALTERNATIVE COMMUNICATION SYSTEM (associated with nonviolent action). A substitute system for public or private communication developed by *opposition groups on a sufficient scale to challenge or bypass the established media and communication systems controlled and perhaps censored by the *opponent *government.

An alternative communication system may include alternative or underground newspapers, radio, television, mobile phones, blogs, websites, or other electronic communications. These communications may be used to spread news throughout the *society or internationally.

These systems may also be used for communications within a *resistance movement, as in spreading information, mobilizing participation in specific actions, and promoting morale.

On a large scale the alternative means can develop into a rival system to politically controlled systems, and thereby constitute a social form of *nonviolent intervention. Alternative means of communication that are not on a scale sufficient to challenge the established system may constitute several *methods of *nonviolent protest and persuasion.

ALTERNATIVE ECONOMIC INSTITUTION (associated with nonviolent action). An economic institution that challenges the established ones and wields power in a *conflict situation. It is a *method of *nonviolent intervention.

Consumers' or producers' cooperatives, for example, would only be such a method when challenging capitalist or *State industries, or when being developed to replace them.

The new institutions may be concerned with production, ownership, or distribution of goods, and may have social and political aims as well as direct economic objectives.

ALTERNATIVE MARKET (associated with civilian-based defense). Substitute channels of buying and selling food and other supplies during *wartime, occupation, or times of *oppression to help meet needs of the populace, to keep goods out of the opponents' hands, or to prevent the *government from establishing complete control over economic life.

In contrast to "black markets" in such crises, which are associated with exploitative prices, alternative markets constitute an economic *method of *nonviolent intervention when their aim is instead political or national.

ALTERNATIVE POLITICAL INSTITUTION (associated with nonviolent action). An organization that conducts certain particular governmental affairs that is not a part of the established and recognized *government. This may develop during the course of a major *nonviolent struggle.

Several such institutions may develop to meet specific needs or to support *resistance measures, and operate concurrently. In a widespread *conflict in which a major issue is the existence of the established *government itself, the newly developed political institution may become so encompassing that it replaces the previous established government. This development may be intended or it may simply happen during the course of the conflict.

See also DUAL SOVEREIGNTY AND PARALLEL GOVERNMENT, GOVERNMENT, and POLITICS.

ALTERNATIVE SOCIAL INSTITUTION (associated with nonviolent action). A new or expanded social institution, frequently an educational or cultural one, that partially or fully replaces an established institution, especially one that is controlled by the *opponents.

Such new institutions may be created to implement the *actionists' principles or program, or launched to increase the effectiveness of other *nonviolent *methods.

A *method of *nonviolent intervention.

ALTERNATIVE TRANSPORTATION SYSTEM (associated with nonviolent action). A substitute transportation system developed during a *conflict to operate temporarily during a *boycott *campaign against the *opponents' system, or to provide an alternative to the opposed established system. This is distinct from regular commercial competition.

A *method of *nonviolent intervention.

ALTRUISM. The concern of individuals, as expressed in action, to give a higher priority to meeting the needs of other persons than to meeting their personal needs. Altruism may be a characteristic of believers in a type of *principled nonviolence.

AMBUSH. In *military conflict an ambush is a planned surprise *attack carried out by forces that have been in hiding.

See also POLITICAL AMBUSH.

AMNESTY. An end by the *State of *punishment or threat of punishment for past illegal behavior. An amnesty may include, for example, release of *political prisoners. Amnesty is sometimes applied as a gesture of political reconciliation, especially during or following a transfer of *control of the *government.

ANARCHISM. A school of political views that repudiates the *State (but not all forms of political organization) as a political institution. Anarchists envision self-organized social and political units to provide for human needs and wants.

The State is blamed for causing *war and *oppression. Its abolition, it is argued, would allow the "inherent goodness" of people to develop without impediment.

Anarchists differ widely on means. Some see a long social evolution as inevitable, while others endorse immediate *direct action. Some favor *violence and others *nonviolent means.

See also SYNDICALISM.

ANARCHY. 1. The Stateless condition of free cooperative institutions toward which anarchists aim.

2. Used disparagingly, utter social chaos, political disorder, and lawlessness.

ANTI-AUTHORITARIAN. Opposed to *authoritarians, either in the sense of strong anti-State views, or, more often, simply being committed to maximum *freedom and minimum regimentation.

ANTI-COUP DEFENSE POLICY (associated with civilian-based defense). A *policy to resist any attempted *coup d'état by planned *noncooperation and *defiance to make it impossible for any usurping group to consolidate or establish *control of the *State and rule the society.

Such a policy may be initiated and organized by the *government or by non-State institutions.

ANTI-MILITARIST. Opposed to *militarism and *military institutions. The term has been especially associated with *social movements and beliefs that have advocated *resistance to military measures, institutions, and activities in order to end *war.

ANTIPATHY. See SOCIAL DISTANCE.

ARBITRARY RULE. Unrestrained governance without fixed limits, rules, procedures, or institutional division of powers, subject only to the discretion of the *ruler.

See also AUTOCRACY, DICTATORSHIP, and TYRANNY.

ARBITRATION. The process by which a person or body not a protagonist in a *conflict settles a dispute by evaluating the claims of the conflicting parties and determining a settlement.

The arbitrator usually is mutually accepted by the conflicting parties, and the proposed settlement may or may not be legally binding. However, compulsory arbitration may be established by law, with set procedures and binding decisions. This may be applied even without advance agreement either to arbitration or to the particular arbitrator.

ARMAMENTS. All resources (i.e., "*weapons") that can be used to wage a struggle or *war against hostile *opponents, whether in a *military war or a *nonviolent struggle.

ARMED FORCES (associated with civilian-based defense). The trained and prepared *defense organizations of a society. These are usually *military forces, but may also be those special *resistance organizations and regular institutions capable of waging *noncooperation and *defiance. The latter may also be called "*civilian-based defense forces" prepared to lead and apply noncooperation and defiance.

ARMS (reconceptualized term). Any physical *weapon used to inflict harm, or any social, economic, psychological, or political *method of action to pressure *opponents in a *nonviolent struggle.

ARMS CONTROL. Explicit agreements or implicit understandings restricting the development, type, size, deployment, or use of *military *weapons, especially those of mass destruction. Such measures may or may not include inspection and enforcement procedures.

In contrast to *civilian-based defense, arms control presumes continued reliance on the military *technique for national *defense, and depends on achievement of agreements and compliance with them.

See also ARMS LIMITATION, ARMS REDUCTION, DISARMAMENT, and TRANSARMAMENT.

ARMS LIMITATION. An *arms control measure to restrict the quantity, type, or use of particular forms of *military *weapons.

See also ARMS REDUCTION and DISARMAMENT.

ARMS RACE. A mutually competitive and cumulative deliberate increase in the *military capacities of two or more *States.

ARMS REDUCTION. The process of scaling down, but not eliminating, particular types of *military weaponry, usually as the result of *negotiation or implicit understandings.

Refers to most types of agreements usually less precisely classed as *disarmament. A type of *arms control.

ARREST. Seizure and *imprisonment of persons by police action, with or without later judicial trial and sentencing, possibly followed by imprisonment or *civil internment.

The arrested persons may be suspected or known to have participated in *resistance actions, or to be members of *resistance organizations. Arrest may also be used to intimidate persons who may become resisters.

*Actionists may at times even deliberately seek arrest and imprisonment to demonstrate *fearlessness, provoke sympathy, arouse attention, or, if the numbers are sufficiently large, to paralyze the institutions of *repression.

See also CIVIL DISOBEDIENCE and SEEKING IMPRISONMENT.

ASSASSINATION. Murder for political motives of individual *government officials, *guerrilla *leaders, political party leaders, *resistance leaders, or other prominent personages. Such killings may be carried out by government personnel, police, *intelligence organizations, members of *opposition movements, *guerrilla campaigns, death squads, or independent actors.

ASSEMBLY OF PROTEST OR SUPPORT. A public gathering of a group of people to express opposition to, or support for, the *policies or acts of a *government or public figure.

Such assemblies are usually held at a place related in some way to the issue—for example, government offices, courts, or prisons. A *method of *nonviolent protest and persuasion.

See also CAMOUFLAGED MEETING OF PROTEST, DEMONSTRATION, DEMONSTRATIVE FUNERAL, PROTEST MEETING, and TEACH-IN.

ASSETS. See SEIZURE OF ASSETS.

ASYLUM. A place of refuge, especially from political *repression. Asylum is usually sought, and formally granted, in an embassy of a foreign *country or in a foreign country itself. The granting of asylum is usually internationally recognized and hence provides genuine safety in most cases. Asylum is historically associated with *sanctuary, which has now become largely symbolic.

ATOMIZATION. The condition under totalitarian systems in which the population is reduced to a mass of isolated individuals, separated from and fearful of each other. The population is organized only by dictatorially controlled organizations and institutions of the system. As a result of this situation the population is impotent and incapable of independent group action and *resistance against the system.

(A totalitarian "system" refers to the unique combination of governance simultaneously by *both* organs of the *State and organs of the official "true" political Party.)

Atomization is the "ideal" condition from the perspective of totalitarian *leaders, because it inhibits organized, collective opposition. However, a totally atomized *society is hard to achieve, as some units of group identification and organization tend to survive. Atomization itself is subject to rapid destruction if and when the population gains a sense of *solidarity, capacity for joint action, and power.

Among the means utilized to atomize the population are (a) destruction of all independent social groups and institutions (*loci of power), and their replacement by bodies centrally directed by the official single Party; (b) *terror; (c) destruction of public and private channels of communication among the population, and their replacement by centrally directed and regulated communication designed to indoctrinate and *control; (d) the institution of a complex system of *control of the society and individuals by organizational and institutional regulation and manipulation; and (e) inducement in people of a sense of the inevitability and rightness of the direction of the totalitarian movement and its leader(s) on the basis of the sole permitted official *ideology.

Hence, "atomize."

See also CIVIL SOCIETY, INFRASTRUCTURE, NONGOVERNMENTAL ORGANIZATION, and TOTALITARIANISM.

ATTACK. Initiation of hostile action by any means, including social, psychological, economic, *military, or political forms, or a combination of these.

Hence, "attacker."

See also AGGRESSION.

ATTACK PREVENTION. A *policy designed to induce potential attackers to cancel planned or anticipated offensive action, especially *military action, against a given country or group.

Attack prevention may be sought by *dissuasion, distraction, encouragement of internal *opposition, positive assistance, or *deterrence (either by military capacity or *civilian-based defense capacity).

AUSTERITY. See POLICY OF AUSTERITY.

AUTARKY. A *policy of national economic self-sufficiency.

A major objective of this policy is to make the *country as invulnerable as possible to *blockade, *international trade embargo, and severance of foreign sources of raw materials and energy supplies.

AUTHORITARIAN. The nature of a political system that is characterized by a rigid and sharply delineated hierarchical distribution of *authority (especially institutionally bestowed authority) closely related to the right of *command and the perceived duty of *obedience. The quality may be present in varying degrees.

An institution or a governmental structure may be described as authoritarian if it has a rigidly structured chain of command and a highly centralized decision-making apparatus. Such a structure is not open to influence from below and suppresses *dissent and *opposition. Authoritarian is thereby the opposite of "democratic."

However, a number of current *governments that can be classified as authoritarian have retained certain formal characteristics of a *liberal *democracy, such as a *constitution, *elections, a legislature that enacts laws, judicial systems that pronounce on major political issues, and even much of the vocabulary of a democratic system. However, not only have these *regimes sometimes seized *control by anti-democratic means, such as a *coup d'état; they also commonly maintain control by anti-democratic political manipulations, such as *rigged elections. They also operate by imposing an authoritarian reality on the hybrid system.

Hence, "authoritarianism."

See also ANTI-AUTHORITARIAN.

AUTHORITY. The perceived quality that leads some individual's or group's judgments, decisions, and recommendations to be accepted voluntarily as right and therefore to be implemented by others through *obedience or *cooperation.

Persons with such perceived authority may have a highly disproportionate influence in determination of *policies, providing *leadership, giving direction or even orders, and settling *conflicts.

Authority is one of the main *sources of political power, but is not identical with power.

Authority may derive from attributed individual qualities, such as superior knowledge, insight, experience, wisdom, and the like. Such perceived superiority may or may not reflect actual qualities and may be attributed to persons who hold no formal institutional position.

Authority may also be bestowed on persons or groups by institutions that possess authority (such as a *State, religious body, school, family, professional association, *military organization, or *resistance organization) through awarding to the individual a position, office, title, or other honor. That person or group may thereby gain a reputation, prestige, and a perceived right to decide certain matters that would never have been granted on the sole basis of actual qualities and merit.

The attribution of authority to a person, group, or institution is neither permanently nor irrevocably bestowed, but it is also not usually rapidly or easily changed or dissolved.

Institutionally bestowed authority may be transferred by the institution to another person or group. Such authority may also be lost if the individual or group is seen to violate that institution's own principles or procedures. Individually gained authority may be weakened, undermined, or lost, if the perception of superiority is significantly lessened or reversed.

Hence, "an authority" or "the authority."

See also AUTHORITARIAN, CHARISMA, and VOLUNTARY SERVITUDE.

AUTOCRACY. A structure of *government in which a single person (an autocrat) occupies the position of *ruler, and makes decisions and issues commands by personal fiat without legal limitations or right of participation by others.

An autocratic ruler may have gained the position through heredity, violent seizure of the *State, or bureaucratic manipulations. Autocracies vary in the degree to which personal control over the society and government is attempted or is successful. This is one form of *dictatorship.

Hence, "autocrat."

See also ABSOLUTISM, BUREAUCRACY, DESPOTISM, DICTATORSHIP, TOTALITARIANISM, and TYRANNY.

AUTONOMY. A condition of *self-determination, self-rule, or *self-government, especially of local, regional, national, linguistic, and cultural groups.

AWARDS. See MOCK AWARDS.

BACKLASH. An unintended and undesired negative *reaction to certain actions by either side in a *conflict whereby the side that took the action loses sympathy or support and the other side gains sympathy or support. This usually happens among *third parties or sections of the population not previously committed to support of either side.

Such reaction is common to serious *violence by resisters, brutal *repression, *terrorism, and other violent acts, which may be rejected by various persons and groups irrespective of their views on the issues in the conflict. However, backlash may also occur as a result of other actions that are offensive.

See also POLITICAL JUJITSU.

BANGING POTS AND PANS. A noisy symbolic form of expressing dissatisfaction with a government by striking pots and pans to make noise. This has been done from within houses, outside houses, or on the streets, as in mass *marches. It has been used in Argentina, Chile, and Serbia. This type of action reduced the chances of violent police retaliation.

This is considered to be a *method of *nonviolent protest and persuasion.

BANKS. See REFUSAL TO PAY RENT OR INTEREST, SEVERANCE OF FUNDS AND CREDIT, and WITHDRAWAL OF BANK DEPOSITS.

BANNERS, POSTERS, AND DISPLAYED PROCLAMATIONS. Prominently displayed written, painted, or printed communications intended to convey a viewpoint or objective to a wider public or to *opponents. A *method of *nonviolent protest and persuasion.

BASE. An area or locality from which *conflict activities are initiated or supported. *Operations may be *violent or *nonviolent. The base may also serve as a source of supplies and medical care, and a place for rest or regrouping.

BATTLE (reconceptualized term). A prolonged clash between opposing *forces, of longer duration than engagements, actions, or skirmishes, and yet shorter than a major phase of a *war or a comparable *conflict.

Although the term is most commonly used in the context of *military conflict, it is also applicable to *civil resistance conflicts and *nonviolent struggle campaigns, as well as in conventional political conflicts.

A battle is most likely to be an implementation of a given long-term *strategy, rather than of a short-term *tactic.

BATTLE PLAN. A preselected intended course of struggle for an anticipated *battle, with the objective of utilizing available *forces with maximum effectiveness to achieve a given objective.

BLACKLIST. Disseminated names of persons, firms, institutions, or *countries to encourage severance of commercial relationships, as in employment and trading, or to discourage initiation of such relationships.

See also BLACKLISTING OF TRADERS, ECONOMIC BOYCOTT, and EMBARGO.

BLACKLISTING OF TRADERS. The prohibition by *government action, during *wartime or during a policy of *embargo, of trade with firms or individuals in order to block indirect transfer of embargoed goods to the opponent *country itself.

A *blacklist of such traders is normally published, and transactions with them prohibited. The list, however, may be unpublished but circulated to potential suppliers, becoming a "graylist," which may delay the prohibited firm in obtaining the embargoed goods elsewhere until a supplier is found who is willing to defy the prohibition by supplying the goods.

A governmental form of *economic boycott.

BLACK MARKET. See ALTERNATIVE MARKET.

BLITZKRIEG. See NONVIOLENT BLITZKRIEG.

BLOCKADE (reconceptualized term). 1. Action by naval forces or other means to prevent supplies from reaching a given destination. Such action may occur during an international *war. It may also be used for the limited purpose of redressing a specific grievance, or may be applied against a country pursuing a *civilian–based defense policy, which depends on foreign supplies of food, fuel, key raw materials, essential commodities, and the like.

See also DEFIANCE OF BLOCKADE and HUNGER BLOCKADE.

2. An attempt by *nonviolent means to sever access to a given location by a mass of human bodies, which may be sitting, standing, or lying down.

See also NONVIOLENT INTERVENTION, NONVIOLENT OBSTRUCTION, and PEOPLE'S BLOCKADE.

BLOCKING OF LINES OF COMMAND AND INFORMATION. The action of subordinates in a chain of *command or other hierarchical structure to impede its operation by quiet obstruction in one of three ways: (a) deliberate failure to relay orders to subordinates, so they never reach those who are intended to carry them out, (b) deliberate ignoring of orders intended for them, instead of either *nonobedience or blatant *disobedience, or (c) deliberate failure to pass information along the channels of communication, especially from the lower echelons upwards, so that the decision makers lack significant data to determine *policies or actions.

Depending on the structure, the withheld information may include data on economic conditions, *public opinion, supplies, *resistance groups, morale of troops, and the like.

BLUE FLU. The method of *reporting "sick" by policemen who are not actually sick, but are often legally prohibited from striking in the usual ways. The name is taken from the dark blue uniforms of police in the United States.

A *method of *strike.

BOYCOTT. A collective refusal to initiate or continue forms of social, economic, or political *cooperation. This is often used as a synonym for *noncooperation.

The word was introduced in 1886 with the refusal by the peasants of Mayo County, Ireland, to continue social and economic relations with one English landlord, Captain Boycott.

See also BOYCOTT OF SOCIAL AFFAIRS, ECONOMIC BOYCOTT, and POLITICAL NONCOOPERATION.

BOYCOTT, ECONOMIC. See ECONOMIC BOYCOTT.

BOYCOTT OF CLASSES IN EDUCATIONAL INSTITUTIONS. See STUDENT STRIKE.

BOYCOTT OF ELECTIONS. The refusal of an *opposition movement to put up candidates for an *election, accompanied by a recommendation that people refuse to vote.

This *method of *political noncooperation is used especially where the opposition believes the coming election will be fraudulently manipulated, where the *authority of the *government conducting the election is repudiated, or where a perceived crucial issue may otherwise be ignored. The boycotters may intend to enlighten the populace, to influence *third parties, or to deprive the ensuing government of *legitimacy, or all of these.

BOYCOTT OF GOVERNMENT DEPARTMENTS, AGENCIES, AND OTHER BODIES.

The refusal to cooperate with *government departments and other divisions, either all of them (because of rejection of the government's *authority) or only particular ones (because of rejection of a particular *policy).

This *method of *political noncooperation may be used either domestically or internationally.

BOYCOTT OF GOVERNMENT EMPLOYMENT AND POSITIONS.

The refusal to assist a *government by working for it. Individuals may either resign from current jobs or positions, or refuse to accept new ones.

The whole *regime (as a *dictatorship or *military occupation) may be seen as *illegitimate, or the action may be directed only at a particular *policy.

Although a large number of people may at times participate, this is not a form of the *strike, which is usually temporary. This *noncooperation is long-term, for the duration of the regime, policy, or *resistance campaign.

Effectiveness depends largely on the numbers, talents, skills, positions, and influence of the boycotters.

BOYCOTT OF GOVERNMENT-SUPPORTED ORGANIZATIONS.

Refusal to join, or resignation from, organizations that are regarded as instruments of the *government that is being opposed.

A *method of *political noncooperation.

BOYCOTT OF LEGISLATIVE BODIES.

A temporary or permanent refusal to participate in a law-making assembly.

Such refusal is especially likely where the legislature is seen to have little real power and instead serves to maintain the *government's prestige and give the false appearance of a functioning *democracy. This type of *boycott may also be used by a national minority against the legislature of the "oppressor" *State.

Minority members of legislatures have also sometimes withdrawn when facing certain defeat, in an effort to make symbolic or newsworthy *protest. At times, of course, the gesture of protest by withdrawal may be counterproductive by simply removing potential critics of the *opponents in the legislature.

BOYCOTT OF SOCIAL AFFAIRS. A group refusal to attend certain gatherings, such as receptions, concerts, and the like, as a means of dissociation from the occasion, certain individuals likely to be present, or the group that organized it.

A *method of *social noncooperation.

BOYCOTT, POLITICAL. See POLITICAL NONCOOPERATION.

BOYCOTT, SOCIAL. See SOCIAL BOYCOTT and SOCIAL NONCOOPERATION.

BRAINWASHING. Treatment of persons, especially *political prisoners or prisoners of *war, by various means to induce them to repudiate their previous political beliefs, *allegiance, and loyalties and to accept new ones.

The means used in such treatment may include some combination of any of the following: rational argumentation, mental and emotional pressures, *propaganda, physical isolation, *torture, and preferential treatment.

BREAKTHROUGH. A major advance, which previously seemed highly unlikely or impossible, that allows an accelerated development of the same factors that achieved the opening.

In the context of *civil resistance and *nonviolent struggle, the term may refer to achievements of either the *actionists or their *opponents. Breakthrough indicates something much less than complete victory, but nevertheless a major advance.

BUMPER STRIKE. A particular type of labor *strike in which workers in several firms that are targets for industrial action selectively withdraw labor at only one firm in the industry at a time. That initial strike is then settled before a new one is begun at another firm.

This enables a concentration of the labor union's organizational and financial strength, while exposing the firm facing the strike to the competition of its rivals that temporarily continue to operate normally.

This *method of strike is closely related to the *detailed strike.

BUREAUCRACY. The administrative organization of formal institutions, especially of the *State. It operates as an apparatus for application of *policies determined by designated officials.

A bureaucracy is hierarchically organized and ordered, and contains highly trained experts and specialists, as well as support staff. It operates by formal regulations, impersonal procedures, and formalized relationships between the bureaucracy and the members of the institution or the citizenry, between various branches of the bureaucracy, and between the bureaucracy and other structural parts of the institution or the State.

Hence, "bureaucratic" and "bureaucrat."

See also BLOCKING OF LINES OF COMMAND AND INFORMATION; BOYCOTT OF GOVERNMENT DEPARTMENTS, AGENCIES, AND OTHER BODIES; BOYCOTT OF GOVERNMENT EMPLOYMENT AND POSITIONS; GENERAL ADMINISTRATIVE NONCOOPERATION; SELECTIVE REFUSAL OF ASSISTANCE BY GOVERNMENT AIDES; and STALLING AND OBSTRUCTION.

BURIALS. See DEMONSTRATIVE FUNERAL, HOMAGE AT BURIAL PLACES, and MOCK FUNERAL.

BUSH WARFARE. An irregular type of *military warfare in which one or both of the contending groups engage in *guerrilla warfare without military fronts or efforts to hold territory.

BUYERS' EMBARGO. See INTERNATIONAL BUYERS' EMBARGO.

CA'CANNY. See SLOWDOWN STRIKE.

CAMOUFLAGED MEETING OF PROTEST. A gathering of *protest held under the (sometimes undisguised) pretense that the gathering is for some other legal and approved purpose.

This may happen when the *regime is a relatively moderate type of *dictatorship, neither *liberal enough to allow open meetings of protest nor tyrannical enough to act ruthlessly against persons attending a gathering that is at least ostensibly legal.

Camouflaged meetings may be held under the guise of organizations for sport, amusement, art, or religion, or simply a social affair, such as a banquet.

A *method of *nonviolent protest and persuasion.

CAMP (reconceptualized term). A temporary or permanent location where *military soldiers or *nonviolent actionists live until needed for *combat.

See also BASE.

CAMPAIGN (reconceptualized term). A coordinated series of *operations—*military, conventional political, *civilian resistance, or *nonviolent action—planned on the basis of a selected *strategy with the objective (s) to be accomplished within contextual limits of time, geography, or political situation.

CAMPAIGN PLAN. A prepared scheme of a series of actions designed to wage a *campaign.

CAPITALISM. An economic system in which all or most of the means of economic production and distribution, such as land, factories, means of transportation, marketing, communication, and the like, are privately owned and operated. The motivating force is to gain economic profits in a largely competitive system.

As capitalism has developed, there has been a change toward major centralization in ever larger corporations, including international ones. There has often also been greater *government involvement in terms of being influenced by the corporations.

Governments have also made efforts to meet social and economic needs that have not been met by, or have been exacerbated by, the capitalist institutions.

CAPITULATION (reconceptualized term).

1. The action of surrendering.
2. The making of the terms of surrender.
3. The document containing the terms of surrender.

Capitulation is usually inevitable following decisive *military *defeat where the struggle has been waged by military means. However, even if military *resistance has been defeated by the *opponents' overwhelming military action, capitulation may yet be avoided by a switch in the *technique of struggle, either to *guerrilla warfare or to *nonviolent struggle.

Where the struggle has all along been waged by *civilian resistance or *civilian-based defense even against military opponents, capitulation would not normally be considered an option. If the struggle has gone badly for the *civilian defenders, a basic change in *strategy could be made for future nonviolent struggle, or even a deliberate period of quiescence initiated to allow time for rest and a buildup of *forces to wage a new *campaign later.

See also DEFEAT and SUCCESS.

CASE (associated with nonviolent action). In the context of discussions of *nonviolent action, a particular conflict in which one of the contenders is applying the *technique of nonviolent action.

CASE HISTORY. An intensive, detailed study of a particular *conflict, bringing together significant data from all available sources, to produce a descriptive historical account as complete as possible.

This includes its background, initiation, the course of the struggle, its final termination, and its aftermath. This descriptive case history may or may not then be supplemented by analyses of the dynamics of the conflict and factors promoting *success or failure, or by testing broader theoretical hypotheses.

CASUALTY (reconceptualized term). An individual who in the course of a struggle—*military or *nonviolent—suffers injury, sickness, capture, *imprisonment, or death. In military struggles deserters are also classed as casualties since they are lost to military duty.

The accounting and comparison of casualties within a particular *conflict and between conflicts therefore requires separate cataloguing and definitions of the precise types of casualties suffered within each conflict.

*Wars, *guerrilla warfare, and acute *nonviolent struggles all share the probability of significant casualties. However, there may be a considerable difference in the extent of such casualties and their impacts on the consequent course of the conflict.

There is probably a general tendency for casualty rates of all types to be significantly higher on the resisters' side when they use *conventional war or *guerrilla warfare, as compared to *nonviolent struggle.

CAUSATION. The process of causing or producing a certain effect or result, whether or not it is intended.

The perception of universal causation assumes that no events simply "happen," but that all are produced by certain prior conditions or events that may be located and identified.

There are various, often conflicting, theories concerning the possible existence of regularities in primary causal factors or conditions, and as to the roles of single-factor and multiple-factor causation.

CENSORSHIP. Any measure taken by institutions or *governments to restrict, regulate, *control, or prohibit the dissemination of information, opinions, or ideas. Such measures may be applied to newspapers, pamphlets, magazines, books, radio, films, television, photographs, private communications, the internet, and other means. Some attempts at censorship may not be fully effective.

The censorship may be applied after the act of dissemination, and hence be punitive, for example, by seizing and destroying remaining copies of publications and punishing those believed to be responsible. Newspapers, other publications, radio stations, and television stations may be closed. Their staffs may be prosecuted, imprisoned, or even murdered.

Censorship may also be preventative, by official prepublication controls that include stopping the transmission or publication of journalists' reports, threats of fines, confiscation of deposits of funds for required "good behavior," threats of *imprisonment, and other means. Advance censorship may be achieved by persuading the controllers of the media to refrain from publishing certain items which are, it is maintained, "in bad taste," "obscene," "racially abusive," "blasphemous," or violations of "*national security."

Tensions may intrinsically exist between the principle of free speech and free press on the one hand, and the necessity of secrecy on matters of key importance to effective *military action, national *defense, or government practices on the other. It has been argued that this tension does not exist when reliance is instead placed on the contrasting *technique of *nonviolent action and the alternative *civilian–based defense policy, which operate in quite different ways.

Censorship has also been applied by nongovernmental bodies, such as religious institutions; for example, it has been used against literature regarded as pornographic or licentious.

During *resistance movements the government in control of the *State, or an institution possessing other means of *repression, may seek to impose full political censorship. At times nongovernmental political parties and other groups have attempted to silence political rivals by bombing, burning, and destroying newspapers, editorial offices, printing plants, bookstores, and radio and television stations operated by political rivals.

Various types of *disobedience and *defiance may be practiced against censorship, including illegal publications. Censorship and control over mail and telephones (to gain information as well as to prevent communication) may lead to the setting up of underground communications.

See also ALTERNATIVE COMMUNICATION SYSTEM, NEWSPAPERS AND JOURNALS OF DISSENT, and RECORDS, RADIO, AND TELEVISION.

CENTRALIZATION. 1. A high degree of concentration of decision-making, *control, direction, administration, or production (or a combination of these) within an institution, *government, or *society. The prime types of centralization are political and economic, or a combination of these.

Hence, "centralize."

2. The process of producing or increasing that concentration, as described above.

See also DECENTRALIZATION.

CHANGES IN DIPLOMATIC REPRESENTATION. See DIPLOMATIC RELATIONS—DELAY AND CANCELLATION, DIPLOMATIC RELATIONS—REDUCED REPRESENTATION, DIPLOMATIC RELATIONS—SEVERANCE OF REPRESENTATION, and DIPLOMATIC RELATIONS—WITHHOLDING OR WITHDRAWAL OF RECOGNITION.

CHARISMA. The perceived special quality with which certain persons are believed to be endowed, giving them extraordinary characteristics and capacities, and often a unique mission. Persons with charisma are regarded as superior to ordinary human beings.

The special qualities may be believed to derive from diverse sources, including supernatural ones, special talents, heroism, and unusual wisdom or insight. Charisma is not limited to religious or spiritual persons. It may also include individuals whose primary orientation is social, political, national, or ideological, including fascist *leaders.

CHARISMATIC AUTHORITY. That type of *authority that derives from *charisma. Charismatic authority is distinguished from traditional authority and legal authority, as Max Weber pointed out, and may in time lose some characteristics and become routinized. The source and nature of accepted authority may significantly influence the issues in a *conflict and the course of a struggle, waged by whatever means. In dictatorial or fascist regimes the ruling ideology tends to endow the *leader with supposed charismatic authority.

CHARISMATIC LEADERSHIP. A type of *leadership derived not from an individual's official position, heredity, *election, or formal status in a hierarchy, but from the personal qualities of the individual, who is perceived to have *charisma.

CITIZEN ARMY. A nonprofessional *military army whose members and officers normally pursue ordinary civilian careers in *peacetime. This type of army is based on universal obligation for men who are citizens and may also include women. This policy is implemented by *conscription, and assumes that a politically active citizenry willingly shoulders military duties when judged to be necessary to reinforce a small professional military corps.

A citizen army is likely to include a relatively short training period, refresher courses, and availability to be called for duty in emergencies. Active duty is often within the country in case of *attack (often met by *territorial defense), but citizen soldiers may on occasion be used outside the country's territory.

CIVIC. Pertaining to political associations and *government affairs.

CIVIC ABSTENTION (associated with civilian-based defense). Withdrawal by citizens from all political associations and from participation in governmental affairs.

See also BOYCOTT OF GOVERNMENT DEPARTMENTS, AGENCIES, AND OTHER BODIES, and BOYCOTT OF GOVERNMENT EMPLOYMENT AND POSITIONS.

CIVIC ACTION (associated with nonviolent action). Deliberate activities by groups of citizens intended to influence policies and their implementation at any level of *government. The means used may include *demonstrations, *letters of opposition or support, *group or mass petition, and *assemblies of protest or support, as well as other legal or illegal *methods of *nonviolent action. Actions identified as "civic" are related to political activities somehow associated with some level of government.

See also CIVIL ACTION.

CIVIC DEFIANCE (associated with nonviolent action). Assertive repudiation of, and resistance to, policies and practices of any level of *government. Civic defiance is based on the claim that it is the citizens' duty to uphold avowed principles of their *society and governmental system when a specific government flaunts these principles.

Civic defiance is applied on the grounds that such *opposition is a duty of the citizenry because of perceived loyalty to the avowed principles.

CIVIC RESISTANCE (associated with civilian-based defense). *Noncooperation with, and *disobedience of, policies and practices of any level of *government, based on the belief that the body in question is violating its avowed moral or political principles.

CIVIC STRIKE. Temporary withdrawal of labor and assistance from a level of *government that is seen to be acting in an unacceptable manner.

CIVIC UPRISINGS. Defiant waging of *nonviolent struggle by diverse *methods intended to coerce or disintegrate the whole current *government or change policies of a particular level of government.

CIVIL. Pertaining to citizens or a *society; peaceful, polite, humane, *nonviolent.

CIVIL ACTION. Activities undertaken by the population and nongovernmental institutions of a *society with the intention of achieving some objective. Diverse means, including *nonviolent action, may be used, but violent means are excluded.

CIVIL DEFENSE. A system of organization, mobilization, and direction of the civilian population of a country which is intended to minimize or counteract the effects of a hostile *military *attack on the country. Civil defense is especially focused on remedial measures against an aerial, rocket, or bombardment attack.

The activities and measures to minimize or counteract the effects of such destructive attacks may include emergency shelter programs; means to counteract chemical, biological, and radiological weapons; a warning system; evacuation; stockpiling of food, water, necessities, and raw materials; fire-fighting and means to deal with other emergency conditions; and provision for emergency repairs and supplies.

This is not to be confused with *civilian defense or *civilian-based defense. However, civil defense measures may be necessary to supplement both military forms of defense and civilian-based defense.

CIVIL DEFIANCE (associated with nonviolent action). Determined, bold, *nonviolent *disobedience and assertive refusal to obey commands, orders, or policies.

The term was used by Albert Luthuli, president of the African National Congress, in reviewing preparations for the 1951 National Congress.

CIVIL DISOBEDIENCE. A deliberate peaceful violation of particular laws, decrees, regulations, ordinances, *military or police commands, or other orders.

These are usually laws that are regarded as inherently immoral, unjust, or tyrannical. (See CIVIL DISOBEDIENCE OF "ILLEGITIMATE" LAWS.) Sometimes however, laws of a largely regulatory or morally "neutral" character may be disobeyed as a symbol of *opposition to wider policies of the *government. (See CIVIL DISOBEDIENCE OF "NEUTRAL" LAWS.)

Civil disobedience may be practiced by individuals, small groups, or masses of people, and the aim may vary widely: (a) The persons disobeying may not wish to disturb the status quo but only to remain true to their deepest convictions ("purificatory civil disobedience"); (b) they may seek to change a particular policy, law, or regulation regarded as immoral or unjust ("reformatory civil disobedience"); (c) in conjunction with other *methods of *nonviolent action, the group may aim to undermine, paralyze, or disintegrate a government regarded as unjust and oppressive and replace it with a new system ("revolutionary civil disobedience"); or (d) civil disobedience may be practiced against a new "*illegitimate" government (of domestic or foreign origin) and in *defense of the previous "*legitimate" government or order ("defensive civil disobedience").

These four types may merge into each other.

See also CIVIC ACTION, LEGITIMACY, NONVIOLENT INTERVENTION, and POLITICAL NONCOOPERATION.

CIVIL DISOBEDIENCE OF "ILLEGITIMATE" LAWS. *Civil disobedience based on the doctrine that when laws or orders are believed to be *illegitimate and immoral, people have a moral responsibility to disobey them. The perceived responsibility to disobey certain laws may be based on a belief that the persons ought instead to obey "higher" laws that they believe are the proper standards of *legitimacy.

In other cases, civil disobedience is justified on grounds that the law or policy violates the national constitution or international law. In such cases, the persons believe, *obedience would make them accomplices to an immoral or unjust act, ultimately regarded as illegal.

An extreme *method of *political noncooperation.

CIVIL DISOBEDIENCE OF "NEUTRAL" LAWS. Violation of laws and regulations that are perceived to be morally "neutral" and not "*illegitimate," as a symbol of opposition to wider policies of the *government. An extreme type of *civil disobedience.

"Neutral" laws or provisions are ones that are simply regulatory, and exist to help the government exercise its *authority, carry out certain lesser functions, or deal with relatively minor matters not affecting health or safety. Such laws neither prohibit "immoral" or antisocial behavior nor inflict an *injustice. They might include, for example, participation in a census or provision of certain other information.

Most proponents of *nonviolent action do *not* regard it as permissible for *nonviolent actionists to disobey laws that prohibit injury to people, but do sometimes consider it permissible to disobey these "neutral" laws. This *disobedience may occur in the advanced stages of a *nonviolent revolutionary struggle, when the resisters have *rebelled against the government itself, either to demonstrate their *rebellion or out of a desire to undermine the government further.

This type of *disobedience may also be applied in cases where the nature of modern government makes it difficult to refuse to cooperate with or to disobey a law directly related to the issue of the struggle. The *actionists may then choose to disobey a regulatory law, as by sitting down inside a public square to object to a certain measure of foreign policy or of *military preparations.

A *method of *nonviolent intervention.

CIVILIAN. One who, or that which, is not *military. This term is used especially in relation to branches of *government, groupings of population, or types of struggle.

In the law of military *conflict (sometimes called international humanitarian law) the term "civilian" is used to refer to those who are not members of military forces.

CIVILIAN-BASED DEFENSE. A policy intended to deter and *defeat foreign *military *invasions, occupations, and internal *usurpations. Usurpations include *coups d'état—with or without foreign instigation and aid.

The term "civilian-based defense" indicates *defense by *civilians (as distinct from military personnel) using civilian means of struggle (as distinct from military and *paramilitary means).

The aim is to deter or to defeat such attempts, not primarily by altering the will of the *usurpers, but by making successful *attacks and usurpations impossible through massive and selective *noncooperation and *defiance by the *society.

The term "civilian" indicates its nonmilitary character, and the term "defense" that it aims at defense of the *independence and democratic character of the society and its principles. Defense is to be achieved by action of the civilian population.

*Deterrence and defense are to be accomplished by social, economic, political, and psychological means of struggle. These are used to wage widespread noncooperation and to offer massive public defiance to attacks. The aim is to deny the attackers their desired objectives, and also to make impossible the consolidation of foreign rule, a *puppet government, or a government of usurpers.

This policy uses nonmilitary forms of struggle, either as a full alternative to military means, or as a supplement to them permanently or during a transition period. Civilian-based defense has sometimes been considered as a policy to supplement military defense, as opposed to replacing it. This combination is likely to be most appropriate where countries pursue *territorial defense or *defensive defense.

Civilian-based defense is thus adoption and adaptation of the *technique of *nonviolent action to form a national defense policy as a practical substitute for (or possibly complement to) military defense and as an alternative to nuclear deterrence.

This noncooperation and defiance may also be combined with other forms of action intended to subvert the loyalty of the attackers' troops and functionaries and to promote their unreliability in carrying out orders and *repression, and even to secure their *mutiny.

Civilian-based defense measures are designed to be applied by the general population, by the particular population groups most affected by the attackers' objectives and actions, and by the institutions of the society, on the basis of advance preparations. Which of these groups are most involved will vary with the attackers' aims— whether they are economic, ideological, political, or other.

*Strategies of civilian-based defense include *nonviolent blitz-krieg, *total noncooperation, and *selective resistance.

This policy has also variously been called "*civilian defense," "nonmilitary defense," and "nonviolent defense." This synonym for civilian defense is especially used in North America. This term may be particularly helpful when the latter may be confused with *civil defense.

Hence, "civilian defender."

See also CIVILIAN-BASED DEFENSE MUTUAL ASSISTANCE PACT and CIVILIAN-BASED DEFENSE TREATY ORGANIZATION.

CIVILIAN-BASED DEFENSE MUTUAL ASSISTANCE PACT (associated with civilian-based defense). An international treaty providing for specified help to be given between the *countries which have adopted *civilian-based defense in part or in full to deal with *security threats.

The specified types of help may be provided in *peacetime or *wartime or both. The aid may include exchange of research results, training programs, participation in *maneuvers, communications facilities, provision for food and other supplies, support for international diplomatic and economic *sanctions, and the like. Such help may be on a bilateral or multilateral basis.

CIVILIAN-BASED DEFENSE TREATY ORGANIZATION (associated with civilian-based defense). An institution that might be established by a *civilian-based defense mutual assistance pact to provide the types of assistance designated by the treaty.

CIVILIAN-BASED RESISTANCE. A synonym for *nonviolent resistance and *civil resistance.

CIVILIAN CONTROL. The political principle that the *civilian branches of *government are superior in position and *command to its *military institutions, as well as the necessary structural arrangements to implement this principle.

CIVILIAN DEFENDERS (associated with civilian-based defense). Resisters who are applying the *methods and *strategies of *civilian-based defense against a *coup d'état or occupation.

CIVILIAN DEFENSE. A direct *defense of the *society, its principles, people, way of life, chosen institutions, and political *autonomy by action of the *civilian population as a whole, and their institutions, using *nonviolent means of struggle. This term is especially used by *advocates of the policy in Britain and India.

A synonym for *civilian-based defense.

CIVILIAN INSURRECTION (associated with nonviolent action). A *nonviolent *uprising by *civilian struggle intent upon bringing about the collapse of the established *government.

This type of struggle can develop very rapidly into a full-scale uprising, employing especially various *methods of *strike and *political noncooperation to paralyze and destroy the *political power of the disliked government within a period of days or a few weeks.

Civilian insurrection is, therefore, to be distinguished from long-term *nonviolent resistance struggles waged at a lower level of intensity over months or years. Civilian insurrection is also distinguished from mass *protests with a more limited aim, for example, of ending particular policies or securing review of contested *election results.

CIVILIAN RESISTANCE (associated with nonviolent action). General and massive *nonviolent resistance by the *civilian population.

This term is used especially to emphasize the large-scale participation of the civilian population, especially in the context of *civilian-based defense.

Hence, "civilian resister."

CIVILIAN STRUGGLE. Social, economic, or political *conflict waged by the *civilian population by means of the *technique of *nonviolent action.

CIVILIAN UPRISING. A synonym for *civilian insurrection.

CIVIL INSTITUTIONS. Those institutions of the *society that are not *military bodies.

CIVIL INTERNMENT. Confinement of people to particular locations (such as *camps) without legal trial, court sentencing, or *martial law measures, as a means of controlling or suppressing a movement of civil unrest of some type.

Hence, "civil internee."

See also CONCENTRATION CAMP, IMPRISONMENT, and INTERNMENT CAMP.

CIVIL LIBERTIES. Personal and social freedoms associated with the individual's relationships to *government, especially freedoms of speech, press, assembly, and organization. Civil liberties may also include freedom of religious belief and worship, freedom to travel, a right to personal privacy, and a right to own and use personal property.

Hence, "civil libertarian."

See also CIVIL RIGHTS and FREEDOM (POLITICAL).

CIVIL RESISTANCE (associated with nonviolent action). Widespread *nonviolent resistance by the *civilian population, usually practiced in conflicts over political issues. The means of action and dynamics are those of *nonviolent action. Civil resistance, however, is usually practiced solely for pragmatic reasons and the term has no connotations of moral *nonviolence or *pacifism. See also *people power.

Hence, "civil resister."

See also CIVILIAN RESISTANCE.

CIVIL RIGHTS 1. Civil liberties that are recognized and enforced by judicial or administrative governmental action, including both liberties of substance and procedural liberties (such as trial by jury) which protect the individual.

2. Liberties secured by prohibition of discrimination based on race, color, creed, and gender in voting, employment, housing, education, health facilities, and welfare.

CIVIL RIGHTS MOVEMENT. Organized activities by members of a group suffering discrimination, and by sympathetic persons, groups, and institutions, aiming to end all forms of discrimination in suffrage, public services, and commercial and social activities, and to achieve full *civil liberties. The means of action used may include *campaigns for legislation, judicial decisions, court appeals, public education, and *nonviolent action.

CIVIL SOCIETY. The totality of independent nongovernmental groups and institutions through which the population meets many of its needs and accomplishes its objectives. These activities may be social, economic, cultural, educational, religious, artistic, pro-independence political, and others that are conducted autonomously from the *State.

The existence and strength of civil society are widely viewed as essential in achieving and maintaining greater freedoms and social *justice and counteracting political and economic *centralization and violations of social justice. The existence of independent organizations provides a basis for *organized resistance in crises.

A strong civil society is regarded as essential for the development and maintenance of a democratic political system.

See also LOCI OF POWER and NONGOVERNMENTAL ORGANIZATION.

CIVIL WAR. An acute *conflict between rival groupings within a *country (usually based in and representing different parts of the country) waged by *military or *paramilitary *forces.

CIVIL WEAPONS (reconceptualized term). Specific *methods of *nonviolent action.

CLASS. See POLITICAL CLASS and SOCIAL CLASS.

CLASS CONSCIOUSNESS. Awareness of one's membership in a group or stratum, such as a *social class or *political class. Such awareness may then contribute to increased participation in action on behalf of one's class in a *class struggle.

CLASSLESS SOCIETY. A *society without structural differentiation of its members into *classes. This is often an ultimate objective of social visionaries, reformers, and revolutionaries.

CLASS STRUGGLE. A *conflict in which a *class in a *subordinate position contends against a dominant class to alter the class relationships, the structure of the *society, and the distribution of benefits deriving from those relationships and that structure of classes.

COALITION. A combination or *alliance of two or more groups or *governments to achieve a positive goal or to *defeat an unwanted change.

COERCION (reconceptualized term). In a *conflict, the blocking of the capacity of one side (A) to implement its will because of preventive actions of the other side (B), despite the continuing efforts of the blocked side (A) to implement its will. The "blocked" side (A) is thus no longer able to act effectively to achieve its objective.

Coercion is thus the elimination of alternatives. In the context of a conflict involving use of *nonviolent action, coercion potentially may be imposed on either side.

Coercion may be imposed as the result of *violence or of paralyzing *noncooperation. Change may thereby be produced or prevented without the agreement of the other side.

Coercion in this sense is distinguished from *compliance under threat, understood as doing the other side's bidding because the group involved is unwilling to endure any longer the consequences of *defiance. These consequences may be the application of extreme violence against them or the denial of wanted or needed assistance.

See also COERCION BY DIRECT PHYSICAL VIOLATION, COMPLIANCE UNDER THREAT, CONSENT, and NONVIOLENT COERCION.

COERCION BY DIRECT PHYSICAL VIOLATION. Procurement of the objectives of a *command by imposing overwhelming physical might on the person to whom the command was given but who refuses to comply.

Such *coercion is sharply distinguished from *obedience, even that obedience which is induced by threat of *punishment.

Coercion by direct physical violation occurs, for example, when a person who was commanded to move from a given spot refuses to do so and then is physically removed by others.

COLD SHOULDER. Systematic *social boycott of certain persons, occupation troops, or functionaries.

This practice may take diverse forms, such as refusal to speak to them, avoiding meeting with them, leaving a location when they enter, becoming silent in their presence, refusal to socialize with them, and the like. German troops were so treated in Denmark and Norway during the Nazi occupations.

See also FRATERNIZATION WITH THE OPPONENTS, ICE FRONT, and SOCIAL NONCOOPERATION.

COLLABORATION (associated with civilian-based defense). During an acute *conflict, *cooperation with, and assistance to, a *government established by a *usurpation (such as a *military *invasion or *coup d'état) or an otherwise oppressive government, such as a *dictatorship.

Collaboration varies considerably in degree. It may include, for example, taking an insignificant job, accepting public office in the new government or being an administrator, providing needed assistance, becoming an informer, acting as a public *advocate of the new government, maintaining essential services such as transport, and many other forms.

Motivations may also be diverse. They may be political, such as a political preference for the usurper's government, a desire to avoid contention, or a desire to become a "peacemaker," or personal, such as cowardice, economic gain, fears for one's family's welfare, or opportunism for personal status, power, or prestige.

Other "indirect collaboration," as it has been called, is carried out by persons who commit acts of *violence and *sabotage within a *nonviolent resistance movement to the detriment of effective resistance, thereby serving a role similar to *agents provocateurs.

Hence, "collaborator."

COLLECTIVE BARGAINING. The process of *negotiation between management representatives and trade unions in an attempt to reach an agreed settlement of unresolved issues. The issues are likely to include disputes over wages, working conditions, and hours.

Such negotiations on labor's side are often backed by an implicit or explicit threat to *strike.

COLLECTIVE BEHAVIOR. A class of noninstitutionalized group conduct characterized by the predominant influence of moods, emotions, impulses, feelings, and irrationality, in contrast to established cultural norms and strategic planning.

Collective behavior may take diverse forms, such as mass hysteria, crowd behavior, collective excitement, or fads.

Not all crowd or mass behavior evidences those characteristics, however. Some cases of large-scale group action are highly orderly and disciplined.

COLLECTIVE DISAPPEARANCE. The severance of all social contact with the *opponents by the population of a small area, such as a village. They remain hidden somewhere within the territory. Hiding distinguishes this *method of *social noncooperation from *protest emigration. Not to be confused with the practice of extremely repressive *governments physically "disappearing" resisters and their supporters.

COLLECTIVE SECURITY (reconceptualized term). A policy designed to prevent *attack by *deterrence, or successful *defense against attack, as a consequence of prepared capacity for joint defense action by member *States of a *military or *civilian-based defense *alliance.

See also CIVILIAN-BASED DEFENSE TREATY ORGANIZATION.

COLLEGE STRIKES AND BOYCOTTS. See ALTERNATIVE SOCIAL INSTITUTION, STUDENT STRIKE, UNITED ATTENDANCE, and WITHDRAWAL FROM GOVERNMENT EDUCATIONAL INSTITUTIONS.

COLONIALISM. 1. The practice of maintaining economic, political, or cultural *domination (or a combination of these) by one *country (or group within that country) over another country and its population. Colonialism may or may not involve settlement in the territory of a significant number of expatriates from the dominant country.

Such a system commonly induces a sense of servitude or inferiority in the people of the *colony as a means of ensuring their *submission and *obedience.

2. The system of *government maintained by dominant colonial governments in their colonies.

Colonialism is regarded as one form of *imperialism.

COLONY. A territory and its population that is ruled politically and controlled economically and militarily by another *country of which it is not an integral part, and from which it differs in significant respects, potentially including economic status, history, culture, or language, or a combination of these.

Hence, "colonial," "colonial power," *colonialism, and "colonist."

COLOR REVOLUTIONS. The series of predominantly *nonviolent popular political *uprisings in the former Soviet bloc in southern Europe and central Asia against *authoritarian *regimes, beginning in 2000. These *revolutions exhibited roughly similar patterns and appeared to model themselves on earlier examples and a shared generalized analysis of how to change an authoritarian political system. The color revolutions were inspired by events in Serbia (the "5th October Revolution," 2000). *Resistance to *rigged elections followed in Georgia (the "Rose Revolution," 2003) and Ukraine (the "Orange Revolution," 2004). The basic concept spread far beyond its region of origin and caused certain Asian authoritarian regimes serious concerns.

Shortly thereafter, several additional movements of *protest and resistance were also called color revolutions, such as the "Cedar Revolution" of 2005 in Lebanon and the "Tulip Revolution" of 2005 in Kyrgyzstan, although some differed significantly in certain respects from the first three examples.

COMBAT. 1. A *fight between contending *forces.

Combat connotes especially sharp or severe struggle, but does not suggest a particular scale of *conflict, nor a particular *technique by which the struggle is waged.

Hence, "small-scale combat," "localized combat," "*military combat," "*civilian combat," and "*nonviolent combat."

2. Opposition to *opponent forces by sharp struggle.

Hence, "combat plan," "combat preparation," and "combat training."

COMBATANT. A person who directly participates in a *fight or *combat, as distinct from persons who take part indirectly, as by carrying out preparations, backup duties, and the like.

In the law of *military *conflict (sometimes called international humanitarian law), the term "combatant" refers to persons who have the right to participate in *hostilities, e.g., by being members of a *State's regular military forces.

COMMAND. An order or instruction backed by the threat or infliction of a *sanction in case of *noncompliance.

See also BLOCKING OF LINES OF COMMAND AND INFORMATION, DISOBEDIENCE, OBEDIENCE, POLITICAL NONCOOPERATION, and VOLUNTARY SERVITUDE.

COMMERCIAL RESISTANCE. *Opposition conducted by deliberate restriction of economic trade in a *conflict between two contestants. These may or may not be independent political units. Commercial resistance may be initiated by merchants, consumers, or *governments.

See also individual forms of ECONOMIC BOYCOTT.

COMMERCIAL WAR. An international *conflict in which each of the contending parties seeks to gain its own advantage and to weaken the other party by economic measures, rather than by *military action.

These measures may include such *methods as *blacklisting of traders, *dumping, *international buyers' embargo, *international consumers' boycott, *international sellers' embargo, *international trade embargo, *preclusive purchasing, *refusal to pay debts or interest, or *seizure of assets, as well as other economic means not classed within *nonviolent action.

COMMUNICATIONS. See ALTERNATIVE COMMUNICATION SYSTEM, BLOCKING OF LINES OF COMMAND AND INFORMATION, CENSORSHIP, and individually listed METHODS of NONVIOLENT PROTEST AND PERSUASION.

COMMUNISM. 1. The doctrine, political system, or practice of a Communist Party, especially those of the Soviet Union and the former Soviet satellite states of Eastern and Central Europe. There have been significant variations between some Communist systems, for example, Maoist China and the Soviet Union. The political dominance of a Communist Party does not always signify Communist economic policies, as in China since the 1980s, where capitalist economics has been encouraged.

See also MAOISM, MARXISM, and MARXISM-LENINISM.

2. Spelled with a small "c," the word refers to a projected higher stage of *society beyond *socialism, in which both dominant economic classes and the *State itself have disappeared.

COMPLIANCE UNDER THREAT (reconceptualized term). The reluctant performance of an act under orders, *obedience to a *command, or fulfillment of a demand, because it was issued with an explicit or implicit threat of an unacceptable serious *punishment for *non-compliance. Or, conversely, abstention from prohibited behavior because of a desire to avoid punishment for *disobedience.

Compliance under threat is commonly but imprecisely described as *coercion, even though an act of will is still involved in compliance. In contrast, coercive acts of will have at times been effectively blocked.

See also COERCION, COERCION BY DIRECT PHYSICAL VIOLATION, CONSENT, NONVIOLENT COERCION, and OBEDIENCE.

COMPLY-IN. See OVERLOADING OF ADMINISTRATIVE SYSTEMS.

COMPROMISE. A settlement of differences in a conflict in which each side makes concessions, giving up a portion of its original aims in exchange for concessions by the other party.

Compromise agreements may at times be motivated by a rational desire to settle a conflict in a fair and reasonable manner. However, compromise may also reflect a recognition by each party that neither is sufficiently strong to win all of its objectives by struggle or threat.

Settlements by compromise may be relatively permanent or may be discarded when the power relationships between the parties alter sufficiently to enable one of them to achieve more of its objectives.

Issues of secondary or minor importance may be far more suitable for this type of settlement than those issues which are perceived to be fundamental to the beliefs, integrity, *social structure, or existence of the group.

Procedures utilized to achieve a compromise include *arbitration, *conciliation, *negotiation, and the like.

CONCENTRATION CAMP. An area in which *civilians are held, usually without trial or judicial sentencing, for purposes of *punishment or because of a policy of "preventive detention" of dissenters against the *regime. Additionally, "undesirables," identified on political, racial, or other grounds, may also be held. Concentration camps may also be used to terrorize inmates or members of the general population who are not in *opposition so that they engage in compulsive *submission.

Concentration camps may vary in the degree to which deliberate maltreatment and *torture are a part of their operation. Deliberate killing of inmates may or may not be a practice in concentration camps.

See also CIVIL INTERNMENT, EXTERMINATION CAMP, IMPRISONMENT, and INTERNMENT CAMP.

CONCILIATION. Resolution of a *conflict by increasing mutual understanding and good will between the parties while reducing *hostility and tensions.

In itself, this approach does not affect the issues at stake nor the ultimate *sanctions of the groups. It does seek to shift the parties away from open struggle and toward more positive influences.

This approach differs significantly, therefore, from *nonviolent action, which is a mode of conducting conflict.

See also ARBITRATION, COMPROMISE, and NEGOTIATION.

CONFLICT. A contest, contention, or dispute between individuals, groups, institutions, or *States, in which the parties involved perceive their respective aims to be in contention or incompatible. The degree to which their respective aims are in contention or incompatible may vary. This variation may influence the choices of the means by which each side will wage the conflict.

Each party is likely to seek to overpower, undermine, weaken, force into *submission, or eliminate the other party as a viable contender, or even to exterminate it.

See also CONFLICT RESOLUTION, DOMESTIC CONFLICT, INTERGROUP CONFLICT, and SOCIAL CONFLICT.

CONFLICT RESOLUTION. A general term referring to the diverse ways in which *conflicts are settled without *violence. These ways may include *arbitration, *conciliation, judicial or legislative action, *negotiation, and other approaches.

CONFLICT STUDIES. A program of academic studies focused on *peace, *war, and *conflict as understood from perspectives in several academic disciplines.

CONFORMITY. Acquiescent behavior in accord with established expectations and norms of a social group. That is, behavior which is similar to, or identical with, the behavior of other members of the *society and the expectations of what is appropriate behavior.

See also NONCONFORMITY.

CONFRONTATION. 1. A clash of opposing *forces, ideas, movements, ideologies, or the like. See also IDEOLOGY.

2. A face-to-face encounter of demonstrators with agents of the *opponents' *government.

CONSCIENTIOUS OBJECTION. The refusal, for moral or religious reasons, to take up *military *weapons, to be inducted into the *military forces, to assist in military preparations, or to participate in warfare.

Such objection may be to all *war (based on *pacifism) or to a particular war ("selective *conscientious objection" based on a type of *selective nonviolence).

Some conscientious objectors accept noncombatant duties within the military forces. Others accept only *civilian tasks as legally accepted alternatives to conscript military training and duty. Still others take a more absolutist position and refuse all *cooperation with military *conscription.

Hence, "conscientious objector."

See also PRINCIPLED NONVIOLENCE and WAR RESISTANCE.

CONSCIOUSNESS RAISING. The process of helping a given population group to develop a fuller and deeper understanding of the social, economic, and political situation in which they live.

CONSCRIPTION. The process of compulsory enrollment and induction of *civilians into duties and responsibilities, usually *military, as part of a comprehensive *government policy of requiring specific duties of whole classes of the population, under penalty of governmental *sanctions.

Military service may be extolled as a citizen duty (see CITIZEN ARMY), but conscription is usually introduced to supplement the permanent military forces, especially in times of crisis or *war, on the assumption that voluntary military recruitment will not provide enough soldiers.

The term may also apply to nonmilitary service, as in times of flood or other natural disasters.

See also CONSCIENTIOUS OBJECTION and NONCOOPERATION WITH CONSCRIPTION AND DEPORTATION.

CONSENT (reconceptualized term). The mental process which, for whatever reason, leads a person to obey a given *command or law, or to provide the *government with *obedience, *submission, and *cooperation.

Consent may then be measured by obedience and compliance, although it is not identical with it. Consent is the intervening mental response between a command and obedience to it.

The subject may consent, and hence obey, because of (a) acceptance of the *authority of the individual or institution issuing the command, (b) indifference to the command (or law, or government), (c) positive approval of it, or (d) fear of the possible *sanction for *disobedience.

It is important, then, to distinguish between "free consent" and "intimidated consent." The consent induced by fear, however, still involves an element of the person's will. The threat of sanctions does not necessarily produce obedience, as many contrary instances testify.

See also COERCION and COERCION BY DIRECT PHYSICAL VIOLATION.

CONSERVATIVE. Persons, groups, *policies, or *doctrines which are intended to maintain and preserve traditional beliefs, mores, and principles, and those institutions and standards of behavior which are believed to embody and apply those beliefs, mores, and principles.

Conservatives may favor change from existing policies and institutions but seek to achieve it gradually without losing valued beliefs, standards, and the like.

Hence, "conservatism."

Since the 1970s, however, conservative beliefs have often been linked to the economic markets, and have therefore been associated with rapid and radical *social change.

CONSISTENT NONCOOPERATION ON A LEGAL BASIS (associated with civilian-based defense). A *strategy for *civilian-based defense against *coups d'état or occupations in which sections of the population persistently continue to perform their usual roles and activities according to their pre-*usurpation legal status and regulations as if the usurping *government did not exist.

These defenders remain at their jobs and carry out their duties under the previously established law, policies, and traditions of their *country, until physically removed by the *usurpers. Such physical removal may follow refusal to obey the usurpers' orders and refusal to cooperate with their *illegitimate efforts to *control and change the *society and its legal principles. This behavior is a crucial aspect of the *work-on without collaboration.

CONSTITUTION. The fundamental framework of a *government, establishing its internal structure and its relationship to the *society and citizenry, including processes for selection of government officials. A constitution may also include set limits on governmental activity, prohibition of arbitrary action, and pledged guarantees of the rights of members of the society.

In some cases, a constitution may primarily take the form of a written document, with the added accumulation of interpretations, amendments, accepted practices, important laws, and the like, based upon or developed from the written constitution.

In other situations a constitution is not recorded in a single document, but instead consists of established practices and traditions as to the form and role of government, laws, and customs, major conventions long accepted by the society, court interpretations, and diverse historical acts or documents that affect the structure of government and its relationship to the society.

Hence, "constitutional."

CONSTITUTIONAL GOVERNMENT. *Government that operates in accordance with an established *constitution in which the governmental officials have reached their positions by established procedures (and not *usurpation), and in which governmental relationships to the *society, limits on government activity, and the rights of individual members of the society are respected and observed.

The constitution can include traditions, laws, court interpretations, historical acts, and key documents.

Constitutions vary in the degree to which they place limits on the activities and procedures of government officials and agencies and make them subject to popular selection and control, and hence nurture a *democracy. Some constitutions may permit autocratic governance, just as some laws may authorize violations of *civil liberties and democratic processes. However, if formal constitutions permit a degree of *authoritarian rule, or if they mask *de facto *dictatorship, they contradict the spirit of *constitutionalism. Written constitutions alone are not a guarantee of constitutional government.

CONSTITUTIONALISM. 1. Adherence to the principles of *constitutional government.

2. An approach to *politics and *government which maintains that political behavior and governmental action should be limited by a combination of (a) political institutions with constitutionally established procedures and limits on governmental action, and (b) voluntary self-restraint by political actors and *rulers in accordance with political norms, standards, and principles of the *constitution.

See also CIVIL LIBERTIES, CONSTITUTIONAL GOVERNMENT, and DEMOCRACY.

CONSTRUCTIVE PROGRAM. The plan for activities and work originally developed by M. K. Gandhi for developing a new *social order through voluntary activities and organizations independent of the *State and other institutions of the old social order. This would simultaneously help to correct certain social ills and build up new institutions intended to play major roles in the nascent social order.

The details of Gandhi's selected programs were not meant for imitation in other *societies. They were intended to address such needs as improved understanding between believers in different religions, decentralized production, sanitation, education, roles of women, needs of peasants and labor, health services, and assistance to students.

Gandhi recommended that constructive program work should precede, accompany, and follow the use of *nonviolent action.

CONSUMERS' BOYCOTT. Refusal in significant numbers by a group of consumers to purchase certain goods or services. It may be organized or spontaneous.

Reasons for such a *boycott may include objections to excessive prices, discrimination in availability, a wider grievance which the boycotted item symbolizes, perceived "immoral" qualities of the item, conditions (especially labor) under which the item has been produced, the use to which profits from it will be put, prejudices of the consumers, and political differences with the manufacturer or seller of the item.

Consumers' boycotts may sometimes involve the publication of "unfair," "black," "closed," or "we don't patronize" lists.

A *method of *economic boycott.

See also INTERNATIONAL CONSUMERS' BOYCOTT and NATIONAL CONSUMERS' BOYCOTT.

CONSUMERS' ECONOMIC ACTION. See CONSUMERS' BOYCOTT, INTERNATIONAL CONSUMERS' BOYCOTT, NATIONAL CONSUMERS' BOYCOTT, NONCONSUMPTION OF BOYCOTTED GOODS, POLICY OF AUSTERITY, REFUSAL TO RENT, and RENT WITHHOLDING.

CONTAMINANT (reconceptualized term). An activity or a situation during a *nonviolent action *campaign that could reduce and possibly destroy the campaign's credibility and effectiveness. The activity or situation may be intended to be counterproductive or may not. The harmful effect occurs because the activity or situation disrupts the workings of the *technique of *nonviolent action and its *mechanisms of change.

Contaminants include *violence, appearance of disunity, a perception of exclusiveness, the presence of foreign nationals in the movement, active participation of *military personnel within the *resistance, an organizational structure that impedes clear decisions and implementation, and *agents provocateurs. The concept "contaminant" and the identification of these activities and situations were introduced by Robert L. Helvey.

CONTINGENCY PLAN (associated with civilian-based defense). A scheme for meeting a particular type of possible danger or for resisting a particular type of *attack by making appropriate decisions and preparations for such action.

Contingency plans may be highly important in *civilian-based defense and other *conflict situations in which opportunity for advance planning exists.

CONTRAVENTION OF LAWS. The breaking or *disobedience of laws.

See also CIVIL DISOBEDIENCE, DISGUISED DISOBEDIENCE, and NONOBEDIENCE IN ABSENCE OF DIRECT SUPERVISION.

CONTROL. Restraint, regulation, curbing, or prevention of certain actions.

CONTROLLED RESPONSE. A deliberately restrained counteraction to an *attack or other hostile action by *opponents, chosen in place of more extreme counteractions. A controlled response may be chosen either in order to prevent the *conflict from getting out of hand or in order to achieve one's objectives more easily.

The term "controlled response" is most often used in a *military context where the *weapons chosen and the severity of their use can be varied to achieve a "flexible response."

The same principle is, however, applicable within forms of *civilian struggle. For example, in *civilian-based defense, the *strategy of *selective resistance is an alternative to *total noncooperation. More generally, the choice of a particular or restricted *method of action in place of wider *resistance—for example, a *general strike or other large-scale noncooperation—would constitute controlled response.

The specific methods of *selective refusal of assistance by government aides, *selective social boycott, and *selective strike illustrate the point. However, selective resistance extends much more widely. It includes certain strategies, *tactics, and methods in which the word "selective" does not appear. Controlled response is closely related to "flexible response."

CONVENTIONAL WAR. *Military war which neither uses *weapons of mass destruction nor is conducted in the manner of *unconventional warfare, such as *guerrilla warfare.

See also WAR.

CONVERSION (associated with nonviolent action). A change of viewpoint by *opponents in the context of a *nonviolent struggle, so that as a consequence of the *actionists' behavior some or many of the opponents positively come to support the actionists' objective.

This does not occur in all nonviolent struggles, and may be restricted to a small minority of cases. Change by conversion may have been influenced by reason, argumentation, and other intellectual efforts, although conversion is more likely to involve the opponents' emotions, beliefs, attitudes, and moral system.

The suffering of the *nonviolent actionists without either retaliation or *submission is regarded as a stimulus that may alter the opponents' perception of the *conflict. This may lead them first to inner conflict and later to a change of feelings and views about the issues.

Conversion is one of four general *mechanisms of change that may operate in *nonviolent action to alter the situation.

See also ACCOMMODATION, DISINTEGRATION, and NONVIOLENT COERCION.

COOPERATION. 1. Joint action by individuals or groups to achieve shared goals.

Variations exist in the degree to which the joint action is valued for itself, or to which it is primarily perceived simply as a means to achieve the common goal.

2. Assistance provided by individuals, groups, and institutions to an individual, a group, or a *government that has requested or *commanded such help.

See also NONCOOPERATION and SUBMISSION.

COOPTATION. The practice, adopted by some *governments, of inducing certain members of the *opposition to become *de facto supporters of the established order by providing them with enhanced status, prestige, or economic benefits.

CORPORATE STATE. The special structure of the *State and the State-party-controlled *society under *fascism, especially Italian fascism. Also called the "Corporative State."

In a Corporate State the populace is claimed to be represented in the legislature on the basis of occupations and professions rather than political subdivisions or geography. However, with the abolition of the earlier political representation, the centrally directed "corporations," organized on the basis of occupations and professions, are used to regiment and control the society and population.

In Nazi Germany a related structure was called *Gleichschaltung.*

CORPORATISM. The political situation in which strong organized interest groups, usually economic ones, strongly influence the formation and implementation of *government *policies.

In the 1930s the term was associated with the Italian *fascist regime. See also CORPORATE STATE.

COUNTERATTACK. An *offensive *operation launched by a defending group which has been subject to an *attack. It may take social, economic, *military, psychological, *civilian, or political forms.

COUNTER-EVENT. A parallel event of a similar type to a *protest, held by the *opponents of the protesters, usually taking place at the same time and usually nearby. It may also be a counter-demonstration, a counter-convention, or a counter-inauguration.

COUNTERFEITING. See POLITICALLY MOTIVATED COUNTERFEITING.

COUNTERGUERRILLA WAR. A combination of *military, *paramilitary, and nonmilitary *operations and activities directed by or on behalf of an established *government against groups waging *guerrilla war intended to undermine or destroy that government. This is a more precise term than *counterinsurgency war.

COUNTERINSURGENCY WAR. The waging of combined *military, *paramilitary, and nonmilitary (including economic, political, and psychological) types of struggle by or on behalf of an established *government against insurgents who are fighting by either conventional military means (a *civil war) or *unconventional warfare.

COUNTERREVOLUTION. Action taken to undermine, *defeat, overthrow, or reverse an attempted or actual *revolution. This occurs when the previous *government has already been removed from power but the usurping government has not yet fully consolidated its own *control and established the intended new political order.

COUNTRY. The territory, *society, institutions, and population ruled by a *State.

See also NATION.

COUP D'ÉTAT. A nonconstitutional seizure of physical and political *control of the *State institutions, usually with use of *military *force or the capacity to use it. In the normal quick coup, secret conspiratorial planning is typical.

The seizure of the State initially focuses on the prime center of *command, decision, and administration (the position of the *ruler), followed by the control and use of communications, and then proceeds to take over the entire State apparatus. In turn, the seizure of the State is seen as the key step to control of the whole *country.

Seizure of the State is usually attempted with the active participation of one or more of the following: a critical part of the security forces (military or police), a political clique, an established ruler seeking dictatorial powers (a self-coup), a section of the ruling elite, the *militia of a political party. By its elite nature a coup is the opposite of a mass popular *revolution.

However, in a few exceptional cases (such as in South Vietnam in 1963), a coup may reflect some of the aims of a preceding *nonviolent movement, or alternatively a coup may be subsequently supported by a nonviolent movement (such as in Portugal in 1974–1975).

Seizure of the actual machinery of command and administration will often begin by action against such key points, such as *government buildings and offices, military and police headquarters, and control centers for communications and transportation. The *usurpers normally intend to maintain order, and to keep the civil service, military forces, local government, and police intact (at least for the time being). Often, various sections of the State will capitulate in the face of perceived overwhelming forces.

Coups normally operate very quickly, in a few hours, but occasionally "slow-motion" or "creeping" coups may stretch out over weeks.

Sometimes coups fail because *noncooperation and *defiance by sections of the government, military forces, or the *civil society, or a combination of these, breaks the intended link between, on the one hand, physical control of government buildings and key centers and, on the other hand, political control of the State, leaving the usurpers isolated. This linkage has been refused in several cases, such as in Germany, France, and the Soviet Union.

Coups may also be imperiled by mass defiance by social institutions, lower-level political institutions, and the population as a whole. Without broad-based *submission of all these, the coup *leadership cannot become a lasting government.

By advance preparations to refuse political, economic, and social *cooperation with the usurpers, *civilian-based defense is intended to deter and *defeat coups d'état.

See also PUTSCH.

COURT ACTION. See CONSISTENT NONCOOPERATION ON A LEGAL BASIS, JUDICIAL NONCOOPERATION, REVERSE TRIAL, and WORK-ON WITHOUT COLLABORATION.

CRAFT STRIKE. A *strike by the workers of a single craft, such as machinists and carpenters, in contrast to a strike in a whole industry.

A craft strike may occur in one or in many shops of a local, regional, national, or international area. Hence, "shop craft strike," "local craft strike," "regional craft strike," and the like.

The craft strike almost always takes place where the union is a "craft union" rather than an "industrial union," which includes all the workers in a plant or industry.

CREDIBILITY. The quality that leads others to believe what one says, especially one's threats and promises. This quality will be evaluated by *opponents in terms of perceived capability and determination to carry out the threats and promises.

The term has been used predominantly in discussions of nuclear *weapons in the context of the effectiveness of diverse types of nuclear threats in deterring *attacks. In a very different way, however, the concept also applies to *civilian-based defense and other *civilian struggle situations. It then relates both to the defenders' ability and willingness to implement the contemplated *civil resistance and to the *government's threats to crush *resistance with extreme *repression.

Perception of determination, capabilities, and willingness to act is critical to establish credibility in *nonviolent struggles.

CULTURAL RESISTANCE. Persistent holding to one's own way of life, language, customs, beliefs, manners, social organization, and ways of doing things despite pressures of another culture. This resistance may protect a culture of indigenous origin or be directed specifically against a culture imposed by a *military occupation or *colonialism.

Cultural resistance may take very undramatic forms, such as teaching one's language to one's children. This may be a form of *microresistance. Only rarely may such resistance be tied to political *resistance or open struggle. When it is, it usually becomes a form of *defiance or *noncooperation.

Such persistent holding to one's own culture may lead to *cultural survival even in highly unfavorable circumstances.

CULTURAL SURVIVAL. The perpetuation of a culture over decades or even centuries. Cultural survival may occur despite the dominance of another culture, *colonialism, or attempts by a foreign *military occupation *regime to subordinate or eradicate that culture.

This phenomenon may or may not be associated with related political or other *resistance. Cultural survival could be limited to *cultural resistance and self-preservation, rather than struggles against the political or *military structure of the dominant group.

CUSTOMS, SOCIAL. See SOCIAL DISOBEDIENCE.

DEBTS. See REFUSAL TO PAY DEBTS OR INTEREST.

DECENTRALIZATION. 1. A wide distribution of decision-making, *control, direction, administration, or production (or a combination of these) within an institution, *government, or *society.

2. The process of widening that distribution and reversing the earlier concentration of such processes.

See also CENTRALIZATION and DEVOLUTION OF POWER.

DECLARATION OF INDEPENDENCE. A public announcement, typically with justifying assertions and arguments, of the intent of a people, usually who regard themselves as a *nation, to institute an independent *government. They assert that they are not to be ruled any longer by the *State that previously claimed their *submission. Instead, they seek *de jure recognition of their new separate status.

DECLARATIONS. See DECLARATIONS BY ORGANIZATIONS AND INSTITUTIONS, DECLARATIONS OF INDICTMENT AND INTENTION, GROUP OR MASS PETITION, LETTERS OF OPPOSITION OR SUPPORT, LITERATURE AND SPEECHES ADVOCATING RESISTANCE, PUBLIC SPEECHES, and SIGNED PUBLIC STATEMENT.

DECLARATIONS BY ORGANIZATIONS AND INSTITUTIONS. Official statements of *opposition to, or support for, *policies, actions, or the *government as a whole issued by organizations and institutions of the *society, such as trade unions, professional societies, political parties, or religious groups.

A *method of *nonviolent protest and persuasion.

DECLARATIONS OF INDICTMENT AND INTENTION. Written or published statements of grievance, or of intention to change a situation, or both, which themselves become significant in affecting people's loyalties and behavior.

A *method of *nonviolent protest and persuasion.

DECOLLABORATION (associated with civilian-based defense). The process of deliberately reversing a condition of *collaboration with a *usurpation *regime of domestic or foreign origin and of eradicating its influence on the *society.

In the course of a conflict, decollaboration may occur as a consequence of a *resistance *strategy designed to induce current collaborators to withdraw assistance to the *usurpers and join the resistance.

After *defeat of the usurpation regime, decollaboration may involve removal of economic, political, or status gains obtained as a consequence of collaboration, and determination of possible additional penalties for collaboration, including *imprisonment. Reintegration plans for former collaborators may also be prepared.

Analysis of the extent and origins of collaboration may contribute to reducing or eliminating it in a future *defense emergency.

DECOLONIZATION. The process of ending a condition of *colonialism and eradicating its economic, social, political, cultural, and psychological influences.

DE FACTO. A Latin term indicating that something exists in reality even though its existence may not be formally or legally recognized.

In the context of *civilian struggles and *nonviolent action, the phrase may indicate changes in power relationships that have occurred but are not yet formally or legally acknowledged.

One example is de facto *independence, as compared to *de jure independence.

DEFEAT. The denial of its objectives to a party in a *conflict.

The determination of defeat or *success, or the degrees thereof, needs to be based on precise criteria, such as an indicated time period and the consequences of the conflict for the substantive issues at stake. Defeat and success cannot usefully be measured by the simple criterion of destruction or crushing of the fighting capacity of the other party.

See also CAPITULATION.

DEFEND (reconceptualized term). To preserve, ward off, protect, minimize harm, and maintain in the face of hostile *attack.

Desire or intent to ward off attackers is an insufficient criterion. The capacity to conduct instrumentally effective action to that end is also required.

DEFENSE (reconceptualized term). 1. Instrumentally effective action to *defend, protect, preserve, and ward off danger.

2. The policy or activities employed to defend a *society or *country against hostile *attack.

*Military means have been widely recognized as the predominant *methods used to provide defense. However, defense and military means need not necessarily be identical. Military means at times have not been able to defend, as distinct from attack, combat, or retaliate. In some situations defense has been provided by nonmilitary means, by *noncooperation, or by other forms of improvised *civilian struggle.

3. *Resistance to attack. The opposite of *offense.

See also CIVIL DEFENSE, CIVILIAN-BASED DEFENSE, CIVILIAN DEFENSE, and DEFENSIVE DEFENSE.

DEFENSE EMERGENCY. A crisis in which a quick *defense response to an *attack, whether of domestic or of foreign origin, is required.

*Contingency plans for rapid mobilization of personnel, materiel, and provisions, as well as strategies for defense against identified types of attack, are required to respond effectively to defense emergencies.

DEFENSE FORCES (reconceptualized term). The body, group, or institution applying *force in *defense against an *attack, whether the defense is conducted by *military or nonmilitary means.

DEFENSE IN DEPTH. 1. A strategic concept of *conventional war in which, instead of concentrating *military forces at the frontier to meet invading *forces, provision is made for *defense capacity deep within the territory. Defending military forces may be organized into successive, mutually supporting lines or perimeters of scattered, relatively self-sufficient strongholds.

The objective of such layers and strongholds is to be able to absorb and gradually weaken the *attack, while remaining able not only to prevent *capitulation but also to continue the fight and prepare for taking the *offensive.

2. The *strategic concept of defense in depth extended to the level of *grand strategy and applied in semi-military or nonmilitary ways to provide defense against *invasion and occupation. This type of defense may also be applied against certain other types of attack by means which diffuse the defense capacity either throughout the territory, or throughout the society's institutions, or a combination of these.

This may be attempted by *civilian-based defense, *guerrilla warfare, or a combination of the two.

DEFENSIVE. Operations designed to withstand or repulse a hostile *attack. The opposite of *offensive.

DEFENSIVE DEFENSE. Restructured *military forces along strictly *defensive lines. The chosen military weaponry is designed and configured solely for defensive use, and the military forces possess no organizational capacity to conduct sustained *counterattacks into the attackers' home *country. This posture has also been called "nonoffensive defense" and "nonprovocative defense."

DEFIANCE. Determined, bold *disobedience and assertive refusal to obey *commands, orders, or *policies.

DEFIANCE OF BLOCKADE. *Nonviolent *defiance of a hostile *blockade imposed by the threat or use of *military, naval, or air action in order to bring food and other necessities to the population of the besieged territory.

This economic *method of *nonviolent intervention is especially likely to be used by *third parties to the *conflict.

DE JURE. A Latin term which means according to law or legally recognized.

A change in law or legal recognition may at times follow *de facto changes of power relationships within a *society or between an emerging *government as an independent entity and the government previously in power.

DELAY AND CANCELLATION OF DIPLOMATIC EVENTS. See DIPLO-MATIC RELATIONS—DELAY AND CANCELLATION.

DELIBERATE INEFFICIENCY AND SELECTIVE NONCOOPERATION BY ENFORCEMENT AGENTS (associated with civilian-based defense). Deliberately carrying out orders given by an opposed *government with less than full efficiency by police, soldiers, and other enforcement officials, or a full refusal by them to follow certain orders.

This *method of *political noncooperation may be motivated by political opinions, sympathy for the resisters, or distaste for *repression.

To the degree to which this method is practiced, the government's ability to enforce its will is reduced and the effect of repression lessened.

DELIVERY OF SYMBOLIC OBJECTS. The delivery to the appropriate official or office of something that symbolizes a grievance or an objective of the *actionists. Dead rats, bottles, milk, and ink have been among the objects used in varying contexts.

A *method of *nonviolent protest and persuasion.

DEMILITARIZE. To remove all *military forces, *weapons, and installations from a given area.

DEMILITARIZED ZONE. A defined geographical area in which combatants have been prohibited, by treaty or other agreement, from retaining or establishing *military forces or installations of any type.

DEMOCRACY. A system of organization of societies and institutions, usually *governments, by which the members of the *society or institution have ultimate *control and a high degree of *freedom. A democratic system is usually structured by *election of representatives to governing bodies, such as legislatures and executive positions.

A representative democratic system is usually associated with avowal of the worth of individuals, *civil liberties, *civil rights, electoral procedures, a central role for the legislature, judicial independence, and protection of minority rights. Belief in the importance of consulting public opinion encourages use of referenda, whether initiated by the government or initiated from below, although this can be seen as undermining the role of the legislature.

Democratic elections are conducted on the basis of alternative candidates, free expression of opinions, and secret ballot, with a decision usually determined by majority vote. The complexities of achieving a majority are reflected by a variety of electoral systems. Emphasis on achieving representation for a range of groups and political viewpoints can result in forms of proportional representation.

Representative "*liberal *democracies" tend to be associated with *constitutional government, but representative democracies that give priority to "the will of the people" or "parliamentary sovereignty" may not accept some limitations inherent in strict *constitutionalism.

Exponents of democracy believe people should be the source of ultimate *authority for the conduct and form of government.

In specific situations, however, practice may depart significantly from that ideal as a consequence of *de facto inequitable distribution of power and wealth throughout the society, which can give elites dominance. The term "democratic" has also been used by clearly dictatorial governments to describe themselves, in order to create the appearance of *legitimacy.

Hence, "democratic" and "democrat."

See also CIVIL LIBERTIES, CONSTITUTION, CONSTITUTIONAL GOVERNMENT, DIRECT DEMOCRACY, and FREEDOM (POLITICAL).

DEMOLITION. The destruction by explosives or other means of material objects which are perceived to have economic, political, *military, or symbolic significance in a *conflict. These are usually man-made objects, such as buildings, bridges, railroad tracks, dams, or non-utilitarian items such as symbolically important statues.

Even when there is no risk of injury or loss of life, demolition is not classed within *nonviolent action, but falls in the intermediate area between *nonviolent action and *violence.

DEMONSTRATION. A public action intended to communicate a viewpoint, especially of *protest and *dissent. Such action may be conducted by an individual, but ordinarily it is by a group, which may vary widely in size.

Although at times acts of *violence and *destruction of property may be intended as *demonstrations, more often some *method of *nonviolent action is used. Demonstrations of *nonviolent protest and persuasion are most often used, but so are methods of *social noncooperation, symbolic types of *strikes, forms of *political noncooperation that show rejection of *authority, and at times some methods of *nonviolent intervention.

Hence, "demonstrator."

DEMONSTRATION STRIKE. See PROTEST STRIKE.

DEMONSTRATIVE FUNERAL. A funeral service, or more often a walking funeral procession, conducted in ways to express *protest and moral condemnation of opponents' actions, *policies, or system. Demonstrative funerals or processions are sometimes held for persons killed by their political *opponents, or for persons who died of natural causes but whose lives symbolized values opposed to the current *government.

Protest may be expressed by the participation of massive numbers of people, the types of symbols they carry, or the content of funeral orations or songs.

A *method of *nonviolent protest and persuasion.

DENIAL ACTIVITIES. Types of *resistance in *civilian-based defense, especially by *methods of *noncooperation, intended to prevent the *usurpers from achieving their intended objectives or *opponents from achieving their aim. The objectives might be economic gains or imposition of a *puppet government, for example.

DEPORTATION. The removal of unwanted people from a specified territory by threat or direct use of police, *military units, or special *agents. Individuals, groups, or whole populations may be removed.

The deportees may either be allowed to go elsewhere as they wish, or be transported to specific locations.

The deportees may be regarded as "undesirable" on racial, religious, nationality, or similar grounds. Or they may hold land or other resources desired by the deporting *government. In other cases, the deportees may be wanted as a compulsory cheap labor force. The deportees may also be seen as an actual or potential political *opposition which is not to be tolerated.

See also NONCOOPERATION WITH CONSCRIPTION AND DEPORTATION.

DEPUTATION. Representatives of a group who meet with an official who has some influence or *control over the issue about which the group is protesting. On occasion, deputations may seek consideration or adoption of an alternative *policy.

A *method of *nonviolent protest and persuasion.

DESPOTISM. A type of *dictatorship in which the *ruler, often with perceived complete *authority, and without any constitutional limits or division of powers, arbitrarily dominates the political system and *society.

See also ABSOLUTISM, CONSTITUTIONAL GOVERNMENT, DEMOCRACY, DOMINATION, FREEDOM (POLITICAL), TOTALITARIANISM, and TYRANNY.

DESTRUCTION OF OFFICIALLY ISSUED DOCUMENTS. Destruction of documents provided by, and perhaps technically owned by, the *government or other body, which individuals are required or expected to keep in their possession for long periods of time. Examples are passes, party membership cards, passports, identity cards, and *conscription registration and classification cards.

A *method of *noncooperation and an act of defiance.

DESTRUCTION OF OWN PROPERTY. The voluntary destruction of one's own property in order to demonstrate the intensity of one's feelings of *opposition. All persons are removed to safety in advance to ensure there is no risk of physical harm to anyone. In extreme cases such destruction has even included burning of one's own home.

A symbolic *method of *nonviolent protest and persuasion.

DESTRUCTION OF PROPERTY. Ruination of physical possessions by any means.

DETAILED STRIKE. Any piecemeal work stoppage by those engaged in a dispute.

Where a *strike is to cover a number of factories in a single industry, or conceivably in a number of industries, it may be organized so that the workers in one factory, or industry, after another stop work on succeeding days or weeks. Such action progressively increases the extent of the strike until a settlement is reached or the full work force is withdrawn.

Another variation would be the withdrawal of a certain number of workers each day from the plant, gradually extending it to include the total number of possible strikers.

This *method of strike enables the unions to concentrate their forces on particular points, plants, or firms, while other nonstriking workers either remain at work, or become unemployed by production shut-downs while they are technically not participating. Hence, in some countries, they are eligible for unemployment benefits, and the unions avoid the responsibility of organizing and financially supporting large numbers of unpaid strikers.

The original meaning of "detailed strike" in England was that the workers one by one stopped work or took up other jobs until the employer inquired about their grievance and was informed of their demands.

A method of the strike.

DETERRENCE (reconceptualized term). The process of restraining or preventing potential attackers from committing a hostile act because they anticipate that if they did so, grave consequences would follow. Deterrence is one means of dissuading *opponents from taking *aggressive action.

Usually this term refers to conventional *military deterrence or to nuclear deterrence. However, the expectation of difficulties if the population of an occupied *country engages in serious *resistance may also provide deterrence. The anticipated resistance may be from *guerrilla warfare or *civilian-based defense measures. At times, expected international economic and diplomatic *sanctions may have deterrent effects.

See also DISSUASION and OCCUPATION COSTS.

DEVOLUTION OF POWER. Structural changes in institutions, *societies, or political systems that shift the location where decisions are made from the top of the structures and systems downward, increasing the opportunity for participation in decision-making by the people whom the decisions affect.

See also DECENTRALIZATION.

DICTATORSHIP. A political system in which the position of *ruler is occupied by a person or group claiming the right to control the political system and *society without constitutional limits, division of powers, or opportunities for the population to select the officials, as by *elections.

Basic *civil liberties do not exist and *opposition is dealt with by *repression.

Hence, "dictator" and "dictatorial."

See also AUTOCRACY, CONSTITUTIONAL GOVERNMENT, DEMOCRACY, DESPOTISM, DOMINATION, TOTALITARIANISM, and TYRANNY.

DICTATORSHIP PREVENTION. A systematic program designed both to prevent a *government gradually developing into a *de facto *dictatorship, and also to ensure the *defeat of any attempt to impose a dictatorship by *usurpation.

Components of such a program could consist of institutional restructuring, *devolution of power, political and economic *decentralization, and changes in the production and distribution of food, fuel, water, utilities, and other necessities.

Such changes are designed to maximize the difficulties of any *ruler or would-be ruler in establishing dictatorial controls over the population, social institutions, and the government.

Systematic preparations and training for *resistance by means of *civilian-based defense measures to defeat any attempted usurpation can strengthen dictatorship prevention programs.

DILEMMA DEMONSTRATION. The use of a particular *method of *nonviolent action in a way that permits the *opponents only two undesired options. They must either grant the objective of the *actionists, or inflict extreme *punishments against them that would harm the opponents' public image unacceptably.

The creation of this dilemma is especially feasible where the demands of the nonviolent actionists are widely believed to be justified, and hence severe *repression of them would be met with dismay by *third parties and/or international opinion.

See also POLITICAL JUJITSU.

DIPLOMACY, GENERAL. The practice of conducting international relations between *governments, as by *negotiations, treaties, bilateral and multilateral arrangements, and participation in international organizations. The outcomes of procedures of diplomacy are often influenced by economic, political, and *military realities.

When normal diplomatic procedures need to be bolstered by stronger action, this need not necessarily be military action. Certain diplomatic forms of *protest and *noncooperation may first be applied. When these procedures have not prevented or corrected a more serious crisis, the way is then opened for application of stronger diplomatic forms of *nonviolent struggle, especially certain *methods of noncooperation.

DIPLOMATIC RELATIONS—DELAY AND CANCELLATION. International action by a *government to stall or halt certain *negotiations, meetings, conferences, or the like, as a result of displeasure with the actions or *policies of another government involved.

See also EXPULSION FROM INTERNATIONAL ORGANIZATIONS, DIPLOMATIC RELATIONS—REDUCED REPRESENTATION, DIPLOMATIC RELATIONS—SEVERANCE OF REPRESENTATION, DIPLOMATIC RELATIONS—WITHHOLDING OR WITHDRAWAL OF RECOGNITION, REFUSAL OF MEMBERSHIP IN INTERNATIONAL BODIES, and WITHDRAWAL FROM INTERNATIONAL ORGANIZATIONS.

A governmental *method of *political noncooperation.

See also DIPLOMACY, GENERAL.

DIPLOMATIC RELATIONS—REDUCED REPRESENTATION. Deliberate decrease of official representation of one *government in another *country without breaking diplomatic relations. Such a change may be initiated by the represented government or by the host government. The action is intended to convey disapproval of the *policies of the other government.

This international form of *political noncooperation has various expressions. A government may recall its own diplomat, leaving the post vacant, but relations officially remain intact. Only the ambassador or high commissioner and a few other high diplomatic officials may leave. Consular officials may remain and continue normal work.

Or a government may request that an individual foreign diplomat be replaced. In other instances, a government may place at the head of its consulate or embassy in another country an official with such a low rank that it is perceived as a sign of disapproval of actions or policies of the host country. At other times, a government may close only certain of its offices in a host country, but not all.

The host government may, conversely, request the represented country to close one or more such offices without withdrawing diplomatic representation entirely.

DIPLOMATIC RELATIONS—SEVERANCE OF REPRESENTATION. The breaking of normal diplomatic ties with another *government by decision of one of them. Normally, an entire diplomatic mission departs from the capital of the other *State, and it requests the recall of that State's diplomatic mission from its own capital, or simply orders it to be expelled.

A government may use this form of international action to stall or halt certain *negotiations, meetings, conferences, and the like as an expression of displeasure with the actions or *policies of another government.

If the whole diplomatic staff, including consular officials, is withdrawn, another *country is often asked to represent the country's remaining interests there.

A governmental *method of *political noncooperation.

See also DIPLOMACY, GENERAL.

DIPLOMATIC RELATIONS—WITHHOLDING OR WITHDRAWAL OF RECOGNITION. The refusal or termination of diplomatic recognition of a *government. This is contrary to the general practice of governments, which generally recognize other governments that are effectively in control of the *countries they rule.

Recognition may be withheld because of objections to the way in which that government came into its position, or objections to its basic political character, actions, or *policies. Occasionally, provisional recognition may be granted, on condition that a certain change be made in that government or its policies.

DIRECT ACTION (reconceptualized term). Social, economic, or political action taken by people themselves acting directly (as by a *strike). Direct action is contrasted with indirect action, such as an effort to get someone else to act in favor of one's group (as by lobbying for enactment of a new law), or an effort by *leaders to persuade *opponents to agree to an acceptable settlement (as by *negotiations).

Direct action has historically been promoted in the labor movement, especially by the syndicalists (see SYNDICALISM).

Direct action may be either *violent or *nonviolent, and has also taken the form of *destruction of property. The term in recent years has been largely identified with *nonviolent action.

Hence, "direct actionist."

See also GROUP LOBBYING.

DIRECT DEMOCRACY. A system of direct personal participation in making decisions by members of an institution or *society, rather than simply electing representatives who vote on the issues, as in representative *democracy.

Forms of direct democracy are often linked to mass *civilian resistance or revolutionary situations when *alternative social institutions are required.

DISARMAMENT. 1. The dismantling or complete abandonment of *military capacity by unilateral or negotiated mutual action. In contrast to *transarmament, disarmament is usually perceived as elimination of *defense capacity. The term "complete disarmament" for eliminating military capacity avoids some of the confusion with the simple term "disarmament."

2. The reduction but not elimination of military capacity by unilateral or mutual action. This is usually perceived as a reduction of defense capacity, which might be provided by nonmilitary means.

The term *arms reduction in such cases avoids confusion and is to be preferred.

DISCIPLINE. See NONVIOLENT DISCIPLINE.

DISCLOSING IDENTITIES OF SECRET AGENTS. The publication of the names, perhaps with photographs and certain details, of identified secret police and undercover political *agents working for the *opponents but operating within and against the *resistance movement.

Such publication makes it extraordinarily difficult for those particular persons to continue their activities as secret agents within the resistance movement.

This means of counteraction may be applied to political agents who have infiltrated or have attempted to infiltrate *resistance organizations, and may constitute an alternative to murdering them. Such disclosure was a frequent practice in some Nazi-occupied countries.

A political *method of *nonviolent intervention.

DISGUISED DISOBEDIENCE. *Disobedience of laws, regulations, orders, and the like, carried out so as to look like compliance.

Banned newspapers, for example, may quickly reappear with new names. Young men in Nazi Germany who did not wish to be conscripted into the army claimed medical exemption with the *cooperation of sympathetic doctors. This *method may take other highly diverse forms.

A *method of *political noncooperation.

DISINTEGRATION (associated with nonviolent action). An extreme development in a *nonviolent struggle in which the *opponent *government completely falls apart. This occurs when the previous *noncooperation and *defiance has been massive. As a result, the sources of power to the persons or group that previously occupied the position of *ruler are completely severed, thereby dissolving the ruler's power.

As a result, the old government has fallen completely apart and there is no one with sufficient remaining power even to surrender. This is the most extreme of the four *mechanisms of change of *nonviolent action.

See also SOURCES OF POLITICAL POWER.

DISOBEDIENCE. *Noncompliance with a *command or law, whether deliberate or accidental and whether openly committed or concealed. Disobedience may take both *violent and *nonviolent forms.

Hence, "disobedient."

See also CIVIL DISOBEDIENCE, DISGUISED DISOBEDIENCE, MUTINY, NONOBEDIENCE IN ABSENCE OF DIRECT SUPERVISION, POPULAR NONOBEDIENCE, and POLITICAL NONCOOPERATION.

DISPLAY OF FLAGS AND SYMBOLIC COLORS. The showing or exhibiting of the flag of a national, religious, social, or political group, or the colors of such a group, or a flag or colors that have some other symbolism, such as mourning or disapproval.

A common *method of *nonviolent protest and persuasion.

DISPLAY OF PORTRAITS. The public exhibition of pictures of *resistance heroes or other persons who symbolize the objectives of the action movement, in order to communicate to others one's political loyalties.

DISSENT. Disagreement with established beliefs, ideas, *policies, or institutions, expressed by word or action, usually without *violence.

Hence, "dissenter" or "*dissident."

DISSIDENT. A person who in thought and actions has contrary opinions to those of the political *society in which he or she lives. This term was widely used for individuals and groups who opposed Communist Party regimes in the Soviet Union and other Communist *countries.

DISSUASION. The act or process of inducing a person, a political group, or a *government not to carry out a course of action that has been considered or planned.

Dissuasion may include rational argument, moral appeal, and *deterrence (in the broad sense). Dissuasion is a broader concept than deterrence.

DIVIDE-AND-RULE ACTIVITIES. Covert activities or semi-open manipulation designed by the *government to deflect the attention of population groups away from their grievances, to focus instead on internal ethnic, religious, cultural, or political *conflicts or rivalries.

Divide-and-rule activities are frequently applied by *dictatorships, *military occupations, and colonial *regimes. These activities often involve *agents provocateurs and *infiltration into the *resistance movement.

DOMESTIC CONFLICT. A *conflict taking place within a *society, as distinct from an international conflict.

DOMESTIC EMBARGO. An *economic boycott initiated and enforced by the *government to operate within the *country. For example, a domestic embargo may be directed against a company with racist or sexist practices.

DOMESTIC EMERGENCY. A crisis within a *country affecting public welfare and safety.

Such a crisis may spring from differing sources, including a *military attack, lack of food, water, or fuel, *riot, *blockade of key supplies, arson, *demolition, attempted *coup d'état, *assassination, *guerrilla warfare, or natural disasters.

DOMESTIC GOVERNMENTAL NONCOOPERATION. See NONCOOPERATION BY CONSTITUENT GOVERNMENTAL UNITS and QUASI-LEGAL EVASIONS AND DELAYS.

DOMINATION. 1. A condition in which one group rules over, *commands, or *controls another group, which has been placed in a position of *subjugation.

2. The act or process of producing that condition.

Hence "to dominate."

DRAFT. See CONSCRIPTION.

DRAMA. See PLAYS AND MUSIC AS PROTEST and SKITS AND PRANKS.

DUAL SOVEREIGNTY AND PARALLEL GOVERNMENT. A rival *government operating in the same *country as the *opponent government during a serious struggle with the established government. This rival institution can be a serious challenge to the *authority and *political power of the opposed *regime. The parallel government can threaten to replace the opponents' government, and may do so if it receives overwhelming support from the populace.

This extreme development of *alternative political institutions has only rarely been deliberately initiated and developed.

More commonly, parallel government has been the unanticipated result of *nonviolent *massive resistance or revolutionary struggle. In such cases, it has emerged gradually, sometimes unconsciously, as rival sources of authority, such as *strike or other *resistance organizations, have developed. New institutions may have progressively assumed or taken over certain governmental functions in order to maintain order, conduct resistance, or meet social needs.

A *method of *nonviolent intervention.

DUMPING. The deliberate sale of a commodity on world markets at below-standard prices in order to depress the world price and reduce the earnings or otherwise harm the economy of a rival *country.

Economies that are highly dependent on the export of one or a very few products are especially vulnerable. Even the threat to dump a product may provoke a reaction.

An economic *method of international *nonviolent intervention.

DYNAMICS OF NONVIOLENT ACTION (associated with nonviolent action). The extremely complex general process and interplay of forces in the operation of *nonviolent action during a *conflict intended to achieve the *actionists' objectives despite the opponents' counteractions.

This involves the clash of *forces with the *opponents, the application of the various leverages (psychological, social, ideational, economic, political, and physical) at the disposal of the *nonviolent actionists, and confronting the opponents' means of *control and *repression. These changes can involve the shifting of power relationships, the utilization of *political jujitsu, the potential influences of *third parties, and the overall domestic and international situation. All these in turn act and react on each other in a process of continuous change.

Each particular facet of *nonviolent action may therefore have far-reaching consequences for the course of the whole struggle, vastly exceeding the very specific instance or situation in which it occurs. Operating optimally, all this may give the nonviolent actionists very considerable direct and indirect control over their opponents' available power capacity.

These dynamics of conflict with one side using *nonviolent struggle tend to produce change by four mechanisms: *conversion, *accommodation, *nonviolent coercion, and *disintegration.

DYNAMISM. A process of continuing development and change.

EARTHWRITING. See SKYWRITING AND EARTHWRITING.

ECONOMIC BOYCOTT. The withdrawal of economic *cooperation in the form of buying, selling, producing, or handling of goods and services. Economic boycotts are often combined with efforts to induce others also to withdraw such cooperation. Economic boycott and the *strike are the two subclasses of *methods of *economic noncooperation.

Economic boycotts may be spontaneous, or more often organized, efforts to restrict the buying or selling market, or the production of an individual, group, company, or *country. These methods have been practiced on the local, regional, national and international levels, by persons or groups directly involved in the grievance, and, very importantly, also by sympathetic *third parties in order to express their *solidarity and increase economic pressure. Motivations and objectives have varied from economic and political ones to social and cultural ones.

This type of economic noncooperation has been used most often in labor struggles and national *resistance movements against foreign rule.

Economic boycotts may be *primary boycotts or *secondary boycotts.

The methods of economic boycott, arranged in six subgroupings, are: (a) *action by consumers*: *consumers' boycott, *nonconsumption of boycotted goods, *policy of austerity, *rent withholding, *refusal to rent, *national consumers' boycott, *international consumers' boycott; (b) *action by workers and producers*: *workers' boycott, *producers' boycott; (c) *action by middlemen*: *suppliers' and handlers' boycott; (d) *action by owners and management*: *traders' boycott, *refusal to let or sell property, *lockout, *refusal of industrial assistance, *merchants' "general strike"; (e) *action by holders of financial resources*: *withdrawal of bank deposits, *refusal to pay fees, dues and assessments, *refusal to pay debts or interest, *severance of funds and credit, *revenue refusal, *refusal of government money; and (f) *action by governments*: *domestic embargo, *blacklisting of traders, *international sellers' embargo, *international buyers' embargo, and *international trade embargo.

ECONOMIC INSTITUTIONS. See ALTERNATIVE ECONOMIC INSTITUTION and ALTERNATIVE MARKET.

ECONOMIC INTERVENTION. See ECONOMIC NONVIOLENT INTERVENTION.

ECONOMIC NONCOOPERATION. The suspension of, or refusal to continue, specific types of economic relationships. This *noncooperation may take many forms, which are grouped under the subclasses of the *economic boycott and the *strike.

ECONOMIC NONINTERCOURSE. Deliberate severance of economic trade with a foreign *country during a *conflict, combining *nonimportation and *nonexportation. If the severance is by *government decision, the action is an *international trade embargo.

ECONOMIC NONVIOLENT INTERVENTION. Direct action by economic means which possess also the other general characteristics of *nonviolent intervention.

The *methods of nonviolent intervention taking economic forms are: *alternative economic institutions, *alternative markets, *alternative transportation systems, *defiance of blockades, *dumping, *nonviolent land seizure, *politically motivated counterfeiting, *preclusive purchasing, *reverse strike, *seizure of assets, *selective patronage, and *stay-in strike.

ECONOMIC PARALYSIS. See PARALYSIS.

ECONOMIC RESISTANCE. *Opposition waged by economic means, particularly by the *methods of *strike, *economic boycott, and *economic nonviolent intervention. This may be used in *domestic conflicts and *civilian-based defense struggles.

See also COMMERCIAL RESISTANCE and ECONOMIC WAR.

ECONOMIC SANCTIONS. The application of *punishments against a *country or *State by economic means by decision of a *government or *international organization.

See also COMMERCIAL RESISTANCE, ECONOMIC WAR, INTERNATIONAL BUYERS' EMBARGO, INTERNATIONAL SELLERS' EMBARGO, INTERNATIONAL TRADE EMBARGO, NONEXPORTATION, and NONIMPORTATION.

ECONOMIC SHUTDOWN. A suspension of the economic activities of a city, area, or *country on a sufficient scale to produce economic *paralysis.

This may be achieved through a *general strike by workers, combined with a closing of establishments by management, businessmen, commercial institutions, and small shopkeepers, i.e., a *merchants' "general strike."

This *method thus includes characteristics of both *strikes and *economic boycotts. Tendencies toward an economic shutdown may occur during general strikes when there is wide support for the political objectives among most sections of the population.

Economic shutdowns vary in the extent to which the various types of economic activities are halted.

The economic shutdown is classed among the methods of the strike.

ECONOMIC WAR. An international *conflict conducted by actions intended to harm a *country's economic wellbeing. This goal is pursued by disrupting its foreign or domestic markets, supply of raw materials, food, fuel, manufactured goods, or its financial stability. Economic war can include manipulation of financial controls, currency stability, credit standing, and the like.

See also COMMERCIAL WAR, ECONOMIC RESISTANCE, and INTERNATIONAL TRADE EMBARGO.

EDUCATIONAL INSTITUTIONS. See ALTERNATIVE SOCIAL INSTITUTION, STUDENT STRIKE, UNITED ATTENDANCE, and WITHDRAWAL FROM GOVERNMENT EDUCATIONAL INSTITUTIONS.

ELECTION. The process of selecting representatives or officials of an institution, or selecting a *government, by voting.

See also BOYCOTT OF ELECTIONS, CONSTITUTIONAL GOVERNMENT, MOCK ELECTION, PLEBISCITE, and RIGGED ELECTION.

EMBARGO. An *economic boycott initiated and enforced by a *government.

See also DOMESTIC EMBARGO, INTERNATIONAL BUYER'S EMBARGO, INTERNATIONAL SELLERS' EMBARGO, and INTERNATIONAL TRADE EMBARGO.

EMERGENCY. See DEFENSE EMERGENCY, DOMESTIC EMERGENCY, and MARTIAL LAW.

EMIGRATION. See PROTEST EMIGRATION.

EMPOWERMENT. The process by which a population group that has previously been weak in comparison with dominant social, economic, or political classes or the established *government is able to mobilize its power potential into effective power and exert *control over its present and future. This process has sometimes occurred through greater organizational development and experience in resisting the previously dominant group. Often referred to as "popular empowerment."

See also POLITICAL CLASS and SOCIAL CLASS.

ENFORCEMENT AGENTS. See AGENT, DELIBERATE INEFFICIENCY AND SELECTIVE NONCOOPERATION BY ENFORCEMENT AGENTS, REFUSAL OF ASSISTANCE TO ENFORCEMENT AGENTS, and REPRESSION.

ESCALATION (reconceptualized term). A reciprocal and continuing increase by both parties in the scale or intensity of a *conflict, or in the means by which it is conducted. The increase may be either deliberate or unintended.

The conflict may be extended, for example, to include new areas, population groups, issues, and the like. Or, previous nonparticipants may take sides and join the struggle. Or, the amount, types, or capacity of the *weapons employed (whether *military or *nonviolent) may be increased. Or, a combination of these or similar changes may occur.

Such extensions by each side may stimulate counteractions from the other side in an upward spiral.

See also ARMS RACE.

ESCAPE. See HIDING, ESCAPE, AND FALSE IDENTITIES.

ESCRACHE (associated with nonviolent action). The Spanish name given to a type of *demonstration used in Argentina since 1995. The purpose is to identify to the public certain persons living or working among them who, during the 1976–1983 military dictatorship, were responsible for *torture and other serious *human rights violations, or other crimes, but who remain at *liberty or serve only comfortable house-arrest sentences.

The demonstration usually begins in the neighborhood square and a carnival-type procession proceeds to the home or workplace of the violator. Subsequently, local inhabitants, artists, and popular educators promote knowledge and debate about the period of the dictatorship. The method has spread to parts of Europe, such as Slovenia, where it has also been used to identify human rights violators.

See also ASSEMBLY OF PROTEST OR SUPPORT, HARASSMENT, and OSTRACISM.

ESTABLISHING NEW SOCIAL PATTERNS. See SOCIAL PATTERNS— ESTABLISHING NEW ONES.

ESTABLISHMENT. A term often used to indicate the complex of institutions and persons perceived as the effective "powers that be" in controlling the *society and political system.

See also CONTROL.

ESTABLISHMENT STRIKE. A *strike by all workers in one or more plants or other units operated by a single management, regardless of the workers' crafts or the location of their job.

EVOLUTIONARY CHANGE. Gradual social, economic, or political change occurring incrementally and without major upheavals or disruptions, whether *violent or *nonviolent.

Contrasted with *revolution.

EXCOMMUNICATION. Exclusion of an individual or group from membership and privileges in a religious body by decision of the *leadership of the religious body.

Such action may be applied for purely personal reasons, such as conduct considered morally objectionable. In other instances this *method of *social noncooperation, and also the *interdict, have been used by religious groups in political and social struggles.

Excommunication and interdict were both important political, social, and religious *sanctions in Europe during the medieval period.

EXECUTIVE USURPATION. Action by the current chief executive of a *government (such as president, prime minister, or monarch) in violation of the provisions of the current *constitution or established practices, to expand the executive's *controls and prerogatives at the expense of the other members of the political system.

The executive may falsely claim a *domestic emergency or *international emergency to justify suspension of *constitutional government and the establishment of dictatorial controls over administration, legislation, the judicial system, *military and police actions, and foreign policy.

See also COUP D'ÉTAT.

EXILE. Residence outside of one's normal residential area or *country as a consequence either of *government edict (as a *sanction or as a means of political *control) or of an individual's decision to leave the country to avoid *punishment until a change of government allows safe return.

In some past instances (as in the Russian Empire), people have been sent to live in an isolated and distant location within the country as a means of controlling political *dissidents. Generally, however, the term refers to residence in another country.

EXPULSION FROM INTERNATIONAL ORGANIZATIONS. Cancellation of membership in an international body, usually because the member has violated the *policies or *constitution of the organization.

A *method of *political noncooperation.

EXTERMINATION CAMP. A location with facilities for deliberate killing of persons whom the *government has determined shall die because it has classified them as members of a despised and corrupting group for ideological reasons.

See also CONCENTRATION CAMP.

FABIAN TACTICS. Actions during a *conflict or a *social movement that rely heavily on gradualism and avoidance of sharp *conflict and abrupt changes. The term derives from the late-nineteenth-century Fabian Society established in the United Kingdom.

FALSE IDENTITIES. See HIDING, ESCAPE, AND FALSE IDENTITIES.

FARM WORKERS' STRIKE. A *strike by farm laborers hired for wages.

FASCISM. 1. The political doctrine and system derived from the Italian political movement headed by Benito Mussolini in the 1930s.

It is characterized by glorification and dominance of the *State, a strong single *leader with *charisma, and *hostility to and suppression of doctrines, institutions, and organizations espousing or practicing *democracy, *socialism, or *Communism.

Fascism also included restructuring of the political system as a *Corporate State, with State control of organizations and corporations, utilizing *terror and *repression internally against *opposition, and extolling *war. Private ownership (but not *control) of the economy was retained, and individual freedoms such as *civil liberties were suppressed.

2. The term is widely used more broadly to include such related systems as *Nazism and *Peronismo*, although they are not identical to Italian fascism.

See also DICTATORSHIP and TOTALITARIANISM.

FAST. Deliberate abstention from certain kinds of food or all food. A fast may be undertaken for personal reasons (health, religion, penance, self-purification) or in order to achieve social or political objectives.

Although personal fasts normally do not constitute *nonviolent action, fasts for reasons of religion, penance, and self-purification may under certain circumstances constitute *nonviolent intervention. The fast as psychological intervention may be used deliberately to gain some social or political goal, or simply to make a moral *protest.

Three types of fast are distinguished: the *hunger strike, the *fast of moral pressure, and the *satyagrahic fast (as applied on some occasions by M. K. Gandhi).

FAST OF MORAL PRESSURE. A conscious use of the *fast to exert moral influence on others to achieve an objective.

This type of fast lacks both the avowed intent of forcing the *opponents to grant the objective, as in the *hunger strike, and also lacks the full characteristics of the *satyagrahic fast, but has some characteristics of both. In the West this type of fast is usually undertaken for a limited period of time.

Because of its more moderate aims and limited duration, this type of fast is less likely than the other two to constitute *nonviolent intervention and is likely instead to become a *method of *nonviolent protest and persuasion.

FEAR. Apprehension, dread, and extreme anxiety because of a present or an anticipated event or condition. Fear of extreme *sanctions is likely to produce *intimidation and passivity.

FEARLESSNESS (associated with nonviolent action). The characteristic of not being afraid of what others may do to oneself.

In *nonviolent struggle this means that the *actionists are able to respond to *imprisonment, assaults, or other *sanctions without signs of *fear, and without *submission or retreat from their intended course.

*Nonviolent action, like any type of *conflict in which the *opponents' acts may be injurious (as in infantry *combat in *conventional war), requires fearlessness or the control of fear in order to carry on in the face of actual or potential *repression. Fear may halt the struggle or prompt flight from danger, hence destroying any chance of *success. Fear therefore must be overcome or removed.

Since casualties are generally fewer in *nonviolent than in *violent struggles, control of fear may be easier in the former.

According to the analysis of *political power on which the nonviolent *technique rests, fear lies at the root of all *despotism. Sanctions to induce *obedience and submission are effective only when they are feared. Removal or control of fear therefore enables the populace to withdraw the support on which despotism depends.

Sometimes in nonviolent struggles fear seems to simply evaporate, while at other times conscious efforts by individual participants or the *leaders of the movement are necessary to control fear. The phrase "casting off fear" is sometimes used to describe these situations.

The actionists may then positively seek the sanction (such as imprisonment) as a means of demonstrating their lack of fear, and therefore the impotence of that measure of repression as a means of *control and *intimidation. This allows the struggle to continue for a sufficient period of time to permit the *mechanisms of change to operate.

See also OBEDIENCE.

FEMINISM. A diverse set of theories, analyses, philosophies, and efforts concerned with the need to correct historically entrenched social, political, and economic injustices faced by women in *society as a whole. Feminism also entails the commitment to challenge the *subordinate role of women through political, usually *nonviolent, action.

Within *social movements, *advocates of feminism have challenged male dominance of the movement. Since the 1970s, they have introduced new styles of informal communication and organization, and sometimes insisted on "women only" protests. Feminist *activists have over the past hundred years also initiated new styles of *protest, such as chaining themselves to symbolic buildings.

FIGHT (reconceptualized term). A sharp *conflict with open matching of *forces, whether waged by *violent or *nonviolent means.

FIGHTING FORCES (reconceptualized term). The groups that are conducting a *fight, or are relied upon to do so in a *war, *defense emergency, *guerrilla warfare, or *nonviolent struggle.

FINANCIAL ACTION. See REFUSAL OF GOVERNMENT MONEY, REFUSAL TO PAY DEBTS OR INTEREST, REFUSAL TO PAY FEES, DUES, AND ASSESSMENTS, REVENUE REFUSAL, SEVERANCE OF FUNDS AND CREDIT, and WITHDRAWAL OF BANK DEPOSITS.

FISH-IN. The practice of *civil disobedience of "illegitimate" laws applied against regulations restricting or prohibiting fishing, such as those enacted for environmental reasons. This *method has been especially applied where people believe the regulation deprives them of their traditional livelihood or where racial or other discrimination is involved.

"FLIGHT" OF WORKERS. Historically, a cessation of work by peasants, slaves, or workers combined with leaving their homes to go to some other place, without stating demands or conditions for their return.

The reasons for their flight, however, were often obvious, such as extremely harsh working conditions.

In this precursor of the *strike, this form of collective *resistance by withdrawal seems sometimes to have been intended to be temporary, but in other cases it was apparently meant to be permanent.

A *method of *social noncooperation.

FORCE (reconceptualized term). 1. An application of power, including *sanctions, with the purpose of inducing some action or result. The sanctions may be threatened or imposed, and may be either *violent or *nonviolent.

2. The body, group, or pressure applying force as defined in 1. Usually used in the plural, as in "the forces of law and order" or "the forces of *revolution."

3. Frequently defined in effect as a synonym for "*legitimate use of *violence," giving "force" the positive connotations of bestowed

*legitimacy, while the same actions, if deemed *illegitimate, are termed "violence."

This third definition of "force" hinders rather than assists clear thought, as it identifies the same phenomenon—violence for social or political ends—by two different terms: "force" if it is approved and "violence" if it is disapproved. It therefore contains a built-in moral judgment and is inappropriate as a descriptive or analytical definition.

See also INSTITUTIONALIZED VIOLENCE and POLITICAL VIOLENCE.

FRATERNIZATION WITH THE OPPONENTS (associated with civilian-based defense). Friendly personal behavior by participants in a *civilian struggle toward soldiers, police, or other *agents of the *opponents, while simultaneously trying to influence them and to engage in direct or indirect *propaganda intended to change their behavior.

This usage should be distinguished from its earlier association with *illegitimate personal links to enemy occupiers, as in World War II, when fraternization with *occupation forces was viewed as a betrayal of the *resistance struggle.

The objectives of constructive fraternization may be: to convince individuals that the aims and policies of the opponents they serve are unjust and those of the *nonviolent actionists are right; to convince them that the resisters have no personal *hostility toward them or desire to injure them; to obtain information for the *resistance movement on the opponents' plans, or on the condition or the morale of their personnel; and to induce inefficiency in the implementation of *repression and other measures, leading eventually to *mutiny.

This type of fraternization may accompany a *noncooperation or *disobedience *campaign against those opponents. Fraternization combined with resistance and efforts to achieve the above objectives thereby constitutes an alternative to the *social boycott as a means of undermining the morale and loyalty of these agents of repression, and of conducting the struggle.

FREEDOM OF CONSCIENCE. A right of individuals to believe as they choose and, while also respecting the freedom of conscience of others, to live in accordance with those beliefs.

This right is usually characterized both by its explicit recognition and by an absence of legal or social regulations which require behavior contrary to one's conscience.

FREEDOM (POLITICAL). A political condition in which individuals have maximum opportunities for choice in decisions important to their lives and *society and for personal and social development, and in which individuals and groups have a high degree of opportunity to participate in the operation of the society and the political system and in the shaping of its future.

Such participation may take place through expression of diverse opinions, through involvement in decision-making (especially directly), and through various types of organization and action.

See also LIBERTY.

FREEDOM RIDE. See RIDE-IN.

FREE WILL (reconceptualized term). The belief that human beings can to a significant degree exercise freedom of choice and make their own decisions about their actions. This belief is based upon the view that human thought and action are not entirely predetermined by factors beyond the individual's control.

This perspective stands in contrast to the belief that the individual threatened with *sanctions has no choice but to obey. In exercising free will, an individual can still choose to disobey and risk receiving the threatened *punishment.

FRONT (associated with nonviolent action). In the context of *civilian struggle, a line or arena of active *conflict between opposing *forces. The line or arena may be social, economic, ideational, or political, but it is not, as in *military war, geographical or physical.

The front may be the point of contest over particular *policies, over *control of particular institutions, over loyalties of population groups, or over control of the social, economic, or political structure, for example.

FRONTAL DEFENSE. In *military warfare, the arrangement of defending troops along a geographical line facing attacking enemy troops with the objective of blocking their advance.

FRONTIER ACTION. See RESISTANCE AT FRONTIERS.

FRUSTRATION. 1. Partial or complete obstruction of fulfillment of a felt need.
2. The feelings produced by such obstruction.

FUNDS. See SEVERANCE OF FUNDS AND CREDIT.

FUNERALS. See DEMONSTRATIVE FUNERAL, HOMAGE AT BURIAL PLACES, MOCK FUNERAL, and POLITICAL MOURNING.

GANDHIAN. 1. Possessing characteristics presumed to be in harmony with M. K. Gandhi's philosophy, program, or type of *nonviolent struggle, known as *satyagraha.
2. A formulation developed by others from Gandhi's philosophy, program, or type of struggle, of which he might or might not have approved.

GENERAL ADMINISTRATIVE NONCOOPERATION (associated with civilian-based defense). Refusal, during a *defense emergency or a major political *conflict, by the great majority of the civil servants, staff, and officials in the *government administrative system to cooperate with the government. It may be a usurping *regime or a previously established government that has lost *legitimacy.
A *method of *political noncooperation.
See also BUREAUCRACY.

GENERAL AND COMPLETE DISARMAMENT. Universal negotiated abandonment of *military capacity for potential international use.

See also ARMS REDUCTION, DISARMAMENT, and TRANSARMAMENT.

GENERALIZED STRIKE. A widespread *strike in which less than a majority of the workers in the important industries of the area or *country halt work simultaneously to express a general grievance. A generalized strike is thus less extensive than a *general strike, and may result from a deliberate decision or from an only partially successful attempt to call a general strike.

Grievances leading to a generalized strike have varied widely, but have included *resistance to *government wage regulations and procedures.

GENERAL RESISTANCE (associated with civilian-based defense). Overall *policy, attitudes, and forms of action for *civilian-based defense established by advance guidelines for *resistance. Action based on such a policy may be implemented in case of a *defense emergency by everyone without specific directives from officials or a *leadership group.

General resistance may, for example, include refusal to assist the *usurpers' police to arrest fellow citizens, refusal to join the usurper's political organizations, refusal to assist *propaganda in favor of the usurpers, and the like.

General resistance is contrasted with *organized resistance, which requires specific instructions. The term was introduced by Lars Porsholt.

GENERAL STRIKE. A work stoppage by a majority of the workers in the more important industries of an area or *country, intended to bring the economic life of that area to a complete standstill in order to achieve certain objectives. These objectives may be oriented to economic, political, revolutionary, or *defense issues.

This *method of *strike may be used on a local, regional, national, or international level.

The work stoppage is usually intended to be total, except that certain vital services necessary for health may be exempted, such as provision of food, water, medical care, and sewage disposal.

Calling a general strike is usually seen as a challenge to the *government. It is one method that has been used to oppose a *coup d'état.

GENOCIDE. The attempted or actual annihilation of a whole people who are identified by culture, race, nationality, religion, or other criteria.
See also EXTERMINATION CAMP.

GLEICHSCHALTUNG. The system of restructuring and controlling the *society by institutional reorganization and hierarchical direction in Nazi Germany. The objective was to control completely every aspect of the society's social, economic, and political life and the whole population. This was done by bringing each organization and institution of the society under dictatorial direction. The aim was to determine the society's activities and to *control its members. These dictatorial structures were in turn controlled by an encompassing dictatorial system.

Although the word *Gleichschaltung* literally only means "coordination," the actual system was far more thorough and comprehensive than the Italian fascist model of the *Corporate State, to which it is related.
See also FASCISM, NAZISM, and TOTALITARIANISM.

GO-HOME-EARLY STRIKE. This was used in Denmark during the Nazi occupation. When German officials responded to increased public *opposition and *sabotage with executions, the prohibition of all meetings and public gatherings of more than five, and a nighttime curfew, workers at one factory in Copenhagen responded.

They left work early on June 26, 1944, and sent a message to German headquarters, saying that because the Germans could not guarantee their food supply, they had to leave work early to tend their garden plots. They were not striking, they said, but potatoes and vegetables were more important to them than the German war industry. This action became known as the go-home-early strike.
See also LIMITED STRIKE.

GOING LIMP. See REFUSAL OF ASSISTANCE TO ENFORCEMENT AGENTS.

GO-SLOW. See SLOWDOWN STRIKE.

GOVERNMENT. 1. The political institution or system of a *society by which or through which the society's ultimate domestic and foreign *policies are determined and carried out.

See also STATE.

2. The particular group of policymakers that at a given time occupies the position of *ruler in a State.

3. More generally, the system by which any social group or institution determines its goals and policies and carries them out.

See also AUTHORITY, CONSTITUTIONAL GOVERNMENT, DEMO-CRACY, DICTATORSHIP, DUAL SOVEREIGNTY AND PARALLEL GOVERNMENT, LEGITIMACY, MILITARY GOVERNMENT, NONCOOPERATION BY CONSTITUENT GOVERNMENTAL UNITS, OBEDIENCE, OVERLOADING OF ADMINISTRATIVE SYSTEMS, OVERTHROW OF A GOVERNMENT, POLITICAL POWER, PUPPET GOVERNMENT, QUASI-LEGAL EVASIONS AND DELAYS, REFUSAL TO ACCEPT APPOINTED OFFICIALS, SELECTIVE REFUSAL OF ASSISTANCE BY GOVERNMENT AIDES, SELF-GOVERNMENT, and SOVEREIGNTY.

GOVERNMENT ADMINISTRATIVE SYSTEM. See BOYCOTT OF GOVERNMENT DEPARTMENTS, AGENCIES, AND OTHER BODIES, BUREAUCRACY, and GENERAL ADMINISTRATIVE NONCOOPERATION.

GOVERNMENT ECONOMIC NONCOOPERATION. See BLACKLISTING OF TRADERS, DOMESTIC EMBARGO, INTERNATIONAL BUYERS' EMBARGO, INTERNATIONAL SELLERS' EMBARGO, and INTERNATIONAL TRADE EMBARGO.

GOVERNMENT EMPLOYMENT. See BOYCOTT OF GOVERNMENT EMPLOYMENT AND POSITIONS.

GOVERNMENT IN EXILE. A *government (as in definition 2 above) that, in the face of a temporarily successful *coup d'état or *invasion, has fled abroad to continue certain *operations.

It may then constitute a continuing challenge to the new *illegitimate government, serve as an organizational base to encourage and perhaps even finance *resistance at home, and may take international actions. The aim of the government in exile may be to undermine the usurping *regime and restore the original *legitimate government.

See also PROVISIONAL GOVERNMENT.

GOVERNMENT PERSONNEL. See BLOCKING OF LINES OF COMMAND AND INFORMATION, BUREAUCRACY, DELIBERATE INEFFICIENCY AND SELECTIVE NONCOOPERATION BY ENFORCEMENT AGENTS, GENERAL ADMINISTRATIVE NONCOOPERATION, JUDICIAL NONCOOPERATION, MUTINY, SELECTIVE REFUSAL OF ASSISTANCE BY GOVERNMENT AIDES, and STALLING AND OBSTRUCTION.

GOVERNMENT-SUPPORTED ORGANIZATIONS. See BOYCOTT OF GOVERNMENT-SUPPORTED ORGANIZATIONS.

GRAND STRATEGY. The conception that serves to coordinate and direct all appropriate and available resources (e.g., economic, human, moral) of the *nation or other group to attain its objectives in a *conflict. The master plan for conducting the conflict.

Grand strategy includes consideration of the rightness of the cause of the *struggle group, determination of the social, economic, and political pressures and influences the struggle group will employ, and the conditions under which open struggle will be initiated.

Grand strategy very importantly includes the selection of the *technique of conflict, or ultimate *sanction, which will be used as reserve leverage in open or implied threats during *negotiations and in an open *confrontation of *forces if that occurs. The selected grand strategy sets the basic framework for the selection of more limited *strategies for waging the struggle.

In the course of such matching of forces, grand strategy includes the allocation of general tasks to particular groups and the distribution of resources to them for use in the conflict.

In addition to questions of how to win the immediate conflict, grand strategy includes consideration of how the struggle itself relates to the achievement of the objectives for which the conflict is waged. The probable long-term consequences and the future condition of *peace also fall within grand strategy.

GRIEVANCE GROUP. The general population group whose grievances are issues in the *conflict and are being championed by the *nonviolent actionists.

The proportion of the grievance group actively involved in the struggle will vary, and may change significantly as the conflict develops. The process of *political jujitsu tends to increase that involvement.

GROUP LOBBYING. The gathering of people to visit their legislative representatives in order to urge them to support or oppose a certain measure, in large enough numbers that the assemblage becomes itself a *demonstration.

Lobbying by individuals or small groups is normally only a verbal expression of opinion and not classed as *nonviolent action. However, lobbying by a large group, or a small group of individuals with exceptional status, or persons acting on behalf of many people or institutions, would be classed as group lobbying.

This *method of *nonviolent protest and persuasion may take the form of a large number of individual or small group visits, or a single lobbying by very large numbers of people simultaneously.

GROUP OR MASS PETITION. A written request or supplication seeking the redress of a specific grievance, signed by a large number of individuals, or by a smaller number of representatives acting on behalf of organizations, institutions, or constituencies. Internet petitions signed by many individuals or organized multiple signed postcards with essentially the same message would also be group or mass petitions.

It is the group nature of this action that makes it a *method of *nonviolent protest and persuasion, since individual petitions are simply personal efforts to persuade.

GUERRILLA. 1. A person participating in *guerrilla warfare.

2. Pertaining to guerrilla warfare.

GUERRILLA THEATER. 1. A skit, dramatic presentation, or similar act with a political theme. It is often performed as a disruption of speeches, lectures, meetings, or normal proceedings of some group or institution, or it may take place in the open air or near buildings of special significance.

Its characters are often extreme parodies of people in power whom the organizers regard as responsible for an injustice or other social ill. The action is designed to stimulate publicity and provoke sympathy for the cause favored by the organizers.

2. More generally, a spontaneous style of stage theater, usually with a political theme.

A social *method of *nonviolent intervention.

GUERRILLA WARFARE. A politico-military *technique of struggle that uses psychological, social, political, *paramilitary, and *military forces, usually against an initially more powerful *government or its military forces.

The various types of action adopted by *guerrillas are applied in varying combinations and proportions at different stages of the *conflict. Because of the dominant political component, irregular forces, lack of a definite geographical front, and highly flexible *strategies and *tactics, guerrilla warfare is commonly contrasted with frontal *conventional war.

In the early stages of guerrilla war, nonmilitary popular *agitation and small-scale *violence, *demolitions, and paramilitary action (for example, hit-and-run attacks and avoidance of frontal confrontations) are used.

The aims may be to win and increase political loyalties from the population, to seize or otherwise obtain *weapons, to undermine the morale of the *opponents, and to harass and wear down the opponents' military and police forces.

While themselves committing major acts of violence, and often deliberately provoking extreme *repression, the guerrillas may seek to capitalize on the *backlash against the opponents' larger-scale violent repression of peaceful *protests in order to alienate the population further from the opponents' government and gain international support for their cause.

Over time, the guerrillas aim gradually to weaken the opponents' resolve and capacities, to increase their own political support and institutional base, and to build up their own military forces and equipment to the level of conventional military standards. If victory is not achieved earlier, the guerrillas may aim to be able in the final stage to wage conventional military war with frontal strategies to defeat their enemy. However, many guerrilla struggles do not proceed to that stage because the conditions do not exist for that kind of escalation or because the lower-level *harassment is seen as sufficient to achieve their goals.

Although differing in obvious ways, guerrilla warfare is similar to *nonviolent action in its emphasis on the importance of securing popular support from the population, undermining the morale and resolve of the opponents, wearing down the opponents' attempts to *control the situation, utilizing the opponents' repression to increase *resistance, and certain other points.

In *nonviolent struggle, however, the importance of all those factors is increased, along with the application of inhibiting factors to limit the opponents' repression.

See also FRONTAL DEFENSE.

HANDLERS' BOYCOTT. See SUPPLIERS' AND HANDLERS' BOYCOTT.

HARASSMENT. See NONVIOLENT HARASSMENT.

HARTAL. A temporary voluntary suspension of the economic life of an area, usually a city, by workers, shop owners, and businessmen, in order to demonstrate extreme dissatisfaction. This Indian form of *protest outwardly resembles a temporary, symbolic, citywide *general strike or *economic shutdown.

Although the *hartal* is largely economic, and hence is classed as a *strike, the effect is symbolic protest. The *hartal* is used not to wield economic influence, but to communicate sorrow, determination, revulsion, or moral and religious feelings.

Generally there is greater emphasis in the *hartal* than in the general strike on its voluntary nature, even to the point of the laborers abstaining from work only after they obtain permission from their employers. Shop owners, businessmen, professionals, and the like, participate by closing their stores and offices.

The *hartal* is usually limited to twenty-four hours, but occasionally will run for forty-eight hours or even longer in very serious cases. It is usually citywide or village-wide, although it may occur over a more extended area, even the whole *country, especially during national mourning.

The *hartal* was often used by M. K. Gandhi at the beginning of major struggles to arouse the population and to test *resistance spirit.

HATRED. Enmity, extreme dislike, or detestation, of another person or group, which often occurs in an acute *conflict.

Hatred can coexist with the use of the *nonviolent *technique and has often done so. However, the effectiveness of *nonviolent struggle may be increased when the *actionists are able to refrain from or control the expression of *hostility and hatred.

The absence of showing hatred—combined with the absence of *violence—may increase the psychological impact of the continuing *nonviolent resistance on the opponents and their *agents of *repression. Absence of signs of hatred may not only facilitate operation of the *conversion *mechanism of change, but also the willingness of the *opponents to reach an *accommodation. Such absence also may help to undermine the loyalty of the opponents' police or troops, contributing to *deliberate inefficiency and selective noncooperation by enforcement agents and even *mutiny—which could promote success through the mechanism of *nonviolent coercion.

Hatred of the opponents' policies and actions may be nonviolently expressed through a *social boycott of the opponents' troops and an *ice front, although neither of those require detestation of the agents as persons.

"HAUNTING" OFFICIALS. The action of following and remaining constantly near an official everywhere he or she goes with the intent of reminding him or her of the "immorality" of his or her behavior (as in repressing a *nonviolent resistance movement), and of the determination and *fearlessness of the population.

A *method of *nonviolent protest and persuasion.

HEAL-IN. See OVERLOADING OF FACILITIES.

HIDING, ESCAPE, AND FALSE IDENTITIES. Under certain special circumstances these types of behavior constitute a *method of *political noncooperation. However, they are not usually a part of *nonviolent action as they commonly indicate *fear, which disrupts the operation of the *technique.

Such actions may be considered politically significant noncooperation, for example, when they are applied against a *government that seeks to arrest, intern, and perhaps exterminate particular groups of people, or during massive *repression. Or such actions may constitute *nonviolent resistance when practiced by groups wanted as *hostages or for *reprisals, forced labor, or conscript duty.

Escape by slaves, and helping slaves escape, constitute *resistance. In certain circumstances, members of the *resistance movement might also themselves choose to "disappear." False identities have occasionally been used on a large scale to combat *conscription for forced labor or *deportation.

HIJRAT. See PROTEST EMIGRATION.

HOMAGE AT BURIAL PLACES. A visit to graves by a large number of people, or by a series of individuals and small groups, expressing political *protest and moral condemnation when the dead have been associated with the cause of the current struggle or have been killed by the *opponents.

A *method of *nonviolent protest and persuasion.

See also DEMONSTRATIVE FUNERAL.

HONORING THE DEAD AS PROTEST. See DEMONSTRATIVE FUNERAL, HOMAGE AT BURIAL PLACES, MOCK FUNERAL, and POLITICAL MOURNING.

HONORS. See RENOUNCING HONORS.

HOSTAGE. A person whose safety and perhaps life are threatened in an effort to induce others to take, or refrain from, certain actions. Usually the person has been physically seized and is held by the group making the threat. In the past the person has often been an important *government official kidnapped to draw attention to the kidnappers' grievance. Hostage taking is one method used by groups in *guerrilla warfare and those engaged in *terrorism.

HOSTILITY. 1. Feelings of extreme aversion or antagonism.

2. An action expressing sharp *opposition or antagonism, as in a *war.

See also AGGRESSION, AGGRESSIVENESS, and HATRED.

HUMAN CHAIN. A *demonstration in which a large number of people hold hands in stationary positions, as an alternative to a *march. The focus may be *protest against a specific site, such as a *military *base, or it may be an expression of *solidarity with resisters.

The largest known human chain is the linkage of two million persons in August 1989 in a 650-kilometer line joining the capitals of Estonia, Latvia, and Lithuania in *opposition to continued rule by the Soviet Union.

HUMAN NATURE. The broad behavioral qualities and potentials common to all human beings. These traits derive from the biological characteristics and needs of people, their mental and emotional characteristics and needs, and the requirements and consequences of living in any *society.

Contrary to widespread belief, *violence is not an inevitable expression of "human nature." Although much violence exists, there are also many situations and entire societies that exhibit very limited violence, much peaceful *cooperation, and resolution of *conflict without violence. These examples clearly demonstrate that normal *frustration and the human propensity for *aggressiveness can be channeled into *nonviolent behavior. That this type of behavior has been seen in many societies during many periods of history demonstrates that it is compatible with "human nature."

HUMAN RESOURCES. As a *source of political power, the number of persons who obey the *ruler, cooperate, or provide the ruler with special assistance by their skills and capacities, as well as the proportion of such persons in the general population, and the extent and forms of their organizations.

HUMAN RIGHTS. Historically, "natural rights" or the "rights of man," now termed "human rights," were claims for minimal *liberties and standards of treatment of persons simply because they are human beings.

These liberties and standards have been elaborated in *liberal theory and practice to mean prohibition of *government or private interference, or suppression of people's opportunities to live without discriminatory treatment, to believe as they choose, to express themselves, and to participate in their *societies. Socialist theory has insisted that there are also economic and social rights related to work and welfare.

A core set of widely accepted human rights is identified in the Universal Declaration of Human Rights issued in 1948 by the United Nations General Assembly. Since then, United Nations covenants have specified a wide range of "civil and political rights" and "economic, social, and cultural rights," and the claims of ethnic and national minorities have been given greater recognition in international human rights law.

See also CIVIL LIBERTIES, CIVIL RIGHTS, DEMOCRACY, FREEDOM (POLITICAL), and JUSTICE.

HUMAN SHIELD. A *method of trying to prevent a violent *attack on people or destruction of material objects by creating a human presence at a threatened site.

The method has been particularly associated with opposition to *war, when *civilians from the *State planning to go to war travel to the *country under threat and offer to stay close to likely targets.

The method has also been used in other contexts. For example, in November 2006, hundreds of Palestinians in Gaza stopped the Israeli air force from destroying the home of a suspected *militant by surrounding the home and climbing on the roof.

HUNGER BLOCKADE. Deliberate severance of supply lines for shipment of food into a populated area, used as a means of *repression against a resisting population.

HUNGER STRIKE. A refusal to eat, with the aim of forcing the *opponents to grant demands, but without serious efforts to convert them. This is in contrast to the *satyagrahic fast.

The hunger strike may be undertaken for a set time, for an indefinite period, or until death if the demand is not granted. It is often resorted to by prisoners whose other means of *resistance are limited.

The purpose is to show the opponents and the public the seriousness of the protesters' beliefs in order to encourage the opponents to rethink their position on the issues, and also to gain increased public support for the protesters.

See also FAST and FAST OF MORAL PRESSURE.

ICE FRONT. Systematic *social boycott in all relationships with particular persons, especially *military occupation troops and functionaries.

This *boycott may include refusal to speak with them, or severely limiting speech (for example, speaking only to give wrong directions), "looking through" individuals as though they were not there, refusal to sit beside them, falling silent when they enter a store, and the like.

The term is of Norwegian origin.

See also COLD SHOULDER.

IDEALISM. Thought or actions based on belief in how people or social or political conditions should be, rather than how they actually are. Contrasted with *realism.

IDEOLOGY. A complex system of interdependent beliefs, theories, and ideas about *society and *politics, which provides an interpretation of the past, explains the present unacceptable situation, and prescribes guidelines for action to bring about a desired future state of affairs.

These beliefs provide the framework of a program to make possible the change from the present to the desired future, based on the understanding of reality that the ideology purports to provide.

The ideology is likely to be made into a system of consciously held beliefs, but it may also be unconsciously accepted.

A genuine ideology, such as *Marxism-Leninism or *Nazism, is more fully developed and directive of *policies than more general political outlooks, such as conservatism, that do not prescribe a path for major change.

ILLEGITIMATE. In violation of the accepted sources of *authority in the institution or a social or political system.

For example, a *ruler would be illegitimate who has violated the *constitution by seizing control of the *State without regard to accepted procedures. A decree, order, or law issued by *usurpers would be illegitimate, as would a decree issued in violation of accepted procedures or sources of authority, such as the constitution or acknowledged religious principles.

IMPERIALISM. A system of *domination by the ruling system of one *country over other countries or peoples, for the purpose of achieving some type of aggrandizement of the dominating system.

Imperialist systems may be used to gain economic enrichment, prestige, improved military-strategic position, cultural domination, political glory, or expanded power. The aim may also involve efforts to strengthen the dominant system by providing it with a "mission," and to bring religious or political "salvation" to the people of the dominated country.

The means used to establish and maintain such domination may include some combination of the following: manipulation of established local *rulers; *military conquest and *military occupation;

economic penetration; outright seizures of property and wealth; direct and indirect economic exploitation; local establishment of new imperial-controlled *governments and *State structures; *imprisonment; killings; terrorization; *indoctrination of the indigenous population to accept their assigned *subordinate position; *genocide; expulsion or resettlement of the indigenous population; destruction of the indigenous culture and way of life; rule by separate subordinate administration; and direct annexation.

IMPOUNDING ASSETS. See SEIZURE OF ASSETS.

IMPRESSED LABOR. See NONCOOPERATION WITH CONSCRIPTION AND DEPORTATION and REFUSAL OF IMPRESSED LABOR.

IMPRISONMENT. Incarceration of persons as a means of *control or *punishment, whether for behavior deemed "anti-social" or "criminal," or for political views or actions.

See also CIVIL INTERNMENT, CONCENTRATION CAMP, EXILE, INTERNMENT CAMP, and SEEKING IMPRISONMENT.

INACTION. Doing nothing.

INDEPENDENCE. Self-government; a condition of not being subjected to external rule or *control.

See also DE FACTO and DE JURE.

INDEPENDENT ORGANIZATION. An autonomous self-directed institution not acting under the orders or *control of another body.

See also LOCI OF POWER.

INDIRECT STRATEGY (reconceptualized term). A principle of *strategy based on a view that greater success may often be gained by avoiding direct frontal assault on one's *opponents' centers of strength, using the same means as used by the opponents. Instead, action is taken in oblique ways which the opponents may be unprepared to withstand effectively.

In a *military conflict, for example, instead of sending troops against the opponents' concentration of *military forces, the resisting forces could go around and *attack from the rear. In that location the opponents are likely to be weak, or not expecting an attack.

The principle has been most developed in military strategic thought, but is also applicable in other types of *conflict, including *nonviolent struggle. The use of social, economic, psychological, and political forms of *resistance instead of *violence are more difficult for the opponents' military forces to deal with than military resistance.

The indirect strategic concept was developed especially by Sir Basil Liddell Hart in his book *Strategy: The Indirect Approach.* Nonviolent struggle may be viewed as an extreme application of that principle of strategy.

INDOCTRINATION. A deliberately initiated process of inculcating individuals, groups, or an entire population with a doctrine, belief, *ideology, or idea, usually at the expense of previously held convictions.

This may be done through an educational system, mass media campaigns, religious conversions, or in extreme cases by *brainwashing.

INDUSTRIAL ACTION. See the METHODS of STRIKE and ECONOMIC BOYCOTT.

INDUSTRIAL CONFLICT. *Conflict between labor and management in manufacturing and trade, especially over union recognition, wages and hours, working conditions, and prerogatives of both sides.

Although conflicts are quite often resolved through *negotiations, *conciliation, and *arbitration, negotiators are usually aware that if they fail, each side may resort to stronger means, including *strikes, *economic boycotts, *lockouts, or *violence.

INDUSTRIAL STRIKES. See BUMPER STRIKE, DETAILED STRIKE, ECONOMIC SHUTDOWN, ESTABLISHMENT STRIKE, GENERAL STRIKE, GENERALIZED STRIKE, INDUSTRY STRIKE, LIMITED

STRIKE, REPORTING "SICK" ("SICK-OUT"), SELECTIVE STRIKE, SLOWDOWN STRIKE, STRIKE BY RESIGNATION, SYMPATHETIC STRIKE, and WORKING-TO-RULE STRIKE.

INDUSTRY STRIKE. A *method of *strike involving a work stoppage in all establishments of a specific branch of manufacturing, services, and trade (such as mining, telephone system, printing, or steel production) in a given area. The area may be local, regional, or national.

INFILTRATION (associated with nonviolent action). 1. The process of deliberate, usually covert, gradual entry of individual members of a group (especially a political party or *political police) into an organization or institution. The purpose may be to gain information, alter that body's *policies or effectiveness, or to take *control of its *leadership positions.

2. In *guerrilla warfare, the secret entry of designated persons into specific geographical areas in order to be in a position later to carry out acts of *demolition, *terrorism, or a tactical action in a *guerrilla *campaign.

3. In a *nonviolent campaign, the *opponents may try to infiltrate the movement in order to influence its actions or goals, disrupt the organization, or discredit the movement. This may be done, for example, by provoking or committing *violence in the name of the campaign.

See also AGENT PROVOCATEUR.

INFRASTRUCTURE. In the context of social organization and structure, the lower-level formal and informal institutional and group framework of a *society. The infrastructure is the set of relationships among the diverse institutions of the society, including the *loci of power.

In a *conflict between an established *government and a *resistance or revolutionary movement, the outcome may be crucially influenced by the degree to which the pre-conflict infrastructure remains, or no longer remains, and is autonomous and responsive to the popular will. That can determine the degree to which the infrastructure is able to support or withhold support from either side in the conflict.

See also CIVIL SOCIETY, LOCI OF POWER, NONGOVERNMENTAL ORGANIZATION, and REVOLUTION.

INHIBITORY GESTURE. A motion by the human body, or a part of the body, intended to communicate to potential attackers that it would be better for all if they did not inflict injuries on the protesters.

Demonstrators in *nonviolent *demonstrations have, for example, shown the *opponents' troops or police their empty hands to make clear that they are not carrying *weapons. In some cases a *violent *attack might produce publicity and shifts of *public opinion hostile to the opponents.

INJUSTICE. 1. A condition of extreme inequality in the social, economic, or political system, or a combination of these, in which people's lives are limited, controlled, distorted, or terminated, as a consequence of *oppression by a dominant privileged group. This often involves violations of *human rights and *civil rights.

Injustice involves a denial of people's human dignity and worth, the *control of their lives by others, and the use of subjected people by the dominant group as mere raw material for achieving that group's objectives. *Violence, applied or threatened, always can be expected as an important tool of the dominant group to induce *submission of the dominated group.

2. Treatment of persons that is regarded as arbitrary, inequitable, or unfair.

See also JUSTICE.

INSTITUTIONALIZED VIOLENCE (reconceptualized term). *Violence that has been built into institutions, especially political ones. Prime examples are the *military and police forces that are predicated upon preparations to use violence in a *conflict.

Violence in some form is usually the implicit or explicit final *sanction for enforcement of the laws and edicts of the *State. When milder means are judged inadequate for enforcing laws or maintaining internal *control, police action and *military forces are employed as the means of last resort even in the most *democratic *countries. In dealing with other States, military means are regarded as the means of last resort.

Violence built into the system as its final sanction is usually regarded as *legitimate violence, if the *government itself is accepted as legitimate. This major violence is usually less noticed than much smaller acts of violence which are regarded as *illegitimate. This institutionalized violence which is approved as legitimate is often disguised by the gentler term "*force."

In *dictatorships and other systems of *domination, institutionalized violence is also used by the *ruler or dominant group to maintain *oppression of a subordinated group and the status quo.

INSTITUTIONS AND RESISTANCE. See ALTERNATIVE COMMUNICATION SYSTEM, ALTERNATIVE ECONOMIC INSTITUTION, ALTERNATIVE MARKET, ALTERNATIVE SOCIAL INSTITUTION, ALTERNATIVE TRANSPORTATION SYSTEM, BOYCOTT OF GOVERNMENT DEPARTMENTS, AGENCIES, AND OTHER BODIES, BOYCOTT OF GOVERNMENT-SUPPORTED ORGANIZATIONS, DUAL SOVEREIGNTY AND PARALLEL GOVERNMENT, EXPULSION FROM INTERNATIONAL ORGANIZATIONS, GENERAL ADMINISTRATIVE NONCOOPERATION, NONCOOPERATION BY CONSTITUENT GOVERNMENTAL UNITS, OVERLOADING OF ADMINISTRATIVE SYSTEMS, REFUSAL OF MEMBERSHIP IN INTERNATIONAL BODIES, REFUSAL TO DISSOLVE EXISTING INSTITUTIONS, WITHDRAWAL FROM GOVERNMENT EDUCATIONAL INSTITUTIONS, WITHDRAWAL FROM INTERNATIONAL ORGANIZATIONS, and WITHDRAWAL FROM SOCIAL INSTITUTIONS.

INSUBORDINATION. Deliberate rejection of the status of *subordination. Therefore, *defiance and *disobedience of *commands of supervisors, superordinate officials, or *agents of the established system.

INSURGENCY (reconceptualized term). An organized internal *revolt or *uprising against a *government, such as by *guerrilla warfare.

See also INSURGENCY WARFARE.

INSURGENCY WARFARE. An internal *revolt or *uprising by violent means, which either is not intended to become a *civil war, or has not yet reached that scale.

See also COUNTERINSURGENCY WAR.

INSURRECTION. An *uprising against an established *government, waged by either *violent or *nonviolent means.

See also CIVILIAN INSURRECTION, INSURRECTIONARY STRIKE, and MORAL INSURRECTION.

INSURRECTIONARY STRIKE. A widespread labor *strike, such as a *general strike or *generalized strike, or an *economic shutdown, initiated with the motive of rebelling against the established economic or political system.

INTELLIGENCE. In the context of a *conflict, the understanding of the *opponents' intentions, plans, *operations, and problems resulting from the collection, comparison, evaluation, and analysis of obtainable information, both publicly available and secret. This is especially relevant to the planning and conduct of a struggle against the opponents.

INTELLIGENCE OPERATIONS. Activity designed to collect information on one's *opponents for use in an existing or a potential *conflict. This activity is often institutionalized in the form of secret police, secret services, or spy agencies. In principle, such activity may be practiced by both the established order and the *resistance.

The *operations of intelligence agencies may sometimes extend to monitoring the activities of *nonviolent and *legitimate dissenters, even though the operations are officially directed against foreign *subversion or spying.

In practice, official intelligence organizations sometimes carry out missions quite different from gathering information. These missions may include assisting *coups d'état, conducting *assassinations, and disrupting *resistance organizations and activities. Such activities may occur both in the organization's home *country and in other countries.

INTERDICT. Suspension by religious officials of services, sacraments, canonical burials, or similar rites to the population in a given territory for a specified period of time as a social and religious *sanction.

The application of the interdict may be partially punitive, but it usually has been aimed at compelling a *government or population to rectify specific grievances. These may be either strictly religious or, more often, political.

See also EXCOMMUNICATION.

INTERGROUP CONFLICT. A general term that is inclusive of any type of contention or *opposition between two groups, regardless of the issues that may be at stake or the means by which the *conflict may be conducted.

The means used may be established institutional procedures, *methods of *nonviolent action, *violence, or informal social processes. The scale may be quite limited or extremely large. The term, therefore, refers to a broad field of contention rather than any precise type of situation.

INTERJECTION. See NONVIOLENT INTERJECTION.

INTERNAL WAR. Organized *military struggle between two groups within a given *country.

See also CIVIL WAR, GUERRILLA WARFARE, and INSURGENCY WARFARE.

INTERNATIONAL BUYERS' EMBARGO. The prohibition, by *government decision, of general or particular purchases and importation of goods from a specific *country.

The intent behind the use of this *method of *economic boycott may be, for example, to change a particular *policy of the government of the boycotted country, to force a broader change in the government, or to contribute to its downfall.

See also EMBARGO.

INTERNATIONAL CONSUMERS' BOYCOTT. A *consumers' boycott that is applied simultaneously in several countries against the products of a particular *country because of a grievance against it. The issue involved is normally a broad humanitarian one of international concern, such as a denial of *human rights, that arouses wide support.

This action by consumers is distinguished from *government-initiated *embargoes.

INTERNATIONAL ECONOMIC NONCOOPERATION. See BLACKLISTING OF TRADERS, INTERNATIONAL BUYERS' EMBARGO, INTERNATIONAL CONSUMERS' BOYCOTT, INTERNATIONAL SELLERS' EMBARGO, INTERNATIONAL TRADE EMBARGO, and NATIONAL CONSUMERS' BOYCOTT.

INTERNATIONALISM. 1. Belief that a community of interests among *nations or *States should supersede the individual short-term objectives of each one.

2. Cosmopolitanism, drawing upon the thoughts, tastes, cultures, and the like of several or many *countries and rejecting national limitations.

INTERNATIONAL ORGANIZATIONS. See CIVILIAN-BASED DEFENSE TREATY ORGANIZATION, EXPULSION FROM INTERNATIONAL ORGANIZATIONS, REFUSAL OF MEMBERSHIP IN INTERNATIONAL BODIES, and WITHDRAWAL FROM INTERNATIONAL ORGANIZATIONS.

INTERNATIONAL POLITICAL NONCOOPERATION. See DIPLOMATIC RELATIONS—DELAY AND CANCELLATION, DIPLOMATIC RELATIONS—REDUCED REPRESENTATION, DIPLOMATIC RELATIONS—SEVERANCE OF REPRESENTATION, and DIPLOMATIC RELATIONS—WITHHOLDING OR WITHDRAWAL OF RECOGNITION.

INTERNATIONAL SELLERS' EMBARGO. A refusal, on the basis of *government decision or in compliance with decisions by international organizations, to sell certain, or any, products to another *country or several countries.

The motives for using this *method of *economic boycott range from objections to the existence of the government itself to certain of its actions. These objections may arise from its political orientation, the means it used to come to power or to maintain itself, or a particular *policy or a specific action of the *regime.

In some cases, such as those involving *military *weapons sales, an international sellers' embargo may be an attempt to halt or prevent a *war by stopping such sales to both sides. Or, under the guise of stopping a war, the embargo against both sides may be intended to assist the stronger side by preventing sales of military weapons to the weaker one.

INTERNATIONAL TRADE EMBARGO. A combination of the *international sellers' embargo and the *international buyers' embargo. It involves a total prohibition of all trade with the *opponent *country, or a near-total ban, exempting perhaps medicines and food.

Classed as a *method of *economic boycott.

INTERNMENT CAMP. A place for confinement of prisoners, usually having fewer permanent buildings than regular prisons. It is usually used to confine a particular population group, such as *political prisoners, and normally not regular criminals.

See also CIVIL INTERNMENT, CONCENTRATION CAMP, and IMPRISONMENT.

INTERSOCIETAL CONFLICT. A *conflict between two or more *societies, regardless of the issues at stake and whether or not the *State is an actor in the contention.

INTERSTATE. Arrangements or activities involving two or more *States.

INTERVENTION. See NONVIOLENT INTERVENTION.

INTIMIDATION. The use of *sanctions, or the threat to use sanctions, to induce others to take, or not to take, certain actions because of their *fear of the likely consequences if they do not comply.

See also FEAR.

INTRASOCIETAL CONFLICT. Any *conflict within a single *society, whether on economic, social, religious, or political issues.

INVADERS. The *forces and administration of a *State or other entity that have engaged in an *invasion and consequently occupation of another *country.

INVASION. The entry of the *military forces of one *State into the territory of another *country for purposes of hostile action, occupation, imposition of demands, gaining of political or economic objectives, or the like.

See also CIVILIAN-BASED DEFENSE, MILITARY OCCUPATION, NONVIOLENT INVASION, OCCUPATION COSTS, OCCUPATION FORCES, PREEMPTIVE INVASION, and RESISTANCE AT FRONTIERS.

IRREGULAR WARFARE. *Violent *conflict using organized *combat troops that, in terms of their positions, combat formations, and strategic *operations, do not operate within the pattern of frontal combat that is characteristic of conventional *military warfare. *Guerrilla warfare is the prime example.

JACOBINISM. A school of revolutionary thought and action derived from, but not limited to, the Jacobins of the French Revolution. Adherents of this school are committed to establishing a revolutionary *dictatorship that aims to remake the *society.

This view holds that a self-chosen revolutionary elite has not only the right but the duty to gain *control of the *State apparatus by any means necessary. That elite then has the duty to use *violence, and especially its own minority dictatorship, enforced if need be by *terror, to achieve its goal. The aim is to destroy the old society, and during a transition period to construct in its place a new system to be based on revolutionary ideals.

Hence, "Jacobin."

JACQUERIE. A mass, usually spontaneous, *rebellion of peasants intent on rectifying specific grievances, using various means. Possible aims may include regaining particular lost rights, or demanding, in the name of an *authority (such as a king), the removal of individual officials who are believed to have betrayed the authority or the *ruler's genuine intent. Jacqueries are not attempts to achieve social *revolution or changes in land ownership.

This method takes its name from the French peasant rebellion of 1358.

See also LAND SEIZURE.

JAIL/GAOL. See ARREST, CIVIL INTERNMENT, CONCENTRATION CAMP, IMPRISONMENT, INTERNMENT CAMP, and SEEKING IMPRISONMENT.

JAIL-IN. See SEEKING IMPRISONMENT.

JAMMING. Obstruction of communications. *Governments have often jammed radio broadcasts from outside the *country. The objective has been to prevent one's own population from hearing information or viewpoints regarded as dangerous to the *regime.

Jamming has also become a form of internal popular *protest. For example, large numbers of people may telephone simultaneously in order to jam the switchboards of government offices, or send e-mails constantly with the intention of clogging up official e-mail sites. Jamming can thus be a way of obstructing government business through modern communications.

"Culture jamming" is a *method of turning corporate advertising into a medium for protest, for example, by changing the content of billboards.

See also OVERLOADING OF ADMINISTRATIVE SYSTEMS.

JOURNALS. See NEWSPAPERS AND JOURNALS OF DISSENT.

JUDICIAL NONCOOPERATION. Refusal by members of a judicial system (judges, jurors, or the like) to carry out the will of the *government, to enforce a particular law or *policy that is regarded as unjust, or to impose a penalty that is regarded as excessive.

A jury, for example, may refuse to convict a *political prisoner despite supporting evidence of guilt and pressure from the judge and prosecutor. In other cases, even in a system where it is not the general constitutional practice, a court may defiantly determine that a specific law or policy of the government is unconstitutional and hence invalid.

An entire judicial institution may resign in *resistance to a *usurper's interference with the court's *independence. Alternatively, individuals, such as judges, may defiantly remain in the judicial system but refuse to enforce laws or regulations which they perceive as *illegitimate.

If such *noncooperation is widespread, the *regime is denied an important means of *controlling the population.

JUJITSU. See MORAL JUJITSU, POLITICAL JUJITSU, and POLITICAL KARATE.

JUNTA. A *military council which has formed as a *government as a consequence of a successful *coup d'état.

JUSTICE. 1. A condition of relative equality of members of a *society in mutual treatment and in effective power in the social, economic, and political system. The members are not then dominated by a privileged group, but have instead the opportunity to develop and *control their own lives and to cooperate with others. A system of justice usually defines certain rights for all individuals.

2. A condition of being treated, and treating others, without arbitrariness and with equity and fairness, whether on the basis of law or other standards.

See also CIVIL RIGHTS, HUMAN RIGHTS, and INJUSTICE.

JUST WAR. A theory that *military warfare is justified, politically, morally, or religiously, under certain circumstances. The *conflict may take the form of international military warfare or *violent *revolution. The *war may be conducted by conventional military means or by *guerrilla warfare.

The criteria may include such factors as the cause being good (for example, *defensive, not *aggressive), the *opponents practicing extreme evil, and the apparent absence of other adequate means of countering the opponents' *violence or *oppression.

Explicit just-war theories are prominent in the writings of Christian theologians, Western philosophers, and Mao Zedong, among others.

In addition to the conditions set forth by just-war theology for resort to military conflict (*jus ad bellum*), theological and philosophical discussions of the topic also focus on the means that are believed to be permissible to use in the course of a war (*jus in bello*)—for example, avoidance of unnecessary killing of *civilians.

The development of *weapons of mass destruction has caused some people to conclude that the criteria for a just war can no longer be fulfilled. Those individuals have sometimes sought an alternative *defense policy in *defensive defense, *territorial defense, or *civilian-based defense. Their views have sometimes been called *nuclear pacifism.

KNEEL-IN. See STAND-IN.

LAND SEIZURE. *Direct action by peasants to achieve changes in land distribution by occupying the land they wish to own, by any available means, and claiming ownership.

See also NONVIOLENT LAND SEIZURE.

LEADER. One who effectively provides guidance or *leadership. Leaders are those individuals or groups who provide effective initiatives and guidance, as in ideas, *policies, and directions for action to a group, movement, or institution. Leaders may also symbolize the movement or organization of which they are a part.

There are wide variations in the purposes of leaders, the origins of their *authority, their styles of *operation, the structure of leadership, and the degree of compliance offered to their proposals or recommendations for action.

LEADERSHIP. 1. The ability to provide the initiatives and guidance that are implemented by others, or the quality of providing such initiatives.

2. The position of a *leader.

3. The group that occupies the position of a leader.

Significant variations in leadership derive from the nature of that position, including the sources of *authority for the position itself, the manner by which the persons or groups are selected or accepted as leaders, the degree of concentration of leadership in a small group or its diffusion throughout the *social structure, the degree of structural separation of the leadership from the rest of the *society, the degree of visibility or identifiability of leaders, and the *sanctions they may use to enforce their will, maintain their position, and implement the group's *policies.

These variations and differences in the nonstructural qualities of leaders may be highly influenced by the culture, general social structure, *constitution, traditions, effective power distribution, time period, and other factors.

The choice of *violent action or *nonviolent action as the ultimate sanction relied upon by the leadership and the society is likely to have different effects on the structure of leadership and the distribution of effective power in the society.

Conventional *military means appear to require a rigidly structured and centralized leadership, but in *combat there is a role for junior officers and initiative. In some past *nonviolent conflicts, strong leaders, often charismatic or inspirational, such as M. K. Gandhi and Martin Luther King Jr., have played significant roles. However, in the course of a *conflict, nonviolent action tends to diffuse leadership, spread effective power through the society, and increase the population's *self-reliance.

LEAFLETING. See LITERATURE AND SPEECHES ADVOCATING RESISTANCE.

LEAFLETS, PAMPHLETS, AND BOOKS. Publication and distribution of leaflets, pamphlets, and books are a normal part of political life, especially political debate and activity.

During conditions of political *repression and struggle, when such publications express views critical of existing *policies or challenge the *legitimacy of the *government as a whole, their publication and distribution become more than a simple means of communication; they constitute a *method of *nonviolent protest and persuasion.

The distribution of leaflets is perhaps most commonly used by dissenting groups, but pamphlets and books may also be involved, especially under conditions of not only political but cultural and linguistic *censorship. They may then circulate in manuscript, typescript, illegally published, or smuggled editions, or documents downloaded from websites. Illegally published books were important during the Solidarity struggle in Poland, for example.

See also LITERATURE AND SPEECHES ADVOCATING RESISTANCE and SAMIZDAT. Because of the content and consequences of such advocacy literature, these types of publications are classified separately.

LEGISLATURE. See BOYCOTT OF LEGISLATIVE BODIES.

LEGITIMACY. Validity that comes from being in accord with accepted sources, criteria, and standards of *authority. Legitimacy is an important source of power both for established *governments and for *opposition movements.

The sources of legitimacy may include moral or political principles, a revered origin, tradition, duration over time, and consistency with the *society's accepted procedures, *constitution, or law.

LEGITIMATE. 1. Conforming to recognized principles and accepted standards.

2. A condition derived from *legitimacy.

LENINISM. A synonym for *Marxism-Leninism, used either for brevity or with the implication that the combination of Lenin's *Jacobinism with *Marxism produced an *ideology closer to Lenin's views than those of Marx.

Hence, "Leninist."

LETTERS OF OPPOSITION OR SUPPORT. Letters on political subjects that have been transformed from mere personal communications into public *protest or declarations. This may occur because of the identity of the addressee, the status or the number of the writers or signatories, or the political context that has heightened the significance of the letter. The letter may originally have been addressed to a private individual, a *government official, a newspaper, or any other party.

The letters may be sent by individuals, a group, or many individuals to a particular person or body to communicate a political viewpoint (as a protest) or to declare an intention of taking a political action (such as *resistance or support).

The letters in this category may be revealed to the public by the writer(s) or the recipient, through a "leak," or because the original was an "open letter." Letters may also be revealed to the public by someone placing them on the internet or a blog. Publication of letters of opposition or support may be intended to influence both the addressee and the general public.

A *method of *nonviolent protest and persuasion.

LEVERAGE. A source of pressure or power, which goes further than rational argument, applied to induce someone to act in a desired way.

LIBERAL. Persons or *policies that meet the standards of *liberalism.

LIBERALISM. A broad school of political thought that views individual *liberty as a primary value, and favors reliance on reason and social tolerance. Liberalism, therefore, places a priority on *freedom of conscience, free speech and publication, and maximizing personal choice. In political terms, liberals stress *civil liberties and *human rights, and favor constitutional limits on *government action.

Liberalism is therefore opposed to conservatism and *nationalism that elevate the community above the individual (though liberals have generally supported national *self-government). Liberalism is also opposed to *State *socialism, which seeks to impose economic equality through centralized *control of the economy.

Liberals have, however, long been divided between those who advocate maximum market freedoms and a limited role for the State, and those who argue the State should provide the economic and social conditions for individual development.

See also CONSERVATIVE and CONSTITUTIONAL GOVERNMENT.

LIBERATION. The act or process of achieving the removal of unwanted restrictions, *controls, or *domination. Liberation may, therefore, be a step toward *freedom, which may be developed following liberation from oppressive controls.

LIBERTARIANISM. A school of political opinion that places great emphasis on maximum *liberty and *freedom, general *opposition to the *State as a form of *government, and the desirability of minimal centralized regulation and minimal application of *sanctions. Emphasis is placed on the merit of participatory institutions with high *decentralization and *devolution of power.

The term is sometimes used more narrowly as a synonym for *anarchism to describe an anti-State political view.

Hence, "libertarian."

See also DIRECT DEMOCRACY and PARTICIPATORY DEMOCRACY.

LIBERTY. A condition in which external *controls and restrictions on personal lives and private associations are absent or at a minimum. This refers especially to those controls or restrictions imposed by, or approved by, *governments.

It is generally accepted, however, that the liberty of one person should not impinge on the liberties of others, and some restrictions of law or custom are therefore socially necessary.

Liberty is, for example, the opposite of slavery.

Liberty may be associated with *freedom to participate in making social and political decisions, but this is not a necessary relationship.

See also CIVIL LIBERTIES, CONSTITUTIONAL GOVERNMENT, DEMOCRACY, DICTATORSHIP, DIRECT DEMOCRACY, FREEDOM (POLITICAL), and LIBERTARIANISM.

LIGHTNING STRIKE. See QUICKIE WALKOUT.

LIMITED STRIKE. The refusal to perform certain marginal work (either within or beyond the required working hours) or refusal to work on certain days. The workers continue, however, to perform most of their normal duties in an efficient way.

This form of *strike may involve a refusal, for example, to work overtime, to work longer, or to do more work than is deemed reasonable.

The limited strike has also been called a "running-sore strike." A version of the limited strike used in Nazi-occupied Denmark has been called a *go-home-early strike.

LIMITED WAR. A type of *military *war which is restricted in its scale, *strategies, geographical expanse, or types of weaponry.

LITERATURE AND SPEECHES ADVOCATING RESISTANCE. Literature or speeches that urge people to undertake some form of *nonviolent *noncooperation or *nonviolent intervention. These calls to *resistance can themselves become a *method of *political noncooperation and acts of *defiance, especially where such pronouncements are illegal or denounced as seditious.

See also SEDITION.

LOBBYING. See GROUP LOBBYING.

LOCAL GOVERNMENT NONCOOPERATION. See NONCOOPERATION BY CONSTITUENT GOVERNMENTAL UNITS.

LOCI OF POWER. "Places" in the society where power is located, converges, or is expressed. Loci of power are social groups and institutions that are able to act independently, wield effective social or *political power, or regulate the effective power of others, especially that of the *ruler or other loci. Singular: locus of power.

The precise form and nature of loci of power varies from *society to society and situation to situation. They are, however, likely to be such bodies as families, *social classes, schools, religious groups, cultural and nationality groups, occupational groups, economic groups, towns, cities, provinces and regions, smaller governmental units, independent courts, voluntary organizations, and political parties.

Most often they are traditional, established, formal social groups and institutions. Sometimes, however, the loci of power may be less formally organized and even be recently created or revitalized in the process of achieving some objective or opposing the ruler (for example, the workers' councils in the 1956 Hungarian Revolution).

The capacity of these loci to control the ruler's power will be influenced by the extent of the existence of such loci, the degree of their independence of action, the sources of power that they control, the amount of *social power that they can independently wield or control, and sometimes other factors.

See also CIVIL SOCIETY, INFRASTRUCTURE, and NONGOVERNMENTAL ORGANIZATION.

LOCK-ON. The use of physical, often mechanical, means of various types to impede the removal of persons from a site. British suffragettes sometimes chained themselves to a symbolic site. Protesters against logging of trees and construction of new roads have put arms into tubes that were then coated with concrete, and wrists have been locked to metal bars.

LOCKOUT. Action by an employer to close down temporarily the operation of a particular industrial or other economic unit, as a means of forcing employees to submit to the employer's *policies. Although the lockout is usually applied in industry, it has also been used against agricultural laborers.

The lockout may be applied in a single firm, or by numbers of employers in a kind of sympathetic lockout in an area or industry.

In a particular industrial *conflict it is sometimes difficult to determine whether the stoppage began as a *strike or a lockout.

The lockout itself is clearly a *method of *nonviolent action, although the introduction of public or private police, national guard, or soldiers on behalf of the management introduces *violence into the lockout, as do rioting or personal *attacks by striking workers.

LOGISTICS (reconceptualized term). Activities encompassing the planning, organization, and provision of transport and supply of material goods.

The term is usually applied in the context of *military action, but is also applicable in any *conflict, including *nonviolent struggles, in which transportation and the allocation and distribution of supplies are required.

LYSISTRATIC NONACTION. The refusal of sexual relations, or sexual noncooperation, by women in order to induce men to do, or to cease doing, something. The name of this *method of *social noncooperation is derived from Aristophanes' play *Lysistrata*, in which wives refused sexual relations with their husbands to induce them to stop a *war.

MANIFESTO. A written public declaration, by individuals or a group, of views, intentions, objectives, or a combination of these, that *dissent from the present *policies or system.

MANEUVER (associated with civilian-based defense). 1. A planned movement of *forces to implement a *strategy or *tactic in a *conflict, whether conducted by *military means, *nonviolent struggle, or other *techniques.

2. Large-scale exercises on a local, regional, or *country-wide level as part of the training and preparations for *civilian-based defense, in which an *attack initiating a *defense emergency is acted out and civilian-based defense measures are simulated.

In addition to their training role, credible maneuvers may increase the deterrent effect of the civilian-based defense preparations, and potentially spread know-how of popular *resistance to other countries, including that of the potential attacker.

The term was introduced in this field by Theodor Ebert in the 1960s.

See also DETERRENCE.

MAOISM. The revolutionary *ideology developed from the thought, principles of *strategy, and political views of Mao Zedong.

This ideology emphasizes the dominant role of the peasantry (in place of the proletariat in classical *Marxism), the Communist Party, and the importance of mass *agitation. Maoists have promoted a popular *revolution by a determined politically indoctrinated population, armed with *military *weapons and waging *guerrilla warfare, to enable the Party to seize control of the *State.

MARCH. A group of people walking in *protest or in advocacy in an organized manner to a place which is regarded as significant to the issue involved.

The duration of the march may vary from an hour or so to several weeks, or even longer. Posters and banners may or may not be carried in this *method of *nonviolent protest and persuasion. Leaflets may or may not be distributed to bystanders.

See also PARADE, PILGRIMAGE, and RELIGIOUS PROCESSION.

MARSHALS (associated with nonviolent action). Persons in *nonviolent *demonstrations who help ensure that the demonstrators carry out the intended form of action, keep order, and remain nonviolent.

Marshals may exert influence by example, advice, and general or specific instructions to the demonstrators with whom they are working. Individuals may be selected as marshals on the basis of their experience, calmness, understanding of the nonviolent *technique, and skills in working with people.

See also NONVIOLENT DISCIPLINE.

MARTIAL LAW. Suspension of normal *civilian laws, police procedures, judicial guidelines, and civilian *government, and their replacement by rule by *military government, edicts, and courts martial. The means of rule in this situation include military decrees and military means of enforcement (military tribunals, courts martial, troop action, and military commissions). Personal constitutional rights, including habeas corpus and *civil liberties, are usually suspended.

Martial law has been used to meet special emergencies produced by both natural disasters and political crises, the latter potentially caused by violent *insurrection, *guerrilla warfare, *civilian insurrection, *general strikes, and *nonviolent resistance. Martial law has also been used to intimidate the population after a *coup d'état or foreign *invasion, in order to forestall the development of *resistance.

Procedures for declaring martial law may vary widely. Even when martial law is decreed by the *legitimate government it may or may not be constitutional.

MARXISM. The system of thought about the nature of *society and politics based on the writings of Karl Marx, partly in collaboration with Friedrich Engels. According to Marxism, society and history follow ascertainable laws of operation and development. History is characterized by progress through various stages of economically defined social systems as a result of economic changes and *class struggles.

Material factors are seen as preeminent in determining the nature of a society. *Conflict is seen to play a positive role. In Marxist thinking, the ownership of the means of economic production ensures *control of the political system and thereby defines the ruling class. The struggle against that class by the next rising economic class, created by economic change, is viewed as the driving force in historical development.

Based on the labor theory of the value of material goods, Marxism points to inbuilt exploitation when the owners of the means of production retain profits produced by the labor of another class.

Every class struggle is seen to be also a political struggle. It is believed that with the triumph of the industrial working class (proletariat) over the capitalist class, the conflicts that have characterized history will be ended. A new socialist type of society will thereby be created, based on social ownership of the means of production. Marx posited that socialism would eventually develop into a higher stage of stateless *communism.

Several differing schools of thought and types of political action have claimed to be based on Marxism. These include *social democracy, *Leninism, and *Maoism, among others.

Since the *Communist Manifesto* by Marx and Engels was published in 1848, the changing nature of capitalism, the experiences of Marxist political parties, and the Soviet Union's claims of following Marxist ideology have generated numerous economic, political, and philosophical debates and an enormous literature.

MARXISM-LENINISM. The revolutionary *ideology resulting from the combination of *Marxism with Lenin's Jacobin conception of revolutionary *grand strategy based on a vanguard party.

Hence, "Marxist-Leninist."

See also JACOBINISM and LENINISM.

MARXISTS. Individuals and groups that claim to follow *Marxism.

Marxists have differed widely in their views on the appropriate means for achieving the new *society, ranging from evolutionary and parliamentary democratic means to *violent *revolution and minority *dictatorship.

MASS ACTION. *Demonstrations or other activity characterized by the participation of extremely large numbers of people.

MASSIVE RESISTANCE. Widespread *civil resistance and *noncompliance against *government policies, such as *noncooperation by constituent governmental units and *quasi-legal evasions and delays.

MATERIAL DESTRUCTION. See SABOTAGE.

MATERIAL RESOURCES. One of six *sources of political power.

Material resources include natural and financial resources, the economic system, communication, and transportation.

MEANS-END SCHEMA. The conception that the actions used to obtain a desired social or political goal themselves determine to a significant degree the result that is actually produced, in contrast to the goal originally stated.

According to this view, if the type of action used to obtain a goal departs significantly from the characteristics of the desired goal, the goal will not be achieved. Instead, the result will resemble the means of action that were used. Therefore, it has been argued, *violence and *dictatorship should be repudiated as means to achieve very different political ends, since those means can only contribute to reproducing themselves in different forms.

This means-end conception has been prominent in the writings of such theorists of *nonviolent social change as Aldous Huxley and M. K. Gandhi.

MECHANISM OF CHANGE (associated with nonviolent action). A particular process that may operate during the application of *nonviolent action, in which various factors may interact to produce a successful outcome by one of four ways.

The four mechanisms of change in nonviolent action are *conversion, *accommodation, *nonviolent coercion, and *disintegration.

Particular combinations of influences and interactions may be required in order for a given mechanism to operate, producing a specific type of change. Such influences may derive from, and operate on, the *opponents, the *nonviolent actionists, *third parties, the wider *grievance group, and the *society generally, or a combination of these, affecting capacities, will, and behavior. In a particular *conflict any of the mechanisms may operate partially, instead of fully.

MEDIA. See ALTERNATIVE COMMUNICATION SYSTEM, NEWSPA-PERS AND JOURNALS OF DISSENT, and RECORDS, RADIO, AND TELEVISION.

MEDIATION. The participation by a third person or group in *negotiations between conflicting parties in order to help them reach an agreement.

A mediator may simply facilitate contacts and communication between the two parties, or the mediator may suggest or interpret concrete proposals.

MEETINGS. See ASSEMBLY OF PROTEST OR SUPPORT, CAMOU-FLAGED MEETING OF PROTEST, PROTEST MEETING, REFUSAL OF AN ASSEMBLAGE OR MEETING TO DISPERSE, and TEACH-IN.

MERCHANTS' GENERAL STRIKE. A simultaneous closing of stores and businesses by the merchants in a city or region.

A *method of *economic boycott.

See also ECONOMIC SHUTDOWN, GENERAL STRIKE, and *HARTAL.*

METHOD (associated with nonviolent action). A *specific* form of action within the *technique of *nonviolent action.

Nearly two hundred specific methods have thus far been identi-fied, and many others are likely to emerge from further research and from innovation in ongoing *conflicts.

See also the lists of methods included under ECONOMIC BOY-COTT, NONVIOLENT INTERVENTION, NONVIOLENT PROTEST AND PERSUASION, POLITICAL NONCOOPERATION, SOCIAL NONCOOPERATION, and STRIKE.

MICRORESISTANCE. *Nonviolent resistance by individuals acting alone or in extremely small, often temporary, groups.

This type of activity enables *resistance to continue against *opponents who are applying extreme *repression. Microresistance can operate when the larger organizations and institutions, which are often bases for resistance, have been neutralized, controlled, or destroyed by the opponents. The term was introduced by Arne Næss.

MILITANCY. A propensity or inclination to be combative and ready to conduct a *conflict vigorously, by whatever means.

MILITANT. 1. A person who is strongly committed to a cause and is willing to take action that is believed to contribute to achieving its objective. Typically, a militant has a belligerent attitude and is ready and willing to participate in a fight by whatever means is required.

2. The quality of being combative and ready and willing to participate in a *conflict, whether by *violent or *nonviolent means.

MILITARISM. The glorification and presumption of superiority and rightful dominance of *military ideas, sentiments, symbols, modes of action, institutions, and *command system of organization, at the expense of, and often in *opposition to, their *civilian counterparts.

MILITARIZATION. The structuring, organization, or orientation of a *society around the assumptions, goals, institutions, and requirements of the *military forces. Militarization operates in preference to and dominance over *civilian institutions, which may be deliberately neutralized or subordinated.

Military forces then exercise preponderant influence within the society and *State, and the military conceptions, *command system, and type of *sanctions are preeminent.

MILITARY. 1. Pertaining to the particular means of conducting *conflict, especially international *war, by attempted physical destruction of the enemy's *military forces, key power centers, and resources. This physical destruction is seen as required to achieve the nonmilitary objectives of the conflict.

The destruction is normally applied both to material objects (supplies, factories, cities, bridges, ports, airports, and the like) and also to the enemy's *human resources (*combat *forces and often *civilian population).

Military forces have often been used not for *defense but for *aggression and *intervention in other *countries.

Before the twentieth century, members of the military forces were generally the main *casualties in any war. With changes in military technology, the emergence of *total war in the twentieth century, and the prevalence of *civil wars since 1945, the number of civilian casualties has become a central concern. Many of these casualties have been the unintended consequence of the use of large-scale explosives, and significant numbers have been victims of land mines.

For the development of military fighting capacity, specialized forces are organized, trained, and equipped to be able to operate under central direction to implement a fighting plan in order to achieve the *government's goals. These are usually political goals, at least in part. Except in cases of *military governments, the military forces operate under the direction of the civilian government.

In addition to its actual *combat role, military capacity has also often been seen to have a deterrent effect on possible attacks, and to provide *leverage in *negotiations and international influence in other situations.

Military institutions and action have served many functions in diverse cultures and periods of history. Those which appear to be most prominent today are *attack, *domination, *defense, and *deterrence. Except in cases of extreme *militarism, military means of combat have not been seen as an end in themselves, but as tools for some other end: political, national, economic, religious, and the like.

Military capacity until recently has been commonly associated with the *control of territory—hence an emphasis on conventional defense at frontiers. Military technology, such as missiles and nuclear *weapons, has in recent decades significantly undermined the capacity of military means to protect a *country's own territory.

Traditionally, it has been assumed that only military means were capable of providing effective defense. There have been times, however, when military means have not been able to provide such defense, and other times when defense has been provided by non-military means.

A military system may also serve certain domestic functions, which vary with the country and political system. These internal functions may be especially prominent in *dictatorships. In modern *States and many earlier governments, military forces have on occasion been used against the civilian population to maintain order, to support the government, and to crush *rebellions, *insurrections, and *revolutions, whether those challenges were waged by *violent action or *nonviolent action.

2. All the military forces and institutions collectively.

See also CONVENTIONAL WAR, CIVILIAN-BASED DEFENSE, DEFENSE IN DEPTH, DEMOLITION, PARAMILITARY, and PEACE-KEEPING.

MILITARY FORCES. The main *military fighting institutions of a *society, usually an army, navy, and air force, and in some *countries other branches, such as marines and coast guard. These are specially trained units of the society that are organized and equipped to wage military *war.

MILITARY GOVERNMENT. Direct administration of a *society by the *military forces instead of a civil *government. It is especially likely to occur in an occupied territory following an *invasion, or within a *country following a *military *coup d'état.

There are likely to be three phases in establishing a military government: (a) the initial *attack and the creation of the military government; (b) consolidation of its *control over the society and political system; and (c) long-term military rule.

See also CONSTITUTIONAL GOVERNMENT, MARTIAL LAW, MILITARY OCCUPATION, and STATE OF EMERGENCY.

MILITARY OCCUPATION. Geographical distribution of *military forces and functionaries of a foreign *State in another *country, usually without the advance consent of the *authorities of the occupied country. The purposes of the occupation may vary widely.

The *control of the territory may be accompanied by control of the *society and the political system, and by *submission of the population, but not necessarily.

At times military occupation may be concurrent with political control. At other times military occupation may be confronted with the occupiers' inability to establish effective political control. Lack of control may occur during widespread *guerrilla warfare or during a *nonviolent war of *resistance.

See also CIVILIAN-BASED DEFENSE and DEFENSE IN DEPTH.

MILITARY WAR. *War waged by *military means.

The term is used when it is desired to make a clear contrast with forms of nonmilitary *conflict.

See also COMMERCIAL WAR, ECONOMIC WAR, GUERRILLA WARFARE, NONVIOLENT WAR, POLITICAL WARFARE, and PSYCHOLOGICAL WARFARE.

MILITIA. An organized *military force of *civilians, trained and prepared for *military action in emergencies. Except for training periods, however, they remain in their normal civilian occupations.

MILLENARIAN MOVEMENT. A *social movement that awaits an expected, perhaps imminent, transformation of *society by a force that can neither be fully explained nor deliberately induced by the followers of the movement.

The transformation may be expected as a result of a supernatural intervention or spontaneous popular *mass action.

MILL-IN. A gathering of *nonviolent actionists for a short time in an open space of symbolic significance or in a location related to the grievance (such as the offices of the *opponents). The people remain in the area but keep moving around.

A large number of demonstrators milling around is likely to impede the usual work of people in the area or building. However, deliberate disruption is not an intended part of this *method of *nonviolent intervention.

MOB. An undisciplined crowd of people, acting on emotional impulses and stimuli, who are participating in some common activity. This may be *violence, *destruction of property, looting, celebration, and the like. The mob's behavior is likely to be unstable and subject to rapid change.

Mob behavior differs sharply from *protest crowd action in that the mob lacks organization, designated *leadership, a plan of action, disciplined behavior, and clear objectives.

There are, of course, in-between categories. For example, a crowd may gather spontaneously to protest but remain fairly disciplined. Conversely, an organized protesting crowd may disintegrate into partial mob behavior, especially if the police or troops use violence against the protesters.

MOBILIZATION (associated with nonviolent action). The preparation of a *civilian population for joint action to achieve an identified goal, or the placing of *military *fighting forces in a condition of readiness for *combat, especially in anticipation of an *attack.

MOCK AWARD. A satirical formal presentation given to *opponents in order to publicize grievances against them, and perhaps to appeal to them to correct the grievance. An example is "polluter of the year."

A *method of *nonviolent protest and persuasion.

MOCK ELECTION. An extralegal "*election" or direct popular balloting on a topical issue. This is organized as a means of *nonviolent protest and persuasion.

Special "polling" places for "voting" may be established, or the "votes" may be collected in some other way, such as by house-to-house visits.

A mock election may be used by large minorities, or by majorities when they are restricted from full participation in the regular political system. Or, minorities that have full access to the regular electoral system may use the mock election as an additional means to reach the public about an issue.

MOCK FUNERAL. A staged "funeral" of some principle (such as *justice or freedom) which the demonstrators cherish, and which they accuse the *opponents of violating.

This *method of *nonviolent protest and persuasion may take the form of a mock funeral procession, in which the participants seek to symbolize the seriousness of their *protest, both by a restrained and serious demeanor and by including some of the paraphernalia of a real funeral procession. These may include display of the mourning color (black, usually, but in some *countries white), and the carrying of a casket, which may bear the name of the violated principle, such as "justice."

See also DEMONSTRATION, DEMONSTRATIVE FUNERAL, HOMAGE AT BURIAL PLACES, and POLITICAL MOURNING.

MORAL BLACKMAIL. An attempt to force acceptance of a goal or demand by actions which, if the *opponents refuse to grant the demand, put the opponents in a very awkward position, both in their own eyes and in the opinion of *third parties. The opponents have no desire to grant the demand but also find the consequences of continuing to refuse virtually intolerable. An example would be a fast to the death by a well-known and highly respected individual.

Moral blackmail does not entail *violence, but it inherently produces extremely strong pressure.

See also DILEMMA DEMONSTRATION.

MORAL INSURRECTION. A vigorous uprising against a law, *policy, or *government, fueled by indignation that it violates important standards of what is right on ethical or religious grounds. The means used are accordingly strong *nonviolent means, and the action is conducted with determination but without *violence.

MORAL JUJITSU. A morally and psychologically unsettling process experienced by the individual police or troops who are inflicting *violent *repression on disciplined *nonviolent actionists.

As a consequence of the actionists' persistence in their activity, while remaining nonviolent, the attackers lose their moral balance. Therefore, it has been argued, they need to change their violent behavior in order to regain their equilibrium. In this process, the reactions of *third parties and the violent agents' own self-perception are both important.

Gradations of this reaction may occur. This concept has been associated with a strong belief in *principled nonviolence and the importance of *conversion and *self-suffering. Moral jujitsu is not typical of other approaches to *nonviolent action.

The term was used by Richard Gregg in his book *The Power of Non-violence* and is not to be confused with *political jujitsu.

MORAL RESISTANCE. A type of *principled nonviolence or *pacifism, whose adherents believe that evil should be acted against, but only by *nonviolent and moral means. Individual moral responsibility is emphasized.

Adherents of this type of pacifism may on occasion (but not always) use or approve the use of the *technique of *nonviolent action. However, they usually emphasize education, persuasion, and individual example to achieve their desired ends.

These believers usually seek to improve *society, but lack an overall social analysis and a comprehensive program for *social change. They generally favor gradual social reform through legislation, education, and efforts to influence *government officials on a piecemeal basis.

Many nineteenth- and twentieth-century American and British pacifists held to this type of pacifism.

MOTORCADE. A procession of slow-moving motor vehicles to convey a viewpoint. The vehicles usually bear posters or banners. The motorcade may be combined with a *parade or *march.

A *method of *nonviolent protest and persuasion.

MOURNING. See DEMONSTRATIVE FUNERALS, HOMAGE AT BURIAL PLACES, MOCK FUNERALS, and POLITICAL MOURNING.

MUSIC. See PLAYS AND MUSIC AS PROTEST and SINGING.

MUTINY. Refusal by members of the *military forces or police, or both, to carry out orders. In extreme cases, those persons may even cease to operate as members of their institutions.

Mutiny may especially occur in response to orders to repress a *nonviolent resistance movement by arrests, shootings, and the like. In other cases in which the army itself is in *revolt against its commanders or the *government, mutiny has been the dominant *method applied in the struggle. This is a method of *political noncooperation.

In a *violent struggle the act of mutiny may be followed by the mutinous troops using *violence against their officers and the government. In a *nonviolent struggle such violence is not needed and is undesirable, for the mutiny itself helps immobilize or dissolve the government's organs of *repression and its *military capacity. The mutiny may also increase the extent of *defiance and *noncooperation among *civilians, and help to paralyze the government's ability to continue to rule.

NATION. A large population, usually but not always territorially located, with a sense of self-identity based on such factors as language, culture, tradition, history, customs, race, or religion. They may hope for national *independence or already have *self-government.

See also the distinct and differing concepts of IMPERIALISM and the STATE.

NATIONAL CONSUMERS' BOYCOTT. A refusal by a major part of the people of a single *nation to buy certain or any goods and services from the foreign *country with which they are in *conflict, or to buy any foreign products at all.

This *method of *economic boycott may be practiced by the people of an independent country, or by the population of a subjected nation seeking to regain its *independence.

The general motivation is to strengthen one's own nation relative to the *opponent country.

NATIONAL DEFENSE. See DEFENSE.

NATIONALISM (reconceptualized term). Loyalty to one's own *nation and belief in its right to achieve or maintain self-rule rather than to be under the *domination of an external political system. Nationalism as defined here is the opposite of imposition of rule on others, chauvinism, *imperialism, worship of the *State, *fascism, and *militarism; the term has often been confused with all of these concepts and thus misused. Other types of nationalism, compatible with this definition, have been quite different, including those of Giuseppe Mazzini and M. K. Gandhi.

NATIONAL LIBERATION. The freeing of a *nation from foreign *control established by *colonialism, *imperialism, or *military occupation.

NATIONAL SECURITY (reconceptualized term). The condition in which a *nation or *country is safe from *attack.

National security may exist because there are no dangers, but that situation is rare. It is more likely to be the result of *dissuasion of potential attackers, either by means which cause them no longer to wish to launch hostile activities, or by some form of *deterrence so that the negative consequences of an attack outweigh any expected benefits.

*States also seek security through membership in military alliances or through forms of *collective security, and also by promoting national economic linkages that encourage *cooperation rather than *conflict.

When national security is violated by actual attack, effective means are required in order to defend against the attack and to protect the citizenry. The choice of means that will actually serve these purposes is highly important.

The plea of "national security" to justify internal *repression and violation of *civil liberties is inconsistent with the usage recommended here in that, in this case, the term is used primarily for rhetorical reasons.

See also DEFENSE.

NATION IN ARMS. A nation whose *government has adopted a type of *military *defense policy in which the general population has assigned roles in preparations for a *defense emergency and in the actual conduct of *defense when an attack has occurred.

See also CIVILIAN-BASED DEFENSE, DEFENSE, DEFENSE EMERGENCY, DEFENSE IN DEPTH, DEFENSIVE DEFENSE, and GUERRILLA WARFARE.

NAZISM. The political *ideology of the National Socialist German Workers' Party led by Adolph Hitler.

The beliefs of the ideology prominently included *racism. The Nazis postulated the inequality of peoples, classifying some as sub-human (suitable for elimination), and the Germans as most superior (deserving not only dominance but *Lebensraum* ["living space"] at the expense of other peoples).

Inequality of individuals within each group, including the Germans, was also a basic belief. Democratic political systems were regarded as catering to the inferior and mediocre. Instead, the "leadership principle" was adopted for the *society and political system, with the "most superior" individual (i.e., Hitler) at the pinnacle of *command, and all others obligated to strict *obedience to the Leader. All means of action deemed to be "necessary" were believed to be justified.

Hence, the Nazi ideology's policy requirements: the biological remaking of Europe, the geographical expansion of the Germans, and the restructuring of German society.

See also NAZI SYSTEM and TOTALITARIANISM.

NAZI SYSTEM. The political system developed in Germany by the National Socialist German Workers' Party, dominated by Adolph Hitler, and intended to implement the principles and achieve the objectives of *Nazism.

The system was a combined Party-*State structure of interrelated and often overlapping agencies.

This structure applied minute and comprehensive *controls over the whole *society (*Gleichschaltung*) and individual lives through psychological manipulation, the fervor of the mass movement, *political police, *propaganda, terror, *concentration camps, and *extermination camps for "undesirables." The Nazis launched massive *military *aggression against neighboring States and rivals, eventually controlling much of Europe and parts of North Africa before being defeated. The economic system was largely left in private ownership but was subject to extensive controls.

Despite efforts toward total control, internal *conflicts, inefficiencies, other weaknesses, and various types of *resistance made the system less successful than the Nazis had intended.

See also NAZISM and TOTALITARIANISM.

NEGATIVE PEACE. A condition in which *military *hostilities are not taking place. That condition is sometimes contrasted with, and seen as inferior to, a condition of positive good will and international *cooperation.

The terms "negative peace" and "*positive peace" both have strong ideological or moral overtones.

NEGOTIATION. The process of attempting, through discussions or other exchanges of viewpoints, to reach an agreement or resolve a *conflict without resort to open struggle.

The outcome of negotiations is rarely determined primarily by rational evaluation of the merits of the arguments of each side. Instead, assessment of each side's commitment to the respective negotiating positions, capacities to struggle for its objectives, and willingness and ability to exchange mutual concessions, are likely to be most important in determining the results.

NEUTRALITY. Nonparticipation in a *conflict generally, or more usually in a *military conflict between two *States or groups of States. Neutrality may be declared unilaterally by any *government. It may also be formalized in pacts or agreements in which the neutral party agrees not to enter into any existing or potential conflict.

During the Cold War between the United States and the Soviet Union, in many Third World *countries, neutrality was associated with membership in the group of nonaligned States, and was sometimes designated as "positive neutrality."

NEW SIGNS AND NAMES. Erection of signs where there have been none, or replacement of old street names, with new names of symbolic significance, for example, "renaming" a street during a *military occupation in honor of a *resistance hero.

A *method of *nonviolent protest and persuasion.

See also REMOVAL OF OWN SIGNS AND PLACEMARKS.

NEWSPAPERS AND JOURNALS OF DISSENT. Special legal and illegal periodicals used to promote the views and causes of the groups issuing them.

Articles and advertisements in regular papers and journals may also be used to communicate views, arouse support, and express *opposition.

A *method of *nonviolent protest and persuasion.

See also ALTERNATIVE COMMUNICATION SYSTEM.

NONCOMPLIANCE. Failure to act in accordance with the desires, instructions, or *command of someone or some institution.

See also DISOBEDIENCE and NONCOOPERATION.

NONCONFORMITY. Deviation from established standards of belief or behavior.

NONCONSUMPTION OF BOYCOTTED GOODS. Refusal to use boycotted products that are already in one's possession, even though their use does not require further purchases of the item.

A *consumers' boycott of purchases is a necessary precondition of nonconsumption. Use of this rare *method of *economic boycott facilitates social pressure to make a consumers' boycott effective, since people cannot excuse themselves by saying they had already purchased the items. Nonconsumption was used by American colonials in their *resistance *campaigns against British regulations prior to resorting to *war.

NONCOOPERATION. Deliberate restriction, discontinuance, withholding, or a combination of these, of social, economic, or political *cooperation with *opponent individuals, activities, institutions, or a *government during a *conflict.

The *actionists may reduce or cease cooperation, or withhold new forms of assistance, or both. When conducted by sufficient numbers of people, this slows or halts normal operations of the particular institution, government, or *society. The noncooperation may be spontaneous or planned, and it may be legal or illegal. The degree and precise forms of noncooperation vary.

Noncooperation is the second and largest class of the *methods of *nonviolent action. Noncooperation includes the three subclasses of *social noncooperation, *economic noncooperation (*economic boycotts and *strikes), and *political noncooperation.

NONCOOPERATION BY CONSTITUENT GOVERNMENTAL UNITS.
Official *noncooperation with the central *government practiced by local, provincial, or federated governmental bodies.

This *method of *political noncooperation is especially likely to be used in cases where the smaller units of government are responsive to public opinion, but the central government is not. This method may also be used in cases where a *coup d'état has occurred or the central government is foreign-controlled.

See also QUASI-LEGAL EVASIONS AND DELAYS.

NONCOOPERATION BY ENFORCEMENT AGENTS.
See DELIBERATE INEFFICIENCY AND SELECTIVE NONCOOPERATION BY ENFORCEMENT AGENTS.

NONCOOPERATION WITH CONSCRIPTION AND DEPORTATION.
Refusal either to register for *conscription as ordered, or to report for duty or *deportation (as for forced labor, political incarceration, *military duty, or extermination).

This *method of *political noncooperation is classified separately from other types of *disobedience because it is not the disobedience itself that is important, but the specific refusal to cooperate with a program of conscription or deportation.

NONEXPORTATION. Refusal to export certain or all types of goods to a *country, with the objective of exerting economic pressure on it in the course of a *conflict.

This method of *economic boycott, if applied without *government decision or *control, may be an application of a *producers' boycott, or, if government-sponsored, may be an *international sellers' embargo.

NONGOVERNMENTAL ORGANIZATION. A cultural, professional, political, or social body independent of the formal governmental structure.

The term "nongovernmental organization" is usually applied to voluntary national and transnational bodies, and does not include economic organizations such as factories, companies, retail outlets, and banks.

The existence of strong nongovernmental organizations is regarded as essential for the achievement and maintenance of a democratic political system.

See also ATOMIZATION, CIVIL SOCIETY, INFRASTRUCTURE, and LOCI OF POWER.

NONIMPORTATION. Refusal to import certain or all products of one or more *countries. If practiced as *government *policy, this *method becomes a type of *embargo.

See also NATIONAL CONSUMERS' BOYCOTT.

NONINJURIOUS PHYSICAL RESTRAINT. Restraint imposed only by preventing bodily movement, rather than inflicting injurious acts on a person who is intent on injuring either one's self or other persons. This may be achieved by careful and restrained use of physical strength (for example, muscular strength or body weight), without inflicting harm on the restrained person.

An example would be physically holding a person who is intent on choking another, to prevent movement, as distinct from striking the person with an injurious blow.

A related phenomenon is the removal, without injury to the person, of an object (such as a knife or a gun) from someone's hand.

NONINTERCOURSE. See ECONOMIC NONINTERCOURSE.

NONOBEDIENCE. A generic term covering those *methods of *political noncooperation that involve violation of laws, injunctions, and restraining orders, police or *military *commands, and other orders supported by the *authority of the *State.

See also CIVIL DISOBEDIENCE, DISOBEDIENCE, NONCOMPLIANCE, NONOBEDIENCE IN ABSENCE OF DIRECT SUPERVISION, and POLITICAL NONCOOPERATION.

NONOBEDIENCE IN ABSENCE OF DIRECT SUPERVISION. *Noncompliance with *commands by a population group in situations in which there is no immediate direct supervision and enforcement. The persons violating the command do nothing to call attention to their noncompliance.

For example, when soldiers arrive to enforce an order the population obeys without *protest, but when the soldiers have left the people resume their previous noncompliance.

A form of *political noncooperation.

See also DISOBEDIENCE.

NONRESISTANCE. A type of *principled nonviolence or *pacifism that rejects on moral and religious grounds all physical *violence, whether on individual, group, *State, or international levels.

Nonresisters are usually members of certain Christian groups, such as some Mennonites or Amish, who seek to do what they believe to be their duty to God, and are often "other-worldly" oriented, believing "this world" to be beyond redemption.

In times of *oppression, nonresisters seek to live in accordance with their beliefs and to ignore the political situation as much as possible, without directly challenging it, even nonviolently. In extreme situations, however, nonresisters may resort to *noncooperation to maintain their integrity.

NONVIOLENCE (associated with nonviolent action). 1. Abstention from *violence because of a moral or religious principle. For example, "She believes in nonviolence."

2. The behavior of people using *nonviolent action who neither initiate violence nor retaliate with violence. For example, "The demonstrators maintained their nonviolence."

Hence, "nonviolent."

The term "nonviolence" should not be used as a synonym for the technique of *nonviolent action, because nonviolent action is often practiced for pragmatic reasons and is not necessarily tied to a general belief in abstention from all violence.

See also NONVIOLENT, NONVIOLENT ACTION, NONVIOLENT DISCIPLINE, PACIFISM, and PRINCIPLED NONVIOLENCE.

NONVIOLENT. Existing or functioning without the use of *violence. Always used with a noun that it modifies. The identification of behavior as "nonviolent" is made on the basis of observed behavior, not on the basis of belief, motive, attitude, or self-description.

See also NONVIOLENCE, NONVIOLENT ACTION, and other entries with the word "nonviolent" as part of the term.

NONVIOLENT ACTION. A *technique of conducting *protest, *resistance, and intervention without physical *violence by (a) acts of omission—that is, the participants refuse to perform acts which they usually perform, are expected by custom to perform, or are required by law or regulation to perform; (b) acts of commission—that is, the participants perform acts which they usually do not perform, are not expected by custom to perform, or are forbidden by law or regulation from performing; or (c) a combination of both.

The technique includes a multitude of specific *methods, which are grouped into three main classes: *nonviolent protest and persuasion, *noncooperation, and *nonviolent intervention.

Nonviolent action may be used as a technique of waging active struggle and as a *sanction to achieve certain objectives in *conflict situations where, in its absence, *submission or violence might have been practiced.

Considerable variation exists within the technique, including the individual methods applied; the motivation for *nonviolent behavior; the attitude toward the *opponents; the objectives of the action; the intended *mechanism of change; and the relation of nonviolent action to other techniques of action.

This broad phenomenon of nonviolent action has variously been referred to, in part or in full, by such terms as *civil resistance, *civilian resistance, *nonviolent direct action, *nonviolent resistance, *passive resistance, *positive action, and *satyagraha. *Civilian struggle indicates the vigorous application of nonviolent action.

Nonviolent action is contrasted with *violent action. These are the two main classes of ultimate sanctions. This should not be interpreted as implying that all social and political action can be clearly classed as "violent" or "nonviolent." There are other broad categories, including simple verbal persuasion, peaceful institutional procedures backed by threat and use of sanctions (violent and nonviolent), and material destruction only.

Hence, "*nonviolent actionist."

See also SABOTAGE.

NONVIOLENT ACTIONIST. A person who uses the *technique of *nonviolent action.

NONVIOLENT AIR RAID. Use of airplanes, balloons, or other air transport to enter the air space of the *opponents, without use or threat of *violence or material destruction, in order to bring leaflets, food, or gifts to the population. The intent may be to produce a psychological impact.

A *method of *nonviolent intervention.

See also DEFIANCE OF BLOCKADE.

NONVIOLENT BLITZKRIEG. A *strategy of *civilian-based defense aimed at producing a quick end of an *invasion or *coup d'état. This *strategy provides a short-term *campaign of *total noncooperation with the attackers' *forces and measures, by all sections of the population. If it does not succeed in producing a quick retreat or collapse of the attackers, the strategy could be followed by a long-term struggle using diverse strategies.

This strategy presumes a strong unified will to resist, and would be assisted by prior civilian-based defense preparations, and an absence of serious internal dissension within the defending country.

Typical *methods suitable for a nonviolent blitzkrieg would be the *work-on without collaboration, probably combined with *general administrative noncooperation and widespread *defiance. If the issues are economic, those methods might be combined with a *general strike or an *economic shutdown.

A nonviolent blitzkrieg is contrasted with *selective resistance. It can be used immediately after an *attack, or at the end of a long struggle when the situation appears to warrant a major push toward final victory. The term was introduced by Theodor Ebert in the 1960s.

NONVIOLENT COERCION. A *mechanism of change in a *conflict using *nonviolent action in which the demands of the *actionists are, as a result of their *struggle, achieved against the will and without the agreement of the *opponents.

This may occur as a consequence of any of three processes: (a) the *defiance may become too diversified and massive to be controlled by the opponents' *repression; (b) the *noncooperation may paralyze the social, economic, and political system; (c) the opponents' ability to apply repression may be undermined, as by unreliability and *mutiny of the opponents' police and soldiers.

Despite any one of these possibilities, or a combination of them, the opponents may still refuse to change the *policies or system. Nevertheless the *nonviolent actionists may be able to meet their objectives. The opponents' capacity to exert *control can be taken away. They can be "nonviolently coerced."

Nonviolent coercion and *disintegration are the strongest of the four mechanisms of change by which nonviolent action may be successful.

See also ACCOMMODATION and CONVERSION.

NONVIOLENT CONFLICT. The application of the *technique of *nonviolent action in a *conflict situation.

NONVIOLENT DEFENSE. See CIVILIAN DEFENSE and CIVILIAN-BASED DEFENSE.

NONVIOLENT DIRECT ACTION. *Direct action by *nonviolent means. Generally the shorter synonym *nonviolent action is preferred.

NONVIOLENT DISCIPLINE. Orderly adherence to the intended course of group activities for a *nonviolent action *campaign, including both compliance with predetermined *strategy, *tactics, and *methods of action (if planned in advance), and maintenance of persistent *nonviolent behavior even in the face of *repression.

Prevention of *violence by the *actionists is essential in order for the special processes and *mechanisms of change in this *technique to operate with maximum effectiveness. Nonviolent discipline may result from intuition, experience, training, informal social pressures, or organized *control.

Discipline, in the sense of persistence in continuing the determined course of action despite the *opponents' *sanctions and *repression, is necessary to prevent a rout and collapse of the campaign.

Discipline, in the sense of carrying out the predetermined strategic and tactical plan, is necessary if the nonviolent *combat *forces are to have maximum effectiveness. Such discipline is also necessary because unplanned actions can diffuse *resistance forces, create confusion, lead to abandonment of the selected strategy and tactics, and produce an outbreak of violence by resisters, all of which would benefit the opponents.

NONVIOLENT HARASSMENT. Action similar to, but significantly stronger and more persistent than, "*haunting" officials and *taunting officials. Threats of bodily harm are excluded.

These psychological *methods of *nonviolent intervention may include publication of names, photographs, and descriptions of the persons to be harassed. The action may include persuading hotels to refuse the harassed persons lodging, closely following the persons night and day, and repeatedly reminding the persons and the public of the objectionable nature of their activities.

Because such activities may easily slide into threats or acts of physical *violence, and may be illegal, extreme *nonviolent discipline is required for their effective use.

NONVIOLENT INSURRECTION. A popular *uprising by *nonviolent means.

NONVIOLENT INTERJECTION. The placing of one's body as a barrier between a person and the objective of that person's work or activity. Such action makes the actor physically vulnerable.

Nonviolent interjection occurs, for example, when an individual moves between a soldier or policeman and a person being apprehended or attacked, or when a person moves into the path of a vehicle. A single person or a small group of people may lie in front of a tank, truck, or train, hoping to induce the driver to refuse to move the vehicle at the risk of inflicting injury or death on those who have interposed themselves (which has occurred).

This *method of *nonviolent intervention is distinguished from *nonviolent obstruction, in that the interposing demonstrators can be overcome, removed, or surmounted (as by persons or vehicles simply proceeding over the bodies). Nonviolent interjection does not apply a major or insurmountable physical barrier, but instead emotional pressure to induce the impeded persons (soldiers or drivers) to desist from their activity, or at least not to continue it at the price of injuring or killing the demonstrators.

This method may take the forms of individual nonviolent interjection or small group nonviolent interjection.

NONVIOLENT INTERVENTION. Direct interference in a situation by *nonviolent means, as distinguished from both symbolic *protest and *noncooperation. The intervention is most often physical, such as a *sit-in, but may be psychological, social, economic, or political.

The action involves seizing the initiative and stepping into the situation disruptively. These methods are regarded as the most militant *methods of *nonviolent action.

Methods of nonviolent intervention may (a) disrupt and potentially destroy the established behavior patterns, *policies, relationships, or institutions that are seen as objectionable; (b) establish new behavior patterns, policies, relationships, or institutions that are preferred; or (c) both.

The methods of nonviolent intervention, arranged in five groups, are:

- *psychological nonviolent intervention*: *self-exposure to the elements, *fast, *reverse trial, *nonviolent harassment;
- *physical nonviolent intervention*: *sit-in, *stand-in, *ride-in, *wade-in, *mill-in, *pray-in, *nonviolent raid, *nonviolent air raid, *nonviolent invasion, *nonviolent interjection, *nonviolent obstruction, *nonviolent occupation;
- *social nonviolent intervention*: *social patterns—establishing new ones, *overloading of facilities, *stall-in, *speak-in, *guerrilla theater, *alternative social institution, *alternative communication system;
- *economic nonviolent intervention*: *reverse strike, *stay-in strike, *nonviolent land seizure, *defiance of blockade, *politically motivated counterfeiting, *preclusive purchasing, *seizure of assets, *dumping, *selective patronage, *alternative market, *alternative transportation system, *alternative economic institution; and
- *political nonviolent intervention*: *overloading of administrative systems, *disclosing identities of secret agents, *seeking imprisonment, *civil disobedience of "neutral" laws, *work-on without collaboration, and *dual sovereignty and parallel government.

NONVIOLENT INVASION. Deliberate and unconcealed *nonviolent entry into a forbidden area.

This action may be used to demonstrate the *actionists' rejection of the right of the *government or agency to exercise *sovereignty or general *control over that area, or their denial of the *opponents' right to use it for a particular purpose. This *method of *nonviolent intervention involves *civil disobedience and the risk of severe *repression.

NONVIOLENT LAND SEIZURE. The *nonviolent expropriation of land by people who occupy and use it without the owner's permission, with the intent of producing a *de facto change of possession and *control. It is usually intended that this de facto change will be recognized later as a *de jure change in ownership.

Usually such land seizures are carried out by landless peasants against large landowners, frequently the same owners for whom the peasants have previously worked, or sharecropped, or from whom they have rented land.

In some instances landless peasants may seize land owned by the *government. In certain other cases, the seizure may be attempted against the government by the previous owners, from whom the land has recently been confiscated as a *punishment for some other *resistance, such as tax refusal.

A *method of *economic nonviolent intervention.

NONVIOLENT OBSTRUCTION. A group of people placing their bodies to prevent a particular activity, or to close down an establishment, so as to create a formidable physical barrier. The obstructers refuse to leave the area despite orders to do so and maintain *nonviolent discipline.

There is a risk of arrest, injury, or death of the obstructers, as with *nonviolent interjection, but the impact is not primarily psychological, as it is with that *method. The impact of nonviolent obstruction is instead associated with actual physical blocking that is difficult to overcome.

This blocking occurs when the interposition is undertaken by large numbers of people, or when they are so placed that it is physically impossible for work to proceed, or for a vehicle to pass, even if the obstructers are injured or killed in limited numbers.

This obstruction is likely to be temporary, however, unless (a) numbers are exceedingly large over a long period, and cannot be dispersed or removed by the means which the *opponents are able and willing to apply; (b) the opponents are unwilling simply to arrest or kill all the demonstrators; (c) the obstructed workers or enforcement officials are, or become, sympathetic to the demonstrators; or (d) the opponents are induced to halt the project by public opposition to the activity or establishment, or to the *repression of the obstructers.

The borderline between nonviolent interjection and nonviolent obstruction, both *methods of *nonviolent intervention, is not always clear.

NONVIOLENT OCCUPATION. Refusal of *nonviolent actionists to leave a particular place and their insistence on remaining there over time. In addition, they may defiantly use the facilities or land, for example, by holding lectures or religious services, or by constructing homes or farming the land.

This form of *nonviolent intervention may be used either after a *nonviolent invasion or a *nonviolent land seizure, or alternatively by people ordered to abandon their own property. Nonviolent occupation may involve technical trespass and violation of other laws.

NONVIOLENT POSITIONAL WAR. A *strategy of *civilian-based defense in which *resistance is concentrated at certain social, economic, or political points or on certain issues, rather than attempting *total noncooperation.

This strategy is equivalent to "positional war" in *military strategy. Within civilian-based defense this strategy is synonymous with *selective resistance or resistance at key points.

NONVIOLENT PROTEST AND PERSUASION. A large class of *methods of *nonviolent action that are largely symbolic acts of peaceful *opposition or attempted persuasion. These acts extend beyond verbal expressions of opinion, but stop short of *noncooperation and *nonviolent intervention.

These methods may show that the protesters approve or disapprove of something, such as a particular action, law, *policy, or a whole *government. These methods simply express a point of view, and are distinguished from the imposition of social, economic, or political pressures directly. These methods, therefore, do not actually resist or disrupt the policy or practice in question.

The methods in this class may be intended primarily to influence the *opponents, to communicate with the public, onlookers, or *third parties, or to influence the wider *grievance group to induce its members to join the *protest or *resistance. These methods may also be used to support some other activity, such as collection of funds for famine victims, or to pressure someone else to act to deal with the grievance. *Demonstrations of nonviolent protest and persuasion may precede or accompany acts of noncooperation or nonviolent intervention, or may be used in their absence.

The methods of nonviolent protest and persuasion, arranged in nine groups, are:

- *formal statements*: *public speeches, *letters of opposition or support, *declarations by organizations and institutions, *signed public statement, *declarations of indictment and intention, *group or mass petition;
- *communications for a wider audience*: *slogans, caricatures, and symbols, *banners, posters, and displayed proclamations, *leaflets, pamphlets, and books, *newspapers and journals of dissent, *records, radio, and television, *skywriting and earthwriting;
- *group representations*: *deputation, *mock award, *group lobbying, *picketing, *mock election;
- *symbolic public acts*: *display of flags and symbolic colors, *wearing of symbols, *prayer and worship, *delivery of symbolic objects, *protest disrobing, *destruction of own property, *symbolic lights, *display of portraits, *paint as protest, *new signs and names, *symbolic sounds, *symbolic reclamation, *rude gesture;
- *pressures on individuals*: "*haunting" officials, *taunting officials, *fraternization with the opponents, *vigil;
- *drama and music*: *skits and pranks, *plays and music as protest, *singing;
- *processions*: *march, *parade, *religious procession, *pilgrimage, *motorcade;

- *honoring the dead*: *political mourning, *mock funeral, *demonstrative funeral, *homage at burial place;
- *public assemblies*: *assembly of protest or support, *protest meeting, camouflaged meeting of protest, *teach-in; and
- *withdrawal and renunciation*: *walkout, *silence, *renouncing honors, and *turning one's back.

NONVIOLENT RAID. A *march to a designated point of symbolic or strategic importance by volunteers, who then demand possession of the site. Such nonviolent raids are not usually conducted with the expectation of actually gaining possession, but are intended to challenge and symbolically defy the established *government.

This *method of *nonviolent intervention usually involves *civil disobedience and the risk of severe *repression. Such a raid may on occasion be used deliberately to induce severe repression, including brutalities, with the hope of producing a *backlash against the *opponents, supporting the *nonviolent actionists, and contributing to *political jujitsu.

In an extremely advanced stage of a nonviolent revolt, however, large masses of people may surround such "seized" points (as government buildings or a factory) and use *nonviolent obstruction in an attempt to prevent their recapture.

Nonviolent raids have also been attempted to gain possession of merchandise rather than a place.

NONVIOLENT RESISTANCE. *Nonviolent action conducted largely by *methods of *noncooperation, such as the various forms of *strike, *economic boycott, and *political noncooperation. It thus mainly involves refusal to perform certain acts and is generally a reaction to actions or a *policy of the *opponents.

NONVIOLENT REVOLUTION. 1. The overthrow, or deliberate promotion of the *disintegration, of a given *government or system by means of mass *nonviolent action.

2. A type of *principled nonviolence or *pacifism which aims at basic, or revolutionary, changes in individuals and society, including the whole *social structure.

These changes are to be accomplished by: (a) the improvement of individual lives, (b) promotion of the principles of *nonviolence, *justice, *cooperation, *freedom, and equality for the whole society, (c) the building of an egalitarian, decentralized, and libertarian *social order, and (d) the combating of social evils by nonviolent action, along with the construction of new institutions.

This type of principled nonviolence has been advanced by groups in several countries, but implemented thus far only to a small degree.

Hence, "nonviolent revolutionary."

See also DECENTRALIZATION, LIBERTARIANISM, and REVOLUTION.

NONVIOLENT SANCTIONS. Forms of psychological, social, economic, or political means intended to influence, apply *leverage, achieve objectives, or impose *reprisals.

See also NONVIOLENT ACTION and SANCTIONS.

NONVIOLENT STRUGGLE. The waging of *conflict by strong *methods of *nonviolent action, including major *noncooperation and *nonviolent intervention, especially when applied against determined and resourceful *opponents, who respond with *repression and other strong countermeasures.

When these characteristics are present, the term "nonviolent struggle" is virtually synonymous with "nonviolent action."

NONVIOLENT WAR (associated with nonviolent action). Large-scale and intense political struggle waged with *methods of *noncooperation and *nonviolent intervention, especially against *invaders or an established *military occupation.

NONVIOLENT WEAPONS (associated with nonviolent action). A synonym for *methods of *nonviolent action, also called *civil weapons.

NUCLEAR PACIFISM. A belief that rejects support for or participation in a *military *policy that includes nuclear *weapons, even though the same persons do not on principle reject use of conventional military weapons.

NULLIFICATION (associated with nonviolent action). The act of making a statute or *government *policy void, useless, or inefficacious by means of massive *economic noncooperation, or *political noncooperation, or both.

Nullification is especially likely to include such *methods as *revenue refusal, *popular nonobedience, *disguised disobedience, *civil disobedience, *refusal of assistance to enforcement agents, and certain other methods. The term was especially used in American colonial struggles against English laws and policies in the 1760s.

OBEDIENCE. Compliance with, or *submission to, a *command or law. Obedience may arise from either free *consent or *fear of *sanctions.

Free consent may derive from a basically nonrational acceptance of the standards and customs of one's *society, or a basically rational consideration of the positive reasons to give obedience. These may include the merits of the *government generally, or those of the particular command or law.

Obedience may also arise from fear of threatened or imposed sanctions for *disobedience. The person is unwilling to undergo them as the price of disobedience, and hence obeys as a result of what might be called "intimidated consent." This latter type of obedience is distinct from *coercion by direct physical violation.

See also CIVIL DISOBEDIENCE, DISOBEDIENCE, NONCOMPLIANCE, NONOBEDIENCE, NONOBEDIENCE IN ABSENCE OF DIRECT SUPERVISION, and POLITICAL NONCOOPERATION.

OBLIGATION. See POLITICAL OBLIGATION.

OBSTRUCTION. See BLOCKING OF LINES OF COMMAND AND INFORMATION, NONVIOLENT INTERJECTION, NONVIOLENT OBSTRUCTION, NONVIOLENT OCCUPATION, and STALLING AND OBSTRUCTION.

OCCUPATION. See MILITARY OCCUPATION, NONVIOLENT OCCU-
PATION, OCCUPATION COSTS, OCCUPATION FORCES, and
OCCUPIED TERRITORY.

OCCUPATION COSTS. The total losses and expenditures of all types
which may result from a *military occupation.

These may include—especially if the occupation is met by
*nonviolent resistance—direct economic costs, time and energies of
the *occupation forces, detrimental impact on their morale and on
the morale of the attackers' home population, deliberately reduced
efficiency or open *resistance among the occupiers' forces and home
population, alienation of *third parties, and international economic
and political *sanctions.

If the occupation is met with spontaneous *nonviolent resistance
or organized *civilian-based defense, the long-term general spread of
knowledge of how to wage resistance in future *conflicts would be
an additional cost for some *governments. Similar costs might be
incurred if resistance is waged by *guerrilla warfare.

See also CIVILIAN-BASED DEFENSE and DETERRENCE.

OCCUPATION FORCES. All personnel used to consolidate and maintain a *military occupation. These *forces include personnel required
to serve in the *military and police, such as political functionaries,
and personnel required to ensure communications, transportation,
economic activities, and the like.

The numbers and types of these forces will vary from *society to
society and *conflict to conflict. The objectives of the occupation
and the nature of the expected or actual resistance will also have an
effect.

OCCUPIED TERRITORY. The land area in which *invaders have distributed *occupation forces.

*Military occupation of a territory is distinct from political *con-
trol of that territory's population and the institutions of its *society.
Territorial occupation and political control may at times be closely

associated, but in other cases the two may be quite separate. The population of the occupied territory may refuse to acknowledge *defeat, and instead may struggle assertively not only to maintain its own independent institutions, but also to undermine the occupation forces and to increase the *occupation costs to such an extent as to induce withdrawal.

See also CIVILIAN-BASED DEFENSE.

OFFENSE. An *attack by whatever means—*military, political, or economic—in which the attackers' *forces have the initiative.

See also DEFENSE.

OFFENSIVE. *Operations that seek to seize and maintain the initiative in a *conflict and to pursue the *offense. The opposite of *defensive.

OFFENSIVE-DEFENSIVE. *Operations that seek to provide *defense against *attack by taking the *offensive to repel the attackers or otherwise induce a withdrawal.

Although this term has been primarily associated with *military action, it is applicable to *nonviolent action, *guerrilla warfare, and especially *civilian-based defense.

OLIGARCHY. 1. A system of *government in which the position of *ruler is occupied by a small elite.

This elite may derive its position from heredity, wealth, social position, *military command, organizational manipulation, or other sources.

Oligarchical government may be formally structured for elite rule, with or without procedures and controls established for its selection and prerogatives. Or the formal constitutional framework may be broader (as in a *democracy) or narrower (as in a monarchy) while actual *control is in the hands of the elite.

2. A system of *domination of any institution or social group by an elite.

See also AUTOCRACY, ESTABLISHMENT, and POWER STRUCTURE.

ONE-PARTY STATE. A structure of *government in which the *State is controlled by a single political party and usually no other significant parties are legally permitted. If other parties nominally exist, they are in practice committed to the goals and policies of the dominant party. This was the case in some East European States under Soviet *domination, in which small parties acted as "fronts" for the ruling party. In one-party States, the functions of government are carried out through the State apparatus, rather than being divided between a party and the State.

See also ONE-PARTY SYSTEM.

ONE-PARTY SYSTEM. Identical to a *one-party State except that the functions of *government may be performed solely through the *State or through both the State and the party itself (as in Nazi Germany).

See also DICTATORSHIP and TOTALITARIANISM.

OPEN CONFLICT. The situation in which two groups that have differences of belief, perspectives, or goals have moved from peaceful coexistence, or a *conflict limited by conventions, social understandings, or constitutional rules within a framework of broader social agreement, to a *confrontation of *forces.

The confrontation of forces may be expressed by electoral procedures, parliamentary activity, *nonviolent action, or *violent action.

OPENNESS. An operational principle in *nonviolent action that the organization backing the movement shall in almost all circumstances act publicly and without secrecy, that names and activities of *leaders are revealed to the public and the *opponents, that written *protests are signed by those making them, and that action itself is carried out in a manner for all to see, without attempted deceit or hiding.

Openness has usually also meant that the opponents, and often the police, are notified in advance of plans for *demonstrations and similar actions.

Among believers in certain types of *principled nonviolence, the principle of openness has derived from an accepted moral imperative to be "truthful" as well as *nonviolent. For *nonviolent actionists who do not believe in a norm of *nonviolence, openness is intrinsically associated with being "truthful" as well as nonviolent.

For nonviolent actionists who do not believe in a norm of nonviolence, openness is intrinsically associated with creation of the conditions for success, especially with the control of *fear and development of *fearlessness, and with the necessity of *nonviolent discipline among the actionists. Openness, however, does not preclude opponents from applying extreme *repression.

Under conditions of extreme *dictatorship and repression the organization of *nonviolent struggle has necessarily operated with a high degree of secrecy, despite extreme efforts by the *government to place *agents into the *resistance organization and to monitor activities electronically. But even then, there will probably be some acts of open *defiance by selected resisters or large crowds.

OPERATION. An organized action, or series of actions, that is intended to implement a tactical or *strategic plan to achieve the objectives of a *battle or *campaign.

See also TACTIC.

OPERATIONAL PLAN. The scheme of connected *operations being carried out simultaneously or in sequence, designed to achieve certain objectives.

Subordinate plans may be prepared for actions that will gain more limited objectives or positions within an operation.

OPPONENTS. The adversaries in a *conflict, whether a group, institution, *government, *invaders, or, rarely, specific individuals.

OPPOSITION. 1. A group which is hostile to, or is in *conflict with, another group because of contrary interests or objectives. The opposition group may be a political party or *resistance movement, while the group they oppose may be a *government, institution, or dominant elite.

2. Action which expresses antagonism, contrary opinions, or resistance.

Hence, "an act of opposition."

3. A condition of being adverse to, opposed to, hostile to, or against, a viewpoint, *policy, or group.

Hence, "being in opposition."

OPPRESSION. The *domination of one group by another group in order to serve the latter's interests.

The required *submission of the *subordinate group in attitude and behavior may be induced by some combination of psychological influences and powerful political, social, or economic structures.

The submission may to some degree be induced by a dominant belief system or by explicit *propaganda that convinces the oppressed that the system and rule are *legitimate and therefore they ought to submit. More often, perhaps, the oppressors employ *control organizations, economic manipulation, threat or application of *repression and physical *violence (by police, prisons, *military units, or instigated *mob action), and other harsh means.

ORGANIZED RESISTANCE (associated with nonviolent action and civilian-based defense). *Nonviolent resistance activities that are conducted by special directives from a *resistance organization, or that require advance planning and group preparations to be carried out.

In *civilian-based defense analysis, organized resistance is contrasted with both *general resistance and *spontaneous resistance.

See also EXCOMMUNICATION, INTERDICT, LYSISTRATIC NONACTION, SELECTIVE SOCIAL BOYCOTT, and SOCIAL BOYCOTT.

OSTRACISM. A synonym for *social boycott.

See also COLD SHOULDER, EXCOMMUNICATION, ICE FRONT, INTERDICT, LYSISTRATIC NONACTION, and SELECTIVE SOCIAL BOYCOTT.

OVERLOADING OF ADMINISTRATIVE SYSTEMS. Intentional overtaxing and clogging of an administrative system by popular action in the form of excessive compliance. This *method has also in some cases been called a "comply-in."

This method of political *nonviolent intervention may take diverse forms. For example, when people opposed to a particular *policy, or to a whole system, are required to update or correct data on themselves (as for *military *conscription), they may repeatedly provide trivial, irrelevant, or excessive information that vastly exceeds the requirements.

Or, when a complex system of rules and regulations is subject to frequent change, people may make vast numbers of inquiries, or suggestions for changes. Or, people may make an inordinate number of *protests or statements related somehow to the operations or policies of the administrative system.

The resulting overloading of the system may make the normal continuance of operations difficult, or may slow its capacity to deal with its normal activities.

See also JAMMING.

OVERLOADING OF FACILITIES. The deliberate increase of demands for services far beyond the capacity of the department, business, or other institution to provide them. As a result of this *method of *nonviolent intervention, the operation of the institution is slowed down or paralyzed.

This overloading may be initiated by customers, the public, or constituents, or by employees of the institution itself. The objectives sought may include political goals, wage increases, and improved standards of service for the regular users of the facilities.

Medical interns using this method to gain increased pay have admitted far more patients to a hospital than facilities and staff could properly handle—a "heal-in."

See also OVERLOADING OF ADMINISTRATIVE SYSTEMS.

OVERTHROW OF A GOVERNMENT. The bringing down or destruction of a *government by any means, irrespective of the nature of the resulting government.

These means, or processes, may include a mass popular *uprising by a subordinated *political class, a *coup d'état, an *invasion, deliberate *subversion, *terrorism, *guerrilla warfare, and *political noncooperation by officials and employees or by the population, or by both.

See also REVOLUTION and UNDERMINING A GOVERNMENT.

OWNERS' AND MANAGERS' ECONOMIC ACTION. See LOCKOUT, MERCHANTS' "GENERAL STRIKE," REFUSAL OF INDUSTRIAL ASSISTANCE, REFUSAL TO LET OR SELL PROPERTY, and TRADERS' BOYCOTT.

PACIFISM. Belief in *nonviolence as a moral, ethical, or religious principle by persons and groups who consequently refuse participation in all international or *civil wars or *violent *revolutions. Some pacifists on principle also reject additional violent practices, such as corporal *punishment and capital punishment.

Pacifists may support or oppose the use of *nonviolent action. In the latter case they may regard some *methods of nonviolent action as too conflictual, coercive, or provocative of violent responses. Pacifists may also favor a considerable variety of activities and *policies, depending on the type of pacifism in which they believe. Some pacifists, for example, Leo Tolstoy, also reject the *State.

Four types of *principled nonviolence—*active reconciliation, *moral resistance, *nonresistance, and *nonviolent revolution—are classed as pacifism. However, one type of principled nonviolence, *selective nonviolence, is not, as it is based on a nonpacifist principle.

PAINT AS PROTEST. The use of paint in limited ways to communicate symbolically a viewpoint, without inflicting permanent damage on the object, which would be *destruction of property.

Painting out the name of a disliked political *leader on, say, a ship, or alteration of a poster, would fall within this method of *nonviolent action, but paint added to a work of art or building that damaged the original condition would not. Some graffiti would therefore be excluded.

A *method of *nonviolent protest and persuasion.

PAMPHLETS. See LEAFLETS, PAMPHLETS, AND BOOKS.

PARADE. A group of people walking in an organized manner to call attention to their grievance or aim, when the point of termination has no intrinsic significance to the *demonstration. The lack of a significant destination distinguishes this *method of *nonviolent protest and persuasion from the *march.

There are many possible variations on the parade. Banners, leaflets, posters, symbolic objects, and special types of walking, such as moving very slowly, swaying, or dancing, may be used. Music may accompany the walkers, and symbolic items may be carried or carted. Sometimes several individual parades may be combined in special ways, for example by their converging at a central point.

See also MOTORCADE, PILGRIMAGE, and RELIGIOUS PROCESSION.

PARALLEL GOVERNMENT. See DUAL SOVEREIGNTY AND PARALLEL GOVERNMENT.

PARALYSIS (reconceptualized term). A condition of immobility in a social unit or institution, especially a factory, economic system, or *government, produced by the widespread, comprehensive, and persistent *noncooperation of the people whose activities normally maintain its operation.

Paralysis can take the forms of "economic paralysis" (likely to be produced by a *general strike, an *economic shutdown, or a *merchants' "general strike") or "political paralysis" (likely to be produced by a simultaneous application of a considerable variety of the *methods of *political noncooperation by the citizenry, government personnel, government institutions, and constituent governmental units).

PARAMILITARY. Activities that possess certain *military features or characteristics, but lack others.

Therefore, the term indicates: semi-military; irregular military; subsidiary to conventional military *combat or *military forces;

similar to but not identical with regular military action, qualities, institutions, *strategies, and the like.

For example, a paramilitary group uses military *weapons (though often on a small scale), but does so on the basis of irregular authorization or organization, or unconventional strategy.

Hence, paramilitary *forces, paramilitary *operations, and paramilitary *techniques of waging struggle (as by *guerrilla warfare).

PARTICIPATORY DEMOCRACY. A synonym for *direct democracy.

This term may be used to emphasize the quality of participation in deliberations and decision-making over time, and not simply the procedure of voting directly on issues.

PARTISAN. 1. A member of a *paramilitary group. A *guerrilla.

2. A *civilian who, as a member of an organized fighting paramilitary group, opposes a foreign *military occupation by such means as *demolitions and the hit-and-run tactics of *guerrilla warfare.

PARTISAN WARFARE. A synonym for *guerrilla warfare. The term was especially used during World War II for guerrilla warfare against *occupation forces.

PARTITION. The division of a political unit, such as a territory, into separate smaller units.

Partition may be carried out by *governments whose *military forces occupy another *country and then divide it as they wish. Partition may also be carried out by the established *State or other controlling body (such as *invaders or an international organization) in order to halt or prevent internecine civil strife between population groups. Or, population groups that have previously lived within a single State may by mutual agreement determine that they wish to have separate political units.

Partition may also occur as a consequence of a *civil war, or *noncooperation *campaigns combined with development of separate institutions and geographical concentrations of the differing population groups.

PASSIVE RESISTANCE. A particular type of *nonviolent resistance adopted solely on grounds of expediency, in which the resisters' activities are largely responses to the *opponents' initiatives and the resisters use less active forms of *noncooperation. Passive resistance is generally limited to *defensive *strategies.

The absence of *violence is usually motivated by considerations of expediency, the resisters being willing to use violence if able to do so with a reasonable chance of *success. Not to be confused with the general *technique of *nonviolent action, which includes many active *methods and strategies.

PEACE (reconceptualized term). 1. The absence of, or the ending of, *military *hostilities between contending *States or other fighting units (as in a *civil war). This is not simply a temporary truce or ending of *conflict because of overwhelming military might, as in the *pax Romana*.

2. In the context of *civilian-based defense, the absence of acts of international *violence, such as a military *attack or *invasion against a *country with a civilian–based defense policy.

These definitions of peace do not, however, exclude *nonviolent attempts by *governments or private groups to influence other governments or countries, nor the use of nonviolent methods of international conflict, such as *embargoes, diplomatic nonrecognition, and *international economic boycotts.

3. Some advocates of major *social change and of certain types of *principled nonviolence prefer to define "peace" as the condition in which their full objectives, including absence of violence and the presence of harmony, *freedom, and *justice, have been achieved.

See also NEGATIVE PEACE, NONVIOLENCE, PEACETIME, POSITIVE PEACE, WAR, and WARTIME.

PEACE ENFORCEMENT. The use of *military means to prevent or to halt military *hostilities.

See also PEACEKEEPING.

PEACEFUL RESISTANCE. A type of *nonviolent resistance, more active than *passive resistance, in which there is a belief (on religious or democratic grounds) in the *relative* moral superiority of *nonviolent means over *violence. Not to be confused with the general *technique of *nonviolent action.

PEACEKEEPER. A member of an organized intervention *force that is intended by its presence and activities to prevent an outbreak of *violence, or to halt existing *violent *conflict between two groups by their presence or activities. Sometimes peacekeepers have been armed with *military *weapons under varying circumstances and sometimes not.

PEACEKEEPING. A process of attempting to prevent *violent *conflict between two groups that have issues in contention, often by deployment of *military *forces. The initiation of international peacekeeping missions, whether under United Nations or other auspices, is generally with the consent of the parties to a conflict.

PEACE MOVEMENT. A loose and informal configuration or association of individuals, groups, and organizations concerned with *peace and *war, which undertake activities intended to prevent or halt *military warfare, to prevent the deployment of particularly destructive *weapons, and to achieve or maintain peace.

The perspectives of participants in a peace movement on the nature and causes of war and peace, and on the *policies that should be followed, usually vary. The orientation of the constituents is usually anti-military, sometimes being opposed to all military activities and sometimes only to specific ones.

Some participants in a peace movement strongly advocate activities and policies intended to develop "peaceful relationships" of *cooperation, goodwill, *justice, friendship, and the like between groups that are or might come into *conflict. Other participants may be primarily or solely interested in preventing or halting a particular war.

"Membership" in a peace movement is extremely loose, as it is not a single organization, and depends upon mutual recognition by the respective constituents. This mutual recognition is associated with a perception that what they hold in common is at the moment more important than their differences in approach and perspectives.

Policies and activities of a peace movement will vary with the conditions, including the immediacy of war, and the beliefs or *ideology of its participants.

See also NEGATIVE PEACE and POSITIVE PEACE.

PEACE RESEARCH. A movement primarily among social and behavioral scientists to promote and conduct different types of research related to *peace and *war, the broader field of *conflict, and the conditions and factors which they believe contribute to those phenomena.

The peace research movement has developed in various countries since the late 1950s in response to growing concern with the question of peace and war.

PEACE STUDIES. A field of academic study, usually on the college or university undergraduate level, that focuses on issues related to *peace and *war as identified by the instructor or academic committee. The courses are often interdisciplinary.

PEACETIME (associated with civilian-based defense). The opposite of *wartime. In the context of *civilian-based defense, the period when a *country is not being *attacked, meaning that it is at *peace.

The peacetime *policies of a country with a civilian–based defense policy may include both domestic policies aimed at constructive improvements to meet the society's existing needs and domestic policies that would make the *society more worthy of *defense. Such a country may also have special international policies—some to meet the country's existing needs, such as economic development, and others intended to increase the chances of nonviolent international assistance in case of *aggression or a *coup d'état against it.

PEASANT STRIKE. A collective refusal by peasants to continue working on the properties of their landlords, especially in feudal and semi-feudal conditions. Grievances may include economic issues, land ownership questions, and termination of legalized serfdom.

PEOPLE POWER. Predominantly *nonviolent mass popular *protest and *resistance, as applied against a *ruler regarded as tyrannical or corrupt. The term "people power" was first widely used in 1986 by demonstrators and journalists to describe the major *demonstrations against President Ferdinand Marcos of the Philippines when he *rigged an election against a political challenger, Corazon Aquino.

PEOPLE'S BLOCKADE. *Nonviolent interjection in an effort to block a large transport vehicle or vessel. This may take the form of human bodies in front of a train, tank, or truck, or people in canoes, kayaks, or rowboats in front of a large ship.

PERSISTENCE (associated with nonviolent action). Continuation of the intended course of action despite threats of *punishment or actual *repression. In *nonviolent action persistence is necessary if a *nonviolent struggle *strategy is to succeed. This is to be distinguished from mere obstinacy in denial of reality.

See also NONVIOLENT DISCIPLINE.

PERSONAL NONCOOPERATION. See TOTAL PERSONAL NONCOOPERATION, and the diverse METHODS of SOCIAL NONCOOPERATION and POLITICAL NONCOOPERATION that can be applied by individuals.

PETITION. See GROUP OR MASS PETITION.

PHASED CAMPAIGN (associated with nonviolent action and civilian-based defense). As part of the *grand strategy for a long-term *nonviolent struggle, a phased campaign is planned to take place at certain points in order to shift major attention to a different component issue, expand the use of certain specific *methods, or increase the involvement of a certain population group.

PHYSICAL NONVIOLENT INTERVENTION (associated with nonviolent action and civilian-based defense). One class of the *methods of *nonviolent intervention.

See also MILL-IN, NONVIOLENT AIR RAID, NONVIOLENT INTERJECTION, NONVIOLENT INTERVENTION, NONVIOLENT INVASION, NONVIOLENT OCCUPATION, NONVIOLENT RAID, PRAY-IN, SIT-IN, STAND-IN, RIDE-IN, and WADE-IN.

PHYSICAL SELF-INJURY. Self-inflicted physical injury intended as a *protest. For example, in the 1970s in the United States some prisoners cut the tendons in their ankles. In Britain in the 1990s *asylum seekers resisting *deportation sewed their lips together, combining fasting from food and illustrating that their voices of protest had been silenced.

PHYSICAL VIOLENCE. See VIOLENCE.

PICKETING. Standing, sitting, or walking back and forth at a place related to an issue in contention in an effort to express *protest, or to persuade others to do, or not to do, a particular act (such as work, or purchase a product).

Placards may be carried, and leaflets may be distributed. The picketers may try to talk with others as a means of promoting their goal.

Picketing may be used alone as a means of protest against particular *policies or acts, or may be used in association with other methods, such as *economic boycott, *political noncooperation, and even *fasts.

Picketing has been widely associated with *strikes, especially to dissuade possible strikebreakers from accepting the jobs of the strikers, and to induce strikers themselves to refrain from work until a settlement is reached. Picketing may also be intended to inform the public of the strike and the issues, and thereby to enlist wider public sympathy and support.

Picketing varies considerably in duration, location, the degree to which it is intended to be persuasive or obstructive, the numbers of participants (ranging from token to mass picketing), and legality.

PICTURE DEMONSTRATION. A *demonstration which depicts to observers the issues in a *conflict as seen by the organizers.

Such portrayal has been accomplished in various ways, including the planting of seeds in a *symbolic reclamation of a disused *military air field, and a *guerrilla theater production against government allocation of resources, in which an "Uncle Sam" gives very thin slices of a pie to bystanders and a huge slice to a person in military uniform.

A single demonstration may have characteristics of both a picture demonstration and a *dilemma demonstration.

PILGRIMAGE (associated with nonviolent action). 1. Walking organized in a way that conveys serious conviction and concern in order to express moral condemnation, or renewed commitment on a social or political *issue.

2. In a religious context, a journey to a sacred site, which may also have political connotations.

In the context of *nonviolent action, this *method of *nonviolent protest and persuasion may be undertaken by persons who wish to bring a "message" to people, to express penance for some policy or deed of the people or *government, or to dedicate themselves publicly to seeking change.

A pilgrimage is likely to be made to a place significant to the beliefs related to the issue in question. A pilgrimage may also have no specific destination, the aim being simply to walk a given distance or time period, or to come into contact personally with the maximum number of people.

A pilgrimage will last at least several days and perhaps even months. Banners and posters are not usually used, although leaflets may be. In certain cases the walking may be supplemented by use of some means of transportation.

PILLARS OF SUPPORT (associated with nonviolent action). The institutions and sections of a *society that supply a given *government with its needed *sources of political power to maintain and expand its power capacity.

Examples are moral and religious *leaders supplying *authority (*legitimacy), labor groups and business and investment groups supplying economic resources, the police, prisons, and *military *forces supplying *sanctions, and similarly with the other identified sources of political power. The term was introduced by Robert L. Helvey.

PLAYS AND MUSIC AS PROTEST. The performance of particular plays, or of music, such as songs, operas, or concerts, under certain political conditions in which the performance constitutes *protest.

This is especially likely to be the case where the theme of the drama or music has political or national significance.

A *method of *nonviolent protest and persuasion.

See also GUERRILLA THEATER.

PLEBISCITE. A direct balloting by eligible voters of a territory, especially on the future political status of that territory and population, or on the future form of *government. The results of a plebiscite may or may not be accepted as binding by the current governing or administering body, or by other groups with an interest in the outcome.

A plebiscite may be conducted on such issues as whether the unit shall become independent, shall come under the rule of an existing *State, or shall be partitioned. If the parties are willing to accept the outcome, this mode of action may be used to resolve such disputes without *civil war or international *war, and without *nonviolent struggle.

PLURALISM. A view or situation that favors diversity of institutions in decision-making and activities in various fields, rather than an authoritarian policy-making and implementation system.

PLURALISTIC SOCIETY. A *society in which multiple institutions exist with a high degree of *autonomy, rather than operating as a strongly hierarchical and centralized social and political order. Political pluralism may or may not reflect ethnic, cultural, or religious pluralism.

POLARIZATION (associated with nonviolent action). The process by which varying social or political opinions become concentrated into two contrasting, less flexible outlooks. This process sometimes occurs temporarily at the beginning of a *nonviolent conflict.

POLARIZE. To develop two contrasting, firmly held perspectives in place of wider and more pliant views of important issues.

POLICE. See DELIBERATE INEFFICIENCY AND SELECTIVE NONCO-OPERATION BY ENFORCEMENT AGENTS, IMPRISONMENT, POLICE STATE, POLITICAL POLICE, and REPRESSION.

POLICE STATE. A *State in which officially disapproved views are illegal, and expression of such views, as well as action for political change, are punishable by police *methods of *control. Surveillance, *arrest, *imprisonment, and perhaps execution are therefore applied to those who *dissent from the established *government, its beliefs, and its *policies.

*Civil liberties and *civil rights are thus nonexistent or, if lip service is given to them, they are continually violated. Neither members of an *opposition, nor anyone else, has access to an independent judicial system.

POLICY. Planned institutional or governmental coordinated actions intended to achieve chosen objectives.

POLICY OF AUSTERITY (associated with nonviolent action). The voluntary giving up of luxuries as part of a *nonviolent action struggle. This *method contains elements of both symbolic *nonviolent protest and persuasion and of *economic boycott.

The practice of austerity may demonstrate to the *opponents, and to vacillating potential resisters, the depth of the *actionists' feelings on the issue. Austerities may also have certain psychological influences on the people practicing them, such as increasing the intensity of their commitment to the struggle. At times, practicing austerities may help a resisting population through times of economic hardship that may accompany a major *resistance campaign.

Giving up luxuries may weaken the opponents' economic position if the opponents normally supply those items to the protesting population.

POLITICAL AMBUSH (associated with nonviolent action and civilian-based defense). A situation that may occur in a *nonviolent struggle against repressive *opponents, when their ease in deploying police, troops, and functionaries, and in violently attacking nonretaliating resisters, proves to be deceptive. Instead of obtaining an easy victory, the opponents find themselves in a serious political situation from which they cannot easily extricate themselves, and in which they may suffer major political losses. This can be a much longer process than a traditional ambush in a *military *conflict.

The opponents' difficulties may result from some combination of the following: expanded and intensified *civil resistance; more complicated and serious political problems; aggravated and expanded enforcement problems; increased undermining of their *authority; growing *alienation and *opposition from *third parties; heightened internal *dissent among the opponents' usual supporters; more widespread and varied *noncooperation; poor morale, deliberate inefficiencies, and even *mutiny of their police and troops; and noncooperation of their functionaries.

A political ambush may develop as an unintended consequence of the operation of the *dynamics of nonviolent action on a large scale, and especially of the process of *political jujitsu. The situation may, however, be deliberately created or cultivated in order to weaken the opponents' relative power position while increasing their need to resort to *repression.

See also DILEMMA DEMONSTRATION.

POLITICAL BOYCOTT. See POLITICAL NONCOOPERATION.

POLITICAL CLASS. A stratum of the population identified by its relative power position in the political *society, especially related to effective decision-making and control of the *State structure.

See also SOCIAL CLASS.

POLITICAL DEFIANCE (associated with nonviolent action). The strategic application of *nonviolent struggle against *dictatorships. It uses *methods of *protest, *noncooperation, and intervention to challenge the rule of a dictatorial clique.

Political defiance involves mobilizing the power potential of an oppressed population in order to undermine the actual power of a dictatorship.

Political defiance strategists initially identify the current and potential *sources of political power of groups in the *society. Using the methods of *nonviolent action, mobilized societal groups then restrict and sever these sources of the dictatorship's power, such as *legitimacy, passive *submission, *material resources, administration, and *sanctions. Those sources are provided by groups and institutions that act as the dictatorship's *pillars of support. Priority is given to undermining the dictatorship's most vulnerable and important pillars of support.

The name of this process was introduced by Robert L. Helvey.

POLITICAL JUJITSU. Political struggle by *nonviolent action against *violent *repression creates a special, asymmetrical *conflict situation. In it the *nonviolent resisters can use the asymmetry of nonviolent means versus violent action to apply a political version of the Japanese martial art jujitsu to their *opponents. The opponents' violent repression against the *nonviolent actionists throws the opponents off balance politically. This is because, as in jujitsu, the opponents are not met with the same kind of action as they have used, nor with *violence, nor with surrender.

The opponents' repression, when confronted with the discipline, *solidarity, and *persistence of the nonviolent actionists, brings attention to the opponents in the worst possible light. This produces shifts in opinion and power relationships favorable to the nonviolent group.

Shifts of opinion *against* the opponents and *favorable* to the nonviolent actionists are likely to occur among *third parties, the general *grievance group, and even the opponents' usual supporters, both internally and internationally. Those shifts may produce both withdrawal of support for the opponents and growth of active support for the actionists.

Third parties, whose esteem or political and economic *cooperation the opponents may wish to retain, may turn against them. Members of the grievance group who have been inactive may join the *defiance. Sometimes the opponents' usual supporters, functionaries, police, and troops may be sufficiently alienated that they participate in mild internal *dissent. In extreme cases these aides may take part in the stronger forms of *demonstrations, *strikes, *disobedience, *deliberate inefficiency and selective noncooperation by enforcement agents, and even *mutiny. These processes, with variations, may occur both in a conflict against an internal *dictatorship and against a foreign occupation *regime.

When shifts of opinion lead to such actions on a significant scale, the opponents' repression will clearly have weakened their relative power position and contributed to their possible *defeat.

For this to happen, the nonviolent resisters need to refuse to shift to violence, where their opponents are stronger. Violence by the resisters is also likely to undermine the support they have achieved to that point. Instead, they must continue their struggle by only nonviolent means.

The process of political jujitsu differs considerably from *moral jujitsu because it affects total power relationships.

POLITICAL KARATE. Very selective use of *methods of *noncooperation and (more rarely) *nonviolent intervention against the *opponents' vital and vulnerable economic and political points or nerve centers. The purpose is to paralyze or disrupt them and hence seriously affect the whole system, or a significant section of it. That impact is then highly disproportionate both to the number of *actionists involved and to the normal effects of the methods used.

These vulnerable points may be related to a disputed *policy, as a key component without which the policy collapses or is obstructed. Among vulnerable points may be the communications system and the transmission of orders downward and information upward within the opponents' system.

At other times the action may be aimed against the whole system by a concentrated *attack on the opponents' crucial *sources of political power. Those sources may include key aspects of industry, transportation, communication, *bureaucracy, police, or *military *forces. Selective action may seriously undermine the effectiveness of a crucial source of power, and consequently seriously weaken the opponents' power.

Such selective action is likely to require fewer participants than widespread noncooperation. Thus it may reduce *casualties resulting from *repression and, if effective, may operate relatively quickly.

Political karate may be especially useful against extreme *dictatorships during *civilian insurrections or *civilian-based defense struggles, both to maximize the political impact of the *resistance and to minimize the danger to sections of the population not participating in the action.

See also SELECTIVE RESISTANCE.

POLITICALLY MOTIVATED COUNTERFEITING. The deliberate distribution of counterfeit money and documents of economic importance by a private *opposition group or foreign *State. The intent is to disrupt the target country's economy or to cause loss of confidence in its currency.

A *method of *economic nonviolent intervention.

POLITICAL MOURNING. Use of the symbols normally used to mourn the death of an individual, applied instead to express political *opposition and sadness because of particular events or *policies. Sometimes the mourning may begin for actual deceased persons, and then gradually turn into political *protest, as in 1989 in Tiananmen Square, Beijing, China, when students initially only mourned the death of a respected national *leader.

The symbols used in this *method of *nonviolent protest and persuasion include flying flags at half-mast, tolling bells, and wearing of a mourning color or symbol.

See also DEMONSTRATIVE FUNERAL, HOMAGE AT BURIAL PLACES, and MOCK FUNERAL.

POLITICAL NONCOOPERATION. A withdrawal of usual political *cooperation, *obedience, or other participation in the political system. The action may be aimed against a specific regulation, law, *policy, usurping group, or even a foreign *government.

As with *strikes and *economic boycotts, the withdrawal is usually temporary, unless the objective is the *disintegration of the *opponent government or system. In most cases, political noncooperation is corporate, concerted action, not simply isolated acts of individuals.

Most of the *methods of political noncooperation are suited to large group action, and are used to wage political struggle to achieve set objectives. These may be limited ones, such as repeal of a certain law, initiation or defeat of a particular policy, or attainment of *civil rights for some or all citizens.

The objectives may be more ambitious, however, such as to promote *disintegration of a dictatorial *regime, or to defend a *legitimate government against a *coup d'état or *invasion. These ends will usually require *noncooperation by large population groups, government personnel, organizations, institutions, constituent governmental units, or some combination of several of these.

At times a *State may apply international forms of political noncooperation against another State. (See DIPLOMATIC RELATIONS—WITHHOLDING OR WITHDRAWAL OF RECOGNITION.) Other forms may be used by and against international organizations.

Certain types of political noncooperation (such as *civil disobedience of "illegitimate" laws) may, however, be applied by individuals or small groups. This may be intended either to offer simple symbolic *protest, or to personally dissociate the noncooperators from the policy or government on moral grounds, without primary concern for political effectiveness.

The significance and effectiveness of political noncooperation is closely related to the numbers of people or political units participating, to their position within the system, and to the opponents' relative need for their cooperation.

Large-scale and persistent political noncooperation is likely to pose serious problems for any government. This is because all governments require cooperation and obedience of the population, and cooperation from the society's institutions, government employees, functionaries, *agents of *repression, and constituent governmental units. Political noncooperation is one of three subclasses of noncooperation. Political noncooperation may be combined with diverse other methods of *nonviolent action.

The methods of political noncooperation, arranged in six groupings, are:

- *rejection of authority*: *withholding or withdrawal of allegiance, *refusal of public support, *literature and speeches advocating resistance;
- *citizens' noncooperation with government*: *boycott of legislative bodies, *boycott of elections, *boycott of government employment and positions, *boycott of government departments, agencies, and other bodies, *withdrawal from government educational institutions, *boycott of government-supported organizations, *refusal of assistance to enforcement agents, *removal of own signs and placemarks, *refusal to accept appointed officials, *refusal to dissolve existing institutions;
- *citizens' alternatives to obedience*: *reluctant and slow compliance, *nonobedience in absence of direct supervision, *popular nonobedience, *disguised disobedience, *refusal of an assemblage or meeting to disperse, *sit-down, *noncooperation with conscription and deportation, *hiding, escape, and false identities, *civil disobedience of "illegitimate" laws;
- *action by government personnel*: *selective refusal of assistance by government aides, *blocking of lines of command and information, *stalling and obstruction, *general administrative noncooperation, *judicial noncooperation, *deliberate inefficiency and selective noncooperation by enforcement agents, *mutiny;
- *domestic governmental action*: *quasi-legal evasions and delays, *noncooperation by constituent governmental units; and
- *international governmental action*: *diplomatic relations—reduced representation, *diplomatic relations—delay and cancellation, *diplomatic relations—withholding or withdrawal

of recognition, *diplomatic relations—severance of representation, *withdrawal from international organizations, *refusal
of membership in international bodies, and *expulsion from
international organizations.

POLITICAL NONVIOLENT INTERVENTION. See CIVIL DISOBEDIENCE
OF "NEUTRAL" LAWS, DISCLOSING IDENTITIES OF SECRET
AGENTS, DUAL SOVEREIGNTY AND PARALLEL GOVERNMENT,
NONVIOLENT INTERVENTION, OVERLOADING OF ADMINISTRA-
TIVE SYSTEMS, SEEKING IMPRISONMENT, and WORK-ON WITH-
OUT COLLABORATION.

POLITICAL OBLIGATION. The citizen's sense of being morally bound to
obey the laws and regulations of the *government (or *ruler), not
necessarily because of approval of each of them, but because of a
belief that it is right to obey the law.

This belief usually derives from the view that government generally benefits *society, and that rules and laws serve individuals and
society more than would their absence.

Complex problems of the sources and limits of political obligation have been raised by political philosophers, including examination of the sources of the government's *authority to *command, of
the criteria for evaluating a particular government and individual
laws, and of possible limits on a citizen's duty to obey.

Acceptance of political obligation may be compatible with
some forms of *civil disobedience, especially *civil disobedience of
"illegitimate" laws.

POLITICAL PARALYSIS. See PARALYSIS.

POLITICAL POLICE. The section of the police which is especially
assigned to investigate, detect and act against political *dissidents,
political *opposition, and violations of political orthodoxy.

Political police are likely to be a significant *agent of *repression
under *dictatorships and in *societies in which *civil liberties and
*civil rights are being, or have been, abolished. The existence of

political police is normally regarded as inimical to *democracy and *constitutional government.

See also POLICE STATE.

POLITICAL POWER (reconceptualized term). The totality of means, influences, and pressures available to determine and implement *policies for the *society, especially the institutions of *government or the *State, or in *opposition to them. Such power may be directly applied, or may be held and perceived as a reserve capacity, as in *negotiations. In such cases it is no less present.

Political power may be measured by ability to *control the situation, to control people and institutions, or to mobilize people and institutions for some activity.

Political power may be used to enable a group positively to achieve a goal, to implement or change policies, to induce others to behave as the wielders of power wish, to engage in opposition or maintain the established system, policies and relationships, to alter, destroy, or replace the prior power distribution or institutions, or to accomplish a combination of these objectives.

Political power is a special type of *social power applied for political purposes. (*Politics is here viewed broadly and not limited to State activities.) Political power is intrinsic to politics, and is involved, directly or indirectly, in all political action. Such power is also a component of virtually every major contemporary social and political *conflict.

Political power derives from identifiable *sources of political power in the society, including *authority, rewards, and *sanctions. Sanctions, either *violent or *nonviolent, are usually a key element of power. The existence and capacity of political power depend on the continual availability of those sources. Therefore, the power holder is dependent on the *cooperation, assistance, and *obedience of the persons and institutions that supply those sources of power.

It is not always necessary to apply power capacity in *open conflict for it to be effective. The mere ability to wield power in direct struggle may be sufficient to achieve the objective. In those cases, power is present in negotiations as well as in open matching of *forces and *war.

It is important to recognize not only actual power but also power potential.

When the context prevents confusion, the simple term "power" may be used.

See also PILLARS OF SUPPORT, POWERLESSNESS, and SOURCES OF POLITICAL POWER.

POLITICAL PRISONER. A person who has been incarcerated or otherwise confined for political reasons, with or without formal charges and court procedures.

In some *countries, political prisoners constitute an official separate class, while in other countries no formal distinction exists between political and nonpolitical prisoners. Political prisoners may have been formally charged with nonpolitical crimes, or with political acts other than those actually committed.

POLITICAL STARVATION. The condition in which a *ruler finds that the sources of power on which the position depends for its operation and existence are no longer available.

When this happens, that ruler will not be able to continue to operate and the *government is dissolved. As this condition is approaching its zenith, it can be expected that extreme measures of *repression, and even irrational brutalities, may be unleashed by desperate components of the old order in frantic efforts to halt the *disintegration.

POLITICAL VIOLENCE (reconceptualized term). *Violence which is used with the intent to further certain objectives in *politics, whether by the *State, non-State groups, or individuals.

Examples of political violence include *imprisonment, *riots, *guerrilla warfare, *conventional war, nuclear war, *assassination, *coup d'état, *civil war, beatings, injuring, *torture, bombing, *terrorism, and execution.

POLITICAL WARFARE. Acute domestic or international *conflict over political issues waged by disruptive political means, short of *political violence but outside of normal constitutional procedures.

These disruptive means may include domestic or foreign efforts to undermine popular support for the *opponents, to win over uncommitted *third parties, to discredit the objectives and activities of the resisters, to encourage or organize political *demonstrations, to support (or weaken) political parties and other organizations, and to rally or reduce support for a given *government or political group.

POLITICS. The processes by which people are governed or govern themselves, by which social and political *policies are determined and implemented, and through which *conflicts over such policies and between political groups (such as parties or *States) are conducted and resolved, whether by institutionalized procedures or *open conflict.

Motivations and long-term goals are both important in politics, but the primary focus is usually on short- and medium-range objectives and means of action.

Politics as defined here includes, but is not strictly limited to, those activities associated with the State. This broader definition encompasses, for example, public education on political issues and corporate extragovernmental action (either constructive or *resistance) to change social or political practices. The term "politics" also can include non-State governmental action and bodies.

Hence, "political."

POPULAR NONCOOPERATION. Widespread *noncooperation among the general population.

POPULAR NONOBEDIENCE. Conscious violation of a law or regulation by disregarding or ignoring it, as though it did not exist, without blatant *defiance and without desire to attract attention.

This *method of *political noncooperation is not identical to either type of *civil disobedience. The disobeyed law may be accepted as *legitimate and the disobedience is not taken in the context of *rebellion against the whole existing *regime.

This method is usually practiced by significant numbers of people acting individually. If practiced by quite large numbers of people, there may be a low probability of identification and *punishment of individuals breaking the law. In contrast, civil disobedience usually implies an open challenge and willingness to accept the prescribed punishment.

See also DISGUISED DISOBEDIENCE and DISOBEDIENCE.

PORTRAITS. See DISPLAY OF PORTRAITS.

POSITIONAL WAR. See NONVIOLENT POSITIONAL WAR.

POSITIVE ACTION. The term coined by Dr. Kwame Nkrumah (later president of Ghana) during the Gold Coast independence struggle. He wrote that it included the "*weapons" of "*legitimate political *agitation," "newspaper and educational *campaigns" and "as a last resort, the constitutional application of *strikes, *boycotts, and *noncooperation based on the principle of absolute *nonviolence."

POSITIVE PEACE. A condition of active *cooperation and goodwill in conducting the normal activities of the *society, in dealing with existing problems, and in improving social, economic, and political conditions.

The term is associated with belief in *active reconciliation and similar *principled nonviolence.

See also NEGATIVE PEACE and PEACE.

POSTERS. See BANNERS, POSTERS, AND DISPLAYED PROCLAMATIONS.

POWER. See POLITICAL POWER, SOURCES OF POLITICAL POWER, and SOCIAL POWER.

POWERLESSNESS. The condition, sense of being, or feeling of being helpless and lacking the means to *control one's own life, much less to help shape the course of societal, political, and international events. At times a population that has felt powerless has mobilized its power potential into actual power.

See also ALIENATION and POLITICAL POWER.

POWER OF THE POWERLESS. This term was the title given by the Czechoslovak playwright and *human rights advocate Vaclav Havel to his essay written in 1976. Havel stressed that the individuals and small groups who refused to cooperate with the "post-totalitarian" regimes in the Soviet bloc (for example, by refusing to vote in meaningless *elections or sign official declarations) were taking actions that could develop into organized *demonstrations and *strikes. Havel's essay and ideas were widely circulated, especially in Eastern and Central Europe.

Havel made the point, elaborated by other analysts of *nonviolent action, that the population living under oppressive rule are not literally powerless but that they have undeveloped power potential that can be developed into actual power.

POWER STRUCTURE. The formal and informal network of power relationships within a *society or institution that determines actual *policies and actions.

The formal structures of institutions and the distribution of power that they officially allocate may approximate the actual power relationships. However, the official and the actual power distributions are never identical. They may differ widely.

At times the existing informal and noninstitutionalized power capacities and networks may modify, rival, or even surpass the actual power capacities of the official power structure.

See also POLITICAL POWER and SOCIAL POWER.

PRAYER AND WORSHIP. Prayer and worship can be conducted in a manner that expresses moral condemnation and even political *protest.

This expression may be made clear by the content of the prayer or worship service, the immediate situation (as when demonstrators are ordered to disperse), the place (as outside a *government building), or often the occasion (for example, if the day has symbolic significance).

A *method of *nonviolent protest and persuasion.

PRAY-IN. Entry, or attempted entry, by persons belonging to an excluded group to a religious building from which they have been barred, in order to participate equally in the religious service.

In cases where admission has been allowed but seating has been segregated, the *actionists using this *method of *nonviolent intervention sit in pews reserved for others.

PRECLUSIVE PURCHASING. Buying up of supplies of important commodities in world markets in order to make them unavailable to *opponents.

An economic form of *nonviolent intervention.

PREEMPTIVE INVASION (associated with civilian-based defense). An *invasion launched against a *country in order to forestall or preclude certain actions or *policies by the invaded country. In the context of *civilian-based defense, a preemptive invasion may occur in order to prevent development of the full potential of that *defense policy.

In the more usual *military context, preemption is often falsely claimed by aggressors to justify their actions.

PRIMARY BOYCOTT. The direct suspension of economic dealings with the *opponents, or a refusal to buy, use, or handle their goods or services.

This action may be accompanied by efforts to persuade others to do likewise.

See also ECONOMIC BOYCOTT and SECONDARY BOYCOTT.

PRINCIPLED NONVIOLENCE. A group of belief systems which include rejection of *violence on grounds of a principle. This principle may be either an imperative against all violence, or a quite different principle which requires abstention only from a particular type of violence, or from its use in a specific situation.

Some of these belief systems extend their definition of "violence" beyond physical violence to include *psychological violence, *hostility, and even *conflict.

The five types of principled nonviolence are *nonresistance, *active reconciliation, *moral resistance, *selective nonviolence, and *nonviolent revolution.

See also NONVIOLENCE.

PRISONERS. See CONCENTRATION CAMP, IMPRISONMENT, INTERNMENT CAMP, and POLITICAL PRISONER.

PRISONERS' STRIKE. Refusal by prisoners to do work required of them by prison officers.

This *method of *strike may be used for various reasons, including objection to being incarcerated or a desire to improve specific prison conditions.

PROCESSION. See DEMONSTRATIVE FUNERAL, MARCH, MOCK FUNERAL, MOTORCADE, PARADE, PILGRIMAGE, and RELIGIOUS PROCESSION.

PROCLAMATIONS. See BANNERS, POSTERS, AND DISPLAYED PROCLAMATIONS, DECLARATIONS BY ORGANIZATIONS AND INSTITUTIONS, DECLARATIONS OF INDICTMENT AND INTENTION, and MANIFESTO.

PRODUCERS' BOYCOTT. Refusal by producers to sell, or otherwise deliver, their product. This *method may then also be called a "selling *strike." This *economic boycott may involve a refusal by any type of producer, from farmers to manufacturers, even to make or raise the product.

The producers' boycott may be used to boost prices by reducing the quantity of available goods, to support fellow producers faced with a *consumers' boycott, or to contribute to a broader *noncooperation movement against an opposed *government or *military occupation.

PROFESSIONAL STRIKE. A *strike by salaried persons in a particular learned or skilled vocation, or by self-employed persons.

The reasons for a professional strike are usually economic or political. Where the reason is political, the professional strike often occurs as part of a wider *conflict, and could initiate a struggle in which different sections of the population are using other *methods of *nonviolent action.

Professional groups such as lawyers may strike to maintain the principles inherent in their profession or to uphold their professional status. This motive is perhaps more common than economic issues.

PROPAGANDA. Written, oral, pictorial, or internet communications intended to influence the attitudes, opinions, and beliefs of those to whom they are directed. The means of communication may include leaflets, newspapers, radio broadcasts, posters, films, and websites.

PROPERTY. See DEMOLITION, DESTRUCTION OF OWN PROPERTY, DESTRUCTION OF PROPERTY, REFUSAL TO LET OR SELL PROPERTY, SABOTAGE, and VIOLENCE.

PROTEST. Expression of objection and disapproval by words or action.

See also ASSEMBLY OF PROTEST OR SUPPORT, CAMOUFLAGED MEETING OF PROTEST, and the class of METHODS called NONVIOLENT PROTEST AND PERSUASION.

PROTEST DISROBING. The public removal of clothes as a means of expressing one's religious or political disapproval of a *policy or a *government.

A form of *nonviolent protest and persuasion.

PROTEST EMIGRATION (*HIJRA* OR *HIJRAT*). Deliberate migration from the jurisdiction of a *State as an expression of extreme disapproval because the resisters believe it to be responsible for certain *injustices or *oppression.

Such action is a very serious *method of *social noncooperation. However, a protest emigration by very large numbers of people may take on the character of *political noncooperation. Protest emigration may be permanent or temporary. The latter occurs especially where the *opponents need the cooperation of the emigrants.

Voluntary emigration was called *hijra* in seventh-century Arabic. The term *hijra* derives from Muhammad's flight from Mecca to Medina, undertaken instead of *submission to *oppression in Mecca. The concept is called *hijrat* or *hizrat* in India, and also *deshatyaga* (giving up the country). Japanese peasant actions of this type were called "desertions" or *chosan*.

PROTEST MEETING. A gathering of people to express *opposition.

Protest meetings may vary considerably in size and nature, including street meetings, small local meetings, well-organized large meetings, and mass open-air rallies of thousands. They normally include planned programs of speeches.

The meeting itself and the speeches are intended to communicate to the *opponents, the general public, and *third parties the protesters' opinion of the opposed *policy, practice, or *government.

Because most of the people attending a protest meeting agree on the issue, the speeches may also be designed to reinforce commitments to the cause, offer new information, and perhaps stir the protesters to take further action.

This *method of *nonviolent protest and persuasion is widely used. The protest meeting may be used on its own, or along with other *methods, such as *strikes, *economic boycotts, or *civil disobedience.

See also ASSEMBLY OF PROTEST OR SUPPORT, CAMOUFLAGED MEETING OF PROTEST, and TEACH-IN.

PROTEST SONGS. See PLAYS AND MUSIC AS PROTEST and SINGING.

PROTEST STRIKE. A work stoppage for a preannounced short period (a minute, a day, or even a week, for example) to express the views of workers on an economic, political, or other issue. Statements on the issue may be presented, but no demands are made. This is also called a token *strike and a demonstration strike.

The aim of a protest strike is to demonstrate that the workers feel deeply about a particular issue, and that they possess the strength to act more strongly if necessary. Alternatively, this *method may be used to spark the imagination of the workers and to promote the idea of striking on that particular issue.

The protest strike may also be used where workers are unable or unwilling to conduct a long strike, or where a longer work stoppage would be met with more severe retaliation than the workers are prepared to suffer, or where the workers seek to avoid serious damage to the economy.

There may be protest *general strikes, protest *industry strikes, and protest *sympathetic strikes. The protest strike may be varied by combining it with periods of *silence, *stay-at-home days, or other methods.

See also HARTAL.

PROTRACTED STRUGGLE (reconceptualized term). A *conflict waged under conditions in which it cannot be won quickly, and may last months or years.

Protracted struggle by *nonviolent action contrasts sharply with the more common application of nonviolent action in a *civilian insurrection or the *strategy of *nonviolent blitzkrieg in *civilian-based defense.

A protracted struggle is especially likely when the *opponents are extremely powerful, when the *struggle group has not made preparations for the *conflict, or when the opponents possess other major advantages.

The term is adapted from Mao Zedong's 1938 phrase "protracted war." It referred to a projected long Chinese *military and *guerrilla warfare struggle against the Japanese *invasion and *military occupation.

PROVISIONAL GOVERNMENT. A partial and temporary governmental apparatus organized during a major *conflict in which *control of the *State is an important issue. A provisional government may either be based within a section of the territory that it intends to rule, or have its headquarters outside that territory. The latter is especially likely during a foreign *military occupation of the *country.

The provisional government may intend to become the sole *government of the territory, or to pave the way for another government with accepted *legitimacy. Provisional governments are especially likely to be organized during *national liberation struggles or *revolutions.

The degree to which a provisional government has all the characteristics of a government varies. In some cases, the provisional government may be largely a figurehead government, without any real governing apparatus or capacities. In other cases, the provisional government may conduct various administrative and other functions within the territory.

The organization and operation of a provisional government may be a significant factor in influencing the course of the conflict.

See also DUAL SOVEREIGNTY AND PARALLEL GOVERNMENT.

PSYCHOLOGICAL NONVIOLENT INTERVENTION. See FAST, NONVIOLENT HARASSMENT, NONVIOLENT INTERVENTION, REVERSE TRIAL, and SELF-EXPOSURE TO THE ELEMENTS.

PSYCHOLOGICAL VIOLENCE (reconceptualized term). Psychological or social pressures that inflict emotional and psychological injury—for example, falsely telling individuals or a group that they are genetically inferior, that they have an incurable fatal disease, that they will always be failures, or that a loved one will be killed.

Psychological violence is distinct from temporary emotional upset that may be caused by a challenge to established behavior, feelings of *hostility, or the threat or use of physical *violence.

PSYCHOLOGICAL WARFARE. Systematic attempts by either adversary, especially during a *military war, to affect the morale, opinions, emotions, and actions of the population, troops, agents, bureaucrats, and other personnel of the other side. The aim may be to make them less reliable in support for their own side or, at times, to become useful to the side applying psychological warfare.

In the context of a *military occupation, occupation officials may also apply psychological warfare against the population of the occupied territory, neutrals, and even friendly groups.

Psychological warfare may be waged by *propaganda, spreading of rumors, dissemination of information and falsehoods, and the like. In the context of a military occupation, certain political, economic, or repressive measures may also be taken to influence the morale, opinions, loyalties, and daily lives of the general population or the occupiers. These measures may purport, for example, to demonstrate humanitarian concerns but really be designed to weaken support of that side for the *war effort. Acts of severe *repression and brutalities may also be used for their psychological effects, in order to induce insecurity and *fear and to weaken the *resistance.

In the context of a military war, psychological warfare may aim to weaken support for the war and reduce active participation in the war.

See also UNCONVENTIONAL WARFARE.

PUBLIC ASSEMBLIES. See ASSEMBLY OF PROTEST OR SUPPORT, CAMOUFLAGED MEETING OF PROTEST, PROTEST MEETING, REFUSAL OF AN ASSEMBLAGE OR MEETING TO DISPERSE, and TEACH-IN.

PUBLICATION OF NAMES. The public announcement during a *resistance movement of the names of people who are either not participating in the *resistance that is widely supported, or who have become, or are becoming, collaborators.

Publication is usually practiced in order to pressure nonparticipants or collaborators (and, indirectly, others who may be wavering) to join the resistance, or refrain from aiding the *opponents. *Social boycotts and *economic boycotts of recalcitrants or collaborators often follow such publication. This form of identification may be withdrawn when the behavior ceases.

This type of pressure may be especially appropriate during resistance to a foreign *military occupation or *coup d'état. Announcements of names may be made by newspapers, leaflets, posters, radio, and the like.

See also COLLABORATION.

PUBLIC OPINION. Views consciously held by a population, whether openly expressed or not, on matters of general concern. These matters may include standards of behavior, beliefs, the social system, identified problems, or current issues. Such views may support the status quo, or may favor changes of various types. Public opinion may be seriously divided.

Public opinion can influence the way in which the *society and political system operate, including the ways in which problems are solved, issues are dealt with, and *conflicts are resolved. Whether public opinion is important in influencing what actually occurs, and if so to what degree, varies. The role of public opinion may depend on the context, the issues at stake, and the distribution of power.

The factors that help to determine the role of public opinion in cases of conflict include: the specific situation; the social and political context; the nature of the society and the political system; the characteristics of the group, institution, or *government which is opposed; the nature of the issue; the intensity with which the views of the public are held; and the means used by the public to support those views.

In political conflicts, both adversaries often seek to influence and control public opinion in support of their political aims. Broadcast and print media are often used for this purpose.

PUBLIC SPEECHES. Talks or discourses openly delivered in order to express *protest or seek support.

Public speeches may be spontaneous, or they may be delivered as planned parts of *demonstrations. They may also take the form of formal addresses at scheduled meetings, or of sermons during religious services.

A *method of *nonviolent protest and persuasion.

PUNISHMENT. A penalty or suffering inflicted, or threatened, in reprisal for disapproved action or behavior. In a political *conflict, punishment is usually understood as inflicted by a *government.

However, punishment also may be imposed by nongovernmental groups and institutions.

See also SANCTION.

PUPPET GOVERNMENT. A titular and formally acknowledged *government that is controlled and manipulated by the government of a foreign *State or other entity.

A puppet government is especially likely to be set up by a State which has invaded and militarily occupied another *country, but is attempting to rule through the invaded country's own nationals.

A puppet government can also occur in the absence of *invasion and *military occupation when a foreign State is able to manipulate and control the political system of another country. This may be done by explicit or implicit threat of a *military invasion, by manipulation of a political party or other elite group in the country, by powerful economic *leverage, by manipulation of sections of the military *forces or *political police, and by activities of political *agents.

PURIFICATORY CIVIL DISOBEDIENCE. See CIVIL DISOBEDIENCE.

PUTSCH. A *coup d'état carried out by units of the *military forces.

Hence, "putschist."

QUASI-LEGAL EVASIONS AND DELAYS. Efforts by subordinate or constituent units of *government (such as cities, states, and provinces) to evade indefinitely, or to delay as long as possible, compliance with a superior law, order, or court decision, but without directly defying it.

The officials of the subordinate unit may publicly claim compliance, but by various means postpone implementation. The officials may, for example, become involved in minor complexities or fine points that postpone compliance. In other cases, postponement may be accomplished on the grounds that some other law or regulation either must first be complied with, or is inconsistent with the law in question. Or the officials may try to confuse the issue and delay compliance in some other way.

Quasi-legal evasions and delays constitute a form of *political non-cooperation, which is similar to *stalling and obstruction. However, the latter consists of acts of individuals, administrative units within a government, and the like. Quasi-legal evasions and delays, on the other hand, are acts of an entire subordinate governmental unit.

See also NONCOOPERATION BY CONSTITUENT GOVERNMENTAL UNITS.

QUICKIE WALKOUT. Short, spontaneous *protest strikes to "let off steam" or to *protest on relatively minor issues. Quickie walkouts are known as "lightning strikes" in England.

They rarely last more than a few hours or involve more than a few workers in a plant. This type of walkout is one of the forms that *wildcat strikes may take.

QUISLING. A person who collaborates with a foreign occupation *regime. The word comes from the name of the Norwegian fascist Vidkun Quisling, who was the most prominent collaborator during the Nazi occupation of Norway.

See also COLLABORATION.

RACISM. 1. A belief that some human groups are inferior to others on the basis of ancestry or biological characteristics.

2. Discriminatory, unequal, segregated, or similar treatment of the members of a group based on a belief by another group that believes it is racially superior.

RADICAL. 1. A person who believes in *radicalism.

2. The quality of a group, program, or movement based upon radicalism.

RADICALISM. A political outlook or *ideology which holds that the solution to existing social or political problems necessitates departing fundamentally from established approaches, and moving instead toward a quite different comprehensive alternative.

See also RADICAL.

RADIO. See ALTERNATIVE COMMUNICATION SYSTEM and RECORDS, RADIO, AND TELEVISION.

REACTION (associated with nonviolent action). 1. An action in response to some stimulus, event, influence, or the like.

2. A response by a population, group, institution, or *government to a challenge or action of another such body.

In the context of *nonviolent action, the nature of a response to the *actionists is likely to be influenced by the issues, by the way in which the challenge is made, by whether *nonviolent discipline is maintained or *violence breaks out, and by other factors.

See also POLITICAL JUJITSU and REPRESSION.

3. A return, or desire to return, to a preferred previous condition of *society and *politics.

REACTIONARY. 1. Related to, or characterized by, a preference for an earlier condition. A term often associated with conservatism.

2. A person who favors a return to an earlier condition.

REALISM. An approach to social and political life that emphasizes the importance of accepting the current social and often political order as it is, perhaps that it is inevitable.

This approach includes giving full recognition to the extent of *conflict, disorder, *violence, and established *controls in evaluating the present order and planning any changes. Sometimes contrasted with *idealism.

REALPOLITIK. A school of political thought that emphasizes the preeminence of *military power in political and international relations.

REBEL. One who, by any means, revolts against, defies, or deliberately disobeys the established order.

REBELLION. Open mass *defiance, *insurrection, or *resistance to the established *government. Rebellions vary in extent and seriousness.

RECONCILIATION. The reestablishment of friendly and cooperative relationships between persons and groups following an argument or *conflict between them.

RECORDS, RADIO, AND TELEVISION. These media can become instruments of *nonviolent protest and persuasion. They may be used to convey ideas, discuss issues, present positions, communicate *resistance messages and instructions, and the like, through music, speeches, declarations, or other means.

When used to resist attempts at *censorship, or to break existing *controls, the use of these media would be a form of *nonviolent intervention.

See also PROPAGANDA.

REFORM. An actual or proposed change in an institution or social system intended to correct or ameliorate a limited *social problem or *injustice, without major alteration of the existing institutions or distribution of power.

REFORMATORY CIVIL DISOBEDIENCE. See CIVIL DISOBEDIENCE.

REFUGEE. A *civilian who has left home or native *country in order to seek safety from immediate or probable dangers, such as *war, persecution, bombings, and the like.

REFUSAL OF AN ASSEMBLAGE OR MEETING TO DISPERSE. Deliberate *noncompliance by a formal meeting, or an informal gathering, with official or unofficial demands that it disperse.

This *method of *political noncooperation may be closely related to *popular nonobedience or to *civil disobedience of "illegitimate" laws.

REFUSAL OF ASSISTANCE TO ENFORCEMENT AGENTS. Refusal for political reasons to help police in performance of their duties. This often occurs under *military occupations and domestic *dictatorships.

This *method includes *noncooperation with requests for information, for help in locating wanted persons, or for assistance in confiscating or disposing of property for unpaid taxes. It may also take the forms of refusal to walk when arrested (going limp), and refusing other types of assistance.

A method of *political noncooperation.

REFUSAL OF GOVERNMENT MONEY. Refusal as a political act to accept a *government's money, either completely or in all but minor transactions. This constitutes a *method of *economic boycott.

In some limited cases, such as during extreme inflation, economic concerns may bolster the political reasons for such action. Refusal of government money may be accompanied by substitution of gold, silver, barter, and the like.

REFUSAL OF IMPRESSED LABOR. Open *noncompliance by a population group to a levy requiring it to supply certain physical labor (as for road construction) to other persons or governmental bodies.

This method of *strike has usually been aimed at the abolition of such levies, rather than the simple improvement of working conditions during the period of service.

REFUSAL OF INDUSTRIAL ASSISTANCE. Economic or political *opposition expressed by the unwillingness of owners, managers, or employed technicians, and the like, to provide economic or technical assistance or advice to *opponents, such as the *government.

A *method of *economic boycott.

REFUSAL OF MEMBERSHIP IN INTERNATIONAL BODIES. Refusal by international intergovernmental institutions to accept a *government as a member.

This governmental form of *political noncooperation may be applied because of political rivalries, disapproval of the government in question on the grounds of its general characteristics or specific *policies, or other reasons. This *method may also be applied in support of an internal *resistance movement.

REFUSAL OF PUBLIC SUPPORT. Deliberate abstention from expressing open support for the existing *government and its *policies. This occurs under particular political circumstances that transform an ordinarily innocuous act into a *method of *political noncooperation.

Under political conditions of organized unanimity and instigated "enthusiasm," persistent silence by individuals may often be dangerously noticeable. Even where the government is not fully totalitarian, some individuals may be expected or ordered to express their public support for it. Their consequent refusal to do so may be regarded as an act of *opposition.

This *method may, for example, take the form of refusal to issue or endorse a declaration of support for the regime, or the form of a *writers' silence.

See also TOTALITARIANISM.

REFUSAL TO ACCEPT APPOINTED OFFICIALS. Refusal by a subordinate political unit to accept a new appointee to an official position.

In cases where the appointee is not persuaded to depart promptly, this *method of *political noncooperation would involve refusal to recognize the person in the official role, and refusal to cooperate with that official in carrying out the duties of the position.

REFUSAL TO DISSOLVE EXISTING INSTITUTIONS. Refusal by political, educational, labor, cultural, or other types of institutions to accept voluntarily their dissolution by *government order.

This can occur when a government seeks to abolish such independent institutions in order to increase its *control of the population, to destroy an *opposition movement, or to restructure the *society on the basis of an ideological preconception.

Using this *method of *political noncooperation, the newly illegal institutions may continue to operate either openly or secretly, and to conduct what normal activities they can, while they collectively resist governmental measures intended to destroy them.

See also BOYCOTT OF GOVERNMENT-SUPPORTED ORGANIZATIONS.

REFUSAL TO LET OR SELL PROPERTY. The refusal of owners of buildings and other property to rent or sell them to members of certain categories of people or groups disapproved by the owner.

A *method of *economic boycott.

REFUSAL TO PAY DEBTS OR INTEREST. Deliberate nonpayment of debts or interest used as a *method of *economic boycott.

This method is especially feasible as a means of *resistance when the debts are owed by the potential resisters to *opponents, or to persons or firms in another *country whose *government is being resisted. It can also be used domestically.

Rarely in these cases, only payment of interest due, not of principal, is refused.

Sometimes a new government may refuse to repay debts incurred by the previous government, especially to foreign governments that supported it.

During the *noncooperation resistance by the American colonies to the British-imposed Stamp Act, George Washington advocated keeping the courts closed so that they could not be used by British merchants to collect debts owed to them by resisting Americans. Washington wrote on September 20, 1765, ". . . the Merchants of G. Britain trading to Colonies will not be among the last to wish for a repeal of it." The merchants then would pressure Parliament to repeal the opposed Stamp Act.

REFUSAL TO PAY FEES, DUES, AND ASSESSMENTS. The deliberate refusal as a *resistance measure by individuals, groups, or *governments to pay fees, dues, or assessments to a private organization, public institution, government, or international body.

A *method of *economic boycott.

REFUSAL TO RENT. The refusal by the potential tenant to rent an available residence, land, or other property, as part of a collective action of *noncooperation.

A *method of *economic boycott.

REGICIDE. The murder for political reasons of the head of *State or *ruler, such as a king, president, or dictator.

See also ASSASSINATION and TYRANNICIDE.

REGIME. A general type of political system, such as representative (including parliamentary), monarchical, dictatorial, and totalitarian systems. Within each general regime there can be a succession of *governments with differing personnel and sometimes differing *policies.

REGIMENTATION. The controlling of an institution, population, or *country in an organized, detailed, and systematic manner, according to a central plan or a central command structure.

REJECTION OF AUTHORITY. See LITERATURE AND SPEECHES ADVOCATING RESISTANCE, REFUSAL OF PUBLIC SUPPORT, and WITHHOLDING OR WITHDRAWAL OF ALLEGIANCE.

RELENTLESS PERSISTENCE. A term widely used in Latin America as the equivalent of *nonviolent action.

RELIGIOUS PROCESSION. A *march or *parade that possesses religious qualities. Religious pictures or symbols may be carried by participants, they may sing religious songs, and the procession may include members of the clergy, monks, nuns, and the like.

This *method of *nonviolent protest and persuasion may be used similarly to the march and parade. The degree of religious motivation, as compared to political and social concerns, may vary.

RELOCATION CAMPS. Fortified locations with restricted entry and exit, for people who have been forcibly resettled in them as part of a *government effort to separate the residents from unwanted influences or *controls, for example, by *guerrilla groups.

See also GUERRILLA WARFARE.

RELUCTANT AND SLOW COMPLIANCE. The delaying of compliance with certain *commands as long as possible, followed by final compliance characterized by a marked lack of enthusiasm and thoroughness.

This form of *political noncooperation is especially used where members of a *grievance group do not feel able to resist unconditionally. When widely practiced, the ability of the *government to carry out its will, although not entirely blocked, is nevertheless slowed and limited.

See also QUASI-LEGAL EVASIONS AND DELAYS.

REMOVAL OF OWN SIGNS AND PLACEMARKS. The removal, alteration, or replacement of house numbers, street signs, placemarks, railroad station signs, highway directions, distance signs, and the like. This *method of *political noncooperation may be intended to misdirect, impede, or delay the movement of foreign troops, police, or others unfamiliar with an area.

This method may be used, for example, to delay the *political police until wanted persons have had time to escape, or until a *resistance meeting place or equipment can be relocated. This method was used in Prague by Czechs resisting Soviet invasion forces in 1968.

RENOUNCING HONORS. The giving up of special honors that have been conferred, or the refusal of new ones that are offered, by the *government or other institution that the *nonviolent actionists oppose.

This *method of *nonviolent protest and persuasion may involve the voluntary renunciation of titles of honor, medals, and honorary offices, and resignation from prestigious societies that are closely identified with the *opponents' cause. Such renunciation may be regarded as an expression of self-sacrifice for the *resistance movement, and as a means of weakening the *authority of the government.

RENT. See REFUSAL TO LET OR SELL PROPERTY, REFUSAL TO RENT, and RENT WITHHOLDING.

RENT WITHHOLDING. Individual or collective refusal by persons renting property to pay their rent, as a means of *protest or *resistance against the landlord.

The withholding may be for only a short period, after which the back rent is paid in full. Or only part of the rent may be withheld. In these cases the withholding becomes a token *demonstration.

If, however, the rent refusers intend to press the issue until their objectives are won, usually they must be willing to face eviction and prosecution.

In some states of the United States, rent withholding is legal in some situations to enforce housing codes and regulations.

This *method of *economic boycott is also called "rent refusal" and "rent strike."

REPORTING "SICK" ("SICK-OUT"). A *method of *strike in which workers stay away from work and report that they are ill (when they are in fact not) to put economic pressure on the employer. They may aim by this action to achieve anything from a slow-down to the equivalent of a full strike.

This *method may be used almost anywhere, but is especially practiced where strikes are prohibited by law, decree, or contract, or where they are not feasible for some other reason, but where sick leave is granted by contract or law.

See also BLUE FLU.

REPRESSION (especially associated with nonviolent action). *Control measures threatened or applied by a *government either to prevent the development or the expression of *opposition, or to punish, crush, or destroy existing opposition.

These measures may include police activities, surveillance, arrests, *imprisonment, crowd control measures, shootings, *terror, *concentration camps, *intimidation, *torture, economic privations, and others. Repression usually involves *violence directly or indirectly.

In very brutal *dictatorships and totalitarian systems, extreme *violent repression may be used against persons not even suspected of *resistance in order to strike extreme *fear, and therefore compulsive *submission, into the general population.

In serious *conflicts in which *nonviolent action is applied against powerful *opponents, repression can normally be expected. A weak *nonviolent resistance movement may be stultified or crushed by repression. However, repression against a strong movement does not necessarily produce submission, but may increase resistance.

This nonviolent *technique operates against violence through its special dynamics without submitting to it or using counter-violence, creating a special asymmetrical conflict situation. *Persistence, *fearlessness, and *nonviolent discipline may neutralize the repression and facilitate *political jujitsu.

When repression is applied against different means of struggle—nonviolent action, *guerrilla warfare, and the like—it is likely to vary in severity, duration, and effectiveness, as well as in the type and extent of *casualties, side effects, and *backlash.

See also DYNAMICS OF NONVIOLENT ACTION.

REPRISAL. Reprisals, which are hostile and often *violent retaliations for certain actions, occur especially in acute *conflicts when important issues are at stake.

The retaliatory acts may be taken by the *government, individual persons, or a private group. The reprisal may be inflicted on individuals, groups, or property. The targeted individuals may be *actionists, their families or friends, or persons with no involvement in the conflict.

Reprisal methods inflicted by the violent *opponents may include *destruction of property, *violence, and at times even *methods of *nonviolent action, such as economic pressures. Reprisals in conflicts appear to be more severe in response to *sabotage and *assassination.

Reprisal methods are more akin to acts of vengeance than to calculated *repression designed to halt the *resistance. They may be deliberately used to create an atmosphere of *terror, but may instead backfire and strengthen the resistance.

RESIGNATION. See BOYCOTT OF GOVERNMENT EMPLOYMENT AND POSITIONS, BOYCOTT OF GOVERNMENT-SUPPORTED ORGANIZATIONS, BOYCOTT OF LEGISLATIVE BODIES, JUDICIAL NONCOOPERATION, STRIKE BY RESIGNATION, and WITHDRAWAL FROM INTERNATIONAL ORGANIZATIONS.

RESISTANCE (reconceptualized term). *Opposition to a *policy, activities, structure, *domination, *aggression, or *attack by *direct action. The opposition may be conducted by social, economic, or political forms of *nonviolent struggle or by *sabotage, *guerrilla warfare, or *military means. Regular institutional procedures are a different type of activity.

Hence, "resister."

See also CIVIL RESISTANCE, CIVILIAN-BASED DEFENSE, CIVILIAN INSURRECTION, GUERRILLA WARFARE, MASSIVE RESISTANCE, NONVIOLENT RESISTANCE, POLITICAL NONCOOPERATION, SABOTAGE, SPONTANEOUS RESISTANCE, and UNDERGROUND MOVEMENT.

RESISTANCE AT FRONTIERS (associated with civilian-based defense). A *strategy of *civilian-based defense in which the *nonviolent defenders place their bodies in the path of invading troops, *military vehicles, and the like, with the aim of halting them by *nonviolent interjection or *nonviolent obstruction.

This strategy, suggested especially by M. K. Gandhi and Vinoba Bhave in India, is intended to offer the attacking *government and individual soldiers the choice either of halting or of advancing by killing many nonviolent volunteers. Success with the strategy depends on moral influence.

More recent analysts of civilian-based defense have strongly criticized this strategy on the basis of its inflexibility, logistical problems, excessive imitation of conventional military *defense, strategic irrelevance, and moral considerations.

Variations on the resistance-at-frontiers strategy include symbolic acts to communicate to invading troops the population's intent to resist, stationing of neutral observers at international boundaries, blocking highways or airports with immobilized automobiles, and the like.

Other strategies of civilian-based defense include *nonviolent blitzkrieg, *selective resistance, and *total noncooperation.

RESISTANCE AT KEY POINTS. See SELECTIVE RESISTANCE.

RESISTANCE GROUP. A limited number of persons who work together in conducting *resistance. Such bodies may operate autonomously or in *cooperation with other groups.

See also CIVILIAN RESISTANCE, NONVIOLENT RESISTANCE, and RESISTANCE MOVEMENT.

RESISTANCE MOVEMENT. A widespread, and usually informally inter-related, network of individuals, informal groups, institutions, and *resistance groups engaged in planned or spontaneous *resistance. The resistance may be directed against an established *government, political system, social patterns, institutions, *usurpation *regime, or *military occupation administration.

See also CIVILIAN-BASED DEFENSE and CIVILIAN INSURRECTION.

RESTRICTED STRIKES. See BUMPER STRIKE, DETAILED STRIKE, LIMITED STRIKE, PROTEST STRIKE, REPORTING "SICK" ("SICK-OUT"), SELECTIVE STRIKE, SLOWDOWN STRIKE, STRIKE BY RESIGNATION, and WORKING-TO-RULE STRIKE.

RETREAT. See STRATEGIC RETREAT and TACTICAL RETREAT.

REVENUE REFUSAL. The refusal voluntarily to provide the *govern-ment with revenue, as a means of *protest or *resistance.

This may involve the refusal to pay income taxes, property taxes (rates), or sales or purchase taxes, or the refusal to purchase certain required licenses (such as for a dog, car, radio, television, etc.). Such refusal may be made either to highlight a particular grievance directly related to the tax or license, or to symbolize a wider grievance against the government. Tax refusal of this type by an individual may be virtually impossible in situations where employers deduct taxes from the employee's income, unless the employer is also refusing economic cooperation with the government.

Revenue refusal may also involve the *boycott of goods whose sale requires a sales or purchase tax. Land or property rents paid to the government may also be refused. Funds for the government (though not technically "revenue") may be refused by boycotting government loans, bonds, and "national savings" accounts. In some cases, taxed items might be sold with the seller refusing to collect or pay the tax.

The refusal to pay taxes or rents to the government is illegal. Where undertaken on a large scale, it may become a severe threat to the existence of the government, either because of the threat to the *State's treasury, or because widespread refusal demonstrates the extent and depth of the population's *defiance of the particular government.

This is a *method of *economic boycott. However, since the revenue is owed to a government, or an agency of it, and is required by statute or regulation, revenue refusal may also be classed as a method of *political noncooperation.

Attempts have sometimes been made to refuse to pay government debts. People have been urged to refuse to pay taxes for that purpose, or resistance and revolutionary groups have warned possible foreign creditors that if they were to loan money to the tottering government, the debt would not be honored when the government falls.

See also REFUSAL TO PAY FEES, DUES, AND ASSESSMENTS.

REVERSE STRIKE. Insistence by workers on working as volunteers on a needed project in order to apply pressure to gain an objective from the *opponents.

For example, employed workers may work harder and longer than they are either required or paid to do, in order to support their demand for pay increases by making it difficult for the employer to deny their requests. They may also continue working after a manufacturing plant has been officially closed.

Alternatively, unemployed workers may insist on doing volunteer work to dramatize the need for jobs, as was done in Sicily in the late 1950s under the inspiration of Danilo Dolci.

The reverse strike constitutes an economic form of *nonviolent intervention, but it is largely psychological in impact. Modifications of the *method have been used by social reformers to demonstrate the need for a slum cleanup *campaign, and by students in the form of *united attendance to show the need for enlarged classrooms and increased faculty.

REVERSE TRIAL. A reversal of the roles of prosecutor and prosecuted in a trial of political *opponents or religious dissenters. By their behavior during the trial the defendants place the *government on trial. The defendants become the prosecutors and the trial is turned into a *demonstration against the government, and becomes a means for those on trial to spread their views.

REVOLT. A synonym for *rebellion.

REVOLUTION. An accelerated change in social, political, or economic life and institutions, or a combination of these, accomplished by mass popular action, which produces, initially at least, a redistribution of power, and does not simply place new personnel into old positions.

This redistribution includes increased participation in decision-making and a popular restructuring of institutions. This restructuring need *not* necessarily be preceded by destruction of the old institutions.

This popular empowerment may not last, however, if the breakdown of the old power structure is not be followed by the institutionalization of the new one and backed by effective capacity for democratic struggle. This fluid situation may open the way for a new minority political, *military, or *intelligence group to establish a new oppressive or dictatorial *government, as occurred in the French and Russian revolutions.

The means of struggle in revolutions differ widely, and include types of *violence, *nonviolent action, *destruction of property, and combinations of these. A revolution usually involves a new source of *legitimacy, or a new perception of an old source of legitimacy.

Revolution is defined here not by the content of espoused beliefs, theories, or *ideology, although these are often important, but by observable behavior and institutional results. The ideational or ideological content of revolutions may differ widely, both in substance and in relative importance.

Hence, "revolutionary."

See also CIVILIAN INSURRECTION, COUNTERREVOLUTION, INSURRECTION, NONVIOLENT REVOLUTION, REBELLION, and *ULTIMA RATIO POPULI*.

REVOLUTIONARY CIVIL DISOBEDIENCE. See CIVIL DISOBEDIENCE.

RIDE-IN. A type of *sit-in adapted to public transportation. This *method of *nonviolent intervention is popularly known in the United States as a "freedom ride," where opponents of segregation persisted in sitting in sections of buses and other vehicles where they were not allowed. These actions occurred as early as 1841 as well as in the 1960s.

Sometimes ride-ins have violated company regulations, or local and state laws. At other times, such actions have been taken to bring local practice into conformity with state or federal law or court decisions.

RIGGED ELECTION. A fake *election in which the form of an election is maintained. However, in place of accurate counting of freely given choices by *legitimate voters, the results are determined by manipulations of various types. Manipulation has included, for example, falsified counting, *intimidation of voters, counting "votes" by deceased persons, buying of votes, and other means.

RIOT. A disorderly action by a crowd of people expressing their feelings or opinions in various boisterous or destructive ways. Riots usually include *destruction of property belonging to others (whether *opponents or not), and sometimes infliction of injury or death on persons who may or may not have had anything to do with the origins of the riot.

Riots may stem from political, economic, and social grievances, or may occur completely without them. Riots in the absence of grievances may occur in association with emotionally charged sporting events, and public drunkenness may contribute to the excesses. Sometimes, actions of the police may provoke crowd rioting. Riots should be distinguished from minor scuffles. In the emotions of the riot, however, the grievances that have triggered the original action may have been forgotten, and destruction may become an end in itself.

Riots in the midst of *nonviolent struggle *campaigns (in which *nonviolent discipline is highly important) have tended to undermine the campaigns, and nonviolent *actionists have on occasion accused *agents provocateurs of initiating the riots in order to help the opponents.

RUDE GESTURE. The use of bodily movements, such as hand gestures or turning one's back, to convey an offensive opinion or deliberate insult in situations of social, political, or international *conflict.

A *method of *nonviolent protest and persuasion.

RULER. The person or group occupying the highest position of *command in the *society and *government, especially that which controls the *State.

See also CONSTITUTIONAL GOVERNMENT, DICTATORSHIP, ESTABLISHMENT, and OLIGARCHY.

SABOTAGE. Acts intended to immobilize, dismantle, damage, or destroy material objects such as equipment, machinery, communications, facilities, means of transportation, and the like. Such acts may be carried out by persons or groups in *conflict with the owner, operator, or beneficiary of those goods or services (including the *State or occupation *regime).

The term covers a wide range of activities. These include (a) acts of immobilization, such as deliberate removal and "loss" (but not damage or destruction) of items, ranging from office files to parts of machines such as vehicles, which only immobilizes them; (b) infliction of physical damage to specific property, especially items associated with the grievance, without injury to persons; and (c) *demolition of targets, such as bridges, trains, and the like, which can endanger persons and risk loss of life, clearly an act of *violence.

Use of more specific terms and descriptions is therefore required when precision is important.

One report claims that the term "sabotage" came into general use around 1897 after a disgruntled French workman threw his wooden shoe (*sabot*) into the machinery of his employer.

SAMIZDAT. A term used in the Soviet Union, in *countries formerly controlled by the Soviet Union, and in China, for the practice of clandestine reproduction and distribution of banned literature. Copies were made a few at a time, by typewriter or by handwriting, and often recopied by hand and further distributed. Where photocopying machines are available they have also been used.

SANCTIONS (reconceptualized term). *Punishments, pressures, and means of action used to penalize, thwart, and alter the behavior of other persons, groups, institutions, or *States. Sanctions are usually punishments or reprisals for failure to behave in the expected or desired manner.

Although "sanction" may be used more specifically as a legal term, the phenomenon itself occurs in a wide variety of social relationships, such as the spanking of a disobedient child or the firing of a disobedient employee, as well as *imprisonment for *disobedience to State laws.

Sanctions may also be applied by the citizenry against the State, by certain nongovernmental groups against others, and by States against each other. Sanctions in domestic and international politics are usually a key source of *political power. In many situations, simply the capacity to wield, or the threat to apply, either *violent or *nonviolent sanctions may induce compliance with the *command.

Sanctions are used by *governments to supplement voluntary acceptance of their *authority and to enforce *obedience.

Other types of sanctions may be applied by the citizenry against an established *ruler, or against a *usurper attempting to seize *control of the State, or by trade unionists seeking to enforce wage increases, for example.

The widespread practice of defining "sanction" also to include positive inducements and rewards to attain one's aims is not followed here. This exclusion is made because clear communication is not facilitated by simultaneous use of a single term to indicate opposite meanings. Instead, such phrases as "positive inducements for obedience" or "rewards for compliance," and the like, may be used to indicate those other concepts.

Many State sanctions involve the threat or actual use of *violence, but other sanctions, especially financial ones, are regularly used. These may include imposition of fines, withdrawal of welfare benefits, and expulsion from jobs and housing. But *nonviolent sanctions by non-State groups and *resistance movements also exist, such as *boycotts, *strikes, and *civil disobedience.

Most violent sanctions are applied basically as punishments for disobedience that has already occurred, not primarily as a means to achieve the aim of the original *command. It is, however, maintained that the threat of punishment for disobedience greatly encourages obedience to the command.

Some violent sanctions, and more often nonviolent sanctions, are used with the primary intent of achieving the original objective which *opponents have refused to grant or to accept. This is often true in the case of *conventional war, *strikes, *political noncooperation, and the like.

A key element in the *operation of *nonviolent action against repressive opponents is the refusal to capitulate or submit in spite of official sanctions and unofficial reprisals.

See also ECONOMIC SANCTIONS.

SANCTUARY (associated with nonviolent action). In the context of *nonviolent action, "sanctuary" is used by persons who, anticipating apprehension or *punishment, take refuge in temples, churches, and other holy places where they cannot be touched by the *opponents without violation of religious, moral, social, or legal prohibitions.

Such violation would put the opponents in a difficult situation, threatening their *legitimacy and potentially alienating their own supporters.

Taking sanctuary in this sense is normally practiced by a group (rarely an individual) whose support or assistance is needed by the opponents.

In certain situations the taking of sanctuary by particular people may indicate a withdrawal of moral support for the *ruler and contribute to the ruler's loss of *authority.

This *method of *social noncooperation can only be used in *societies in which traditional beliefs and taboos are strong. During the Persian constitutional revolution of 1905–1906, Muslim *leaders on occasion took refuge in the holy city of Qum and in the British embassy, symbolizing their withdrawal of legitimacy from the authoritarian shah.

In some societies the general tradition of sanctuary previously existed, as freedom from arrest while in a holy place, but now is not respected. In such cases, groups of protesters nevertheless, when expecting arrest, have sometimes withdrawn to such traditional places as a type of "symbolic sanctuary."

SATYAGRAHA. 1. In India, a synonym for *nonviolent action as practiced by M. K. Gandhi, as in "to launch satyagraha."

2. In India, a particular nonviolent action *campaign, such as "the 1928 Bardoli satyagraha."

3. The type of *principled nonviolence developed by M. K. Gandhi. Derived from Sanskrit, the term roughly means "firmness relying on truth as essence of being." This belief enjoins its adherent, a *satyagrahi, to improve his or her own life, to combat social evils by nonviolent action, and to build a better social order by constructive work.

SATYAGRAHI. A person who participates in a *satyagraha *campaign.

SATYAGRAHIC FAST. A type of *fast refined by M. K. Gandhi for attaining social objectives by arousing the consciences of those against whom the fast is directed. Its characteristics were formulated by him. This type of fast is contrasted with the *hunger strike.

Normally the satyagrahic fast is not directed against *opponents in a *conflict, unless those persons and the *satyagrahi have been personal friends and the latter feels that a trust has been broken. In Gandhi's view the fast may also be used when an opponents' *control and *repression have eliminated other possible means of *protest and *resistance. However, lacking other alternatives, Gandhi thought that prisoners subjected to inhuman treatment might fast for improved conditions, but not for release from prison.

Gandhi believed that considerable spiritual preparation and social service were necessary before one was justified in undertaking a satyagrahic fast. The satyagrahi could then fast to arouse the conscience of former or present friends (an individual, a group, or even millions), but only after other *nonviolent means had been exhausted.

The satyagrahic fast may be for a predetermined time period, or until death if a set demand is not granted. The latter was only to be used in extreme situations. Gandhi insisted, however, that people should not capitulate to anyone who had gone on a fast, unless they were convinced of the rightness of the objective sought.

SCHOOLS. See ALTERNATIVE SOCIAL INSTITUTION, STUDENT STRIKE, UNITED ATTENDANCE, and WITHDRAWAL FROM GOVERNMENT EDUCATIONAL INSTITUTIONS.

SCHWEIKISM. Systematic failure to carry out ordered or expected behavior efficiently. Instead, the response may be procrastination, delays, *reluctant and slow compliance, incomplete obedience, deliberate misunderstandings, and evasion. Both sides in a conflict can employ this *method. This could involve a *government, or sections of a government, resisting an occupation or a *coup d'état.

The term is derived from the satirical novel *The Good Soldier Schweik* by the Czech writer Jaroslav Husek.

SCORCHED EARTH POLICY. The deliberate destruction of buildings, food supplies, crops, water supplies, cities, transportation, facilities, and the like—anything that could be useful to the population or to foreign *invaders. The destruction may also be conducted by foreign invaders to deny the population the means of inhabiting the territory, or the destruction may be conducted by the defending population to deny invaders needed resources.

In case of the latter, such actions are likely to be accompanied by withdrawal of the population into unoccupied territory or other more protected locations. The intent is to make the *military occupation as difficult as possible for the invaders, and to deprive them of any possible economic benefit from the occupation. This policy has been applied in conjunction with *military *defense and *guerrilla warfare.

SECONDARY BOYCOTT. An *economic boycott, usually a *consumers' boycott, against *third parties, in an effort to induce them to support the original economic boycott against the *opponents.

See also PRIMARY BOYCOTT.

SECRET AGENTS. See DISCLOSING IDENTITIES OF SECRET AGENTS.

SECRET POLICE. See POLITICAL POLICE.

SECURITY (reconceptualized term). The condition of being safe. This may occur either because of an absence of dangers, or because of the presence of effective means of protection against possible hostile actions and *attacks.

This definition is in contrast to the widespread claim of "national security" to justify overruling of *civil liberties and democratic constitutional procedures.

SEDITION. Advocacy by printed or spoken word of the overthrow of a *government. As an act of disloyalty, sedition is milder than treason.

Sedition is usually defined by laws, and hence these definitions differ from *country to country. Also, interpretations of laws against sedition vary with the international conditions, often being broader in time of *war or *military occupation.

Hence, "seditious."

SEEKING IMPRISONMENT. *Actionists verbally requesting to be jailed, or acting so as to ensure their own *imprisonment as the primary objective. This activity is distinguished from imprisonment that follows as a secondary consequence of *civil disobedience.

Actionists using this *method may, for example, deliberately break a particular regulation with the express purpose of being imprisoned. When some of the persons have been arrested, those who have not may specifically ask that they also be arrested.

This method is usually applied by several persons or large numbers acting together. This political form of *nonviolent intervention may be used to express *solidarity with individuals already under *arrest. The intent may also be to demonstrate a lack of *fear of arrest, to obtain the release of those already arrested, to clog the courts or fill the prisons, to obtain wider publicity, or to expand the *resistance.

When the objective is to fill the prisons, this method may be called a *jail-in.

SEIZURE OF ASSETS. Impounding or confiscating assets owned by a hostile *State or its nationals during a *conflict.

This economic *method of *nonviolent intervention may take such specific forms as blocking the use of bank accounts and of securities in brokerage accounts, stopping payment of interest or dividends, abrogation of patent or royalty rights, and similar courses of action. The aim normally is to inflict economic loss on the hostile *country.

SELECTIVE NONVIOLENCE. A type of *principled nonviolence characterized by the refusal to participate in *particular* *violent *conflicts, usually international *wars, because of some overriding nonpacifist political or religious principle. In certain other situations, the same persons, guided by the same principle, might be willing to use *violence to accomplish the desired ends.

SELECTIVE PATRONAGE. Promotion of patronage of designated firms, or of products with particular origins, as a means of exerting economic pressure in a *conflict where other firms or products are being boycotted.

This economic *method of *nonviolent intervention has, for example, been used instead of explicitly boycotting other firms, especially to bypass anti-boycott laws, as in some U.S. states. An effect similar to an *economic boycott may be obtained by simply urging people to purchase from particular firms.

Similarly, trade unions have often promoted the purchase of products bearing the union label. This version of selective patronage has been applied in order to support higher wages and improved working conditions, by rewarding companies that have union contracts, and thus shifting business away from those without them.

Selective patronage has also been used by other groups to reward businesses that have pursued a *policy that the group approves, especially one regarded as a financial risk.

Selective patronage *campaigns to promote purchase of the products of one's own *country have also been used by national *independence movements to build up the dependent country economically, and thereby to reduce financial rewards to the imperial country.

SELECTIVE REFUSAL OF ASSISTANCE BY GOVERNMENT AIDES (associated with nonviolent action and civilian-based defense). Individual or collective refusal by *government employees, administrators, officials, *agents, or officers to carry out particular instructions or orders, while informing their superior officers of the refusal.

This *method of *political noncooperation may or may not be announced to the public, but as far as the superior officers are concerned, the refusal is clear and open. This quality distinguishes this method from the more hidden types of evasion and obstruction.

SELECTIVE RESISTANCE (associated with civilian-based defense). A *civilian-based defense *strategy of concentrating *resistance on the *defense of important social, economic, or political institutions, or on certain pivotal issues, especially on those related to basic freedoms, or on both types of issues.

1. Defense of independent social, economic, and political institutions would have a special role in keeping the social and political system out of the *usurpers' control. This would prevent the usurpers from gaining effective *control of the key institutions, including communications and transportation. The maintenance of the independent groups and institutions (*loci of power) would ensure bases for potential resistance to the usurpers. Successful defense of these independent bodies could help to block any attempt to atomize the population. (See also ATOMIZATION.)

The particular points selected for a given *campaign would usually be chosen because they could also have a considerable impact on the future course of the struggle.

2. Another important component of selective resistance is the *defense of the *society's principles, especially basic freedoms and *civil liberties (such as free speech). Along with that is *opposition to efforts to indoctrinate the population with the usurpers' *ideology. (See also INDOCTRINATION.)

3. Finally, selective resistance would aim to communicate to all concerned the issues at stake from the perspective of the defenders.

Concentrated resistance at the right points would be aimed to promote dissension among the *opponents, while maximizing support and participation within the defending population.

Civilian-based defense using this strategy would involve a series of campaigns on specific issues, often conducted in part by particular sections of the population.

Selective resistance may be associated with the *work-on without collaboration. Selective resistance is also called "resistance at key points" and "*nonviolent positional war." The term "selective resistance" is especially useful in contrasting this strategy with *nonviolent blitzkrieg and *total noncooperation. The strategy of selective resistance, if successful, is likely in time to be supplemented or replaced with another strategy involving massive *noncooperation and *defiance.

SELECTIVE SOCIAL BOYCOTT. A type of *social boycott that is restricted to one or more particular types of relationship. This restriction may be the result of a tactical decision, or the boycotted relationship may just happen to be the main point of contact between the particular resisters and the *opponents.

A selective social boycott may take such forms as refusal to shake hands or rejection of personal invitations. In other situations, shopkeepers may be willing to speak to occupation troops, but still refuse to sell them anything.

This latter expression of this *method of *social noncooperation differs from a *traders' boycott in that it is not a refusal to sell the item in question, but to sell it to that particular person.

SELECTIVE STRIKE. A *strike in which workers refuse to do only certain types of work, often because of some political objection, such as shipping certain goods to a disliked *government. The objection is to the nature of the tasks themselves, not to hours, working conditions, or the like.

The intention of the selective strike is thus both to prevent that particular work from being done, and to induce the employer not to ask the workers to do that type of work in the future.

SELF-DETERMINATION. A decision-making capacity that enables a population group, *nation, or *country to decide upon its own broad political future.

This decision may be reached by *plebiscite or other procedure. The political issue may be, for example, whether the unit shall be independent or part of a larger *State, or what type of political system it will adopt.

SELF-EXPOSURE TO THE ELEMENTS. Exposure of one's own body to discomfort or suffering from extreme heat or cold, in order to induce others to change attitudes or take certain action. Such action has also taken the form of taking up a precarious position, such as on prison roofs.

This is a *method of psychological intervention, related to the *fast.

SELF-GOVERNMENT. The process or condition in which members of a group, population, institution, or *nation themselves determine and administer the *policies relevant to that unit. Self-rule.

See also CONSTITUTIONAL GOVERNMENT, DEMOCRACY, DIRECT DEMOCRACY, GOVERNMENT, and SELF-DETERMINATION.

SELF-RELIANCE. The capacity to meet one's needs, and fulfill one's obligations, solely by depending on one's self. This has been regarded by M. K. Gandhi and others as a great advantage during a *nonviolent struggle *campaign.

SELF-SUFFERING. Endurance by *nonviolent actionists of deprivations and injuries resulting from continued *defiance despite *repression, without the actionists' retaliating or capitulating.

The actionists may be willing to pay the price not only to make the *technique of struggle effective, but in some cases to promote *conversion of the *opponents.

The term "self-suffering" and the emphasis on this process are especially associated with the Gandhian tradition within *nonviolent action.

The suffering is likely to be inflicted by the opponents' *agents of repression. More rarely, it may derive from one's own action, as in a *fast. In either case, self-suffering is believed by *satyagrahis to have an unequalled potential to change the opponents' feelings, beliefs, and attitudes, and to bring about their conversion.

See also ACCOMMODATION, NONVIOLENT COERCION, and SOCIAL DISTANCE.

SELLERS' BOYCOTT. See INTERNATIONAL SELLERS' EMBARGO, INTERNATIONAL TRADE EMBARGO, MERCHANTS' "GENERAL STRIKE," PRODUCERS' BOYCOTT, REFUSAL TO LET OR SELL PROPERTY, and TRADER'S BOYCOTT.

SEVERANCE OF DIPLOMATIC REPRESENTATION. See DIPLOMATIC RELATIONS—SEVERANCE OF REPRESENTATION.

SEVERANCE OF FUNDS AND CREDIT. Exertion of economic pressure by cutting off the *opponents' sources of money, such as salaries, appropriations, loans, and investments. Such severance may be made by individuals, firms, or *governments.

A *method of *economic boycott.

SEWING LIPS TOGETHER. See PHYSICAL SELF-INJURY.

SEXUAL NONCOOPERATION. See LYSISTRATIC NONACTION.

SHAREHOLDERS' ACTION. This *method has been used in *opposition to *policies of major corporations. In order to apply it, individuals purchase a very small number of shares and thereby acquire the right to attend annual meetings of the firm and to raise questions about corporate policies. They may also engage in more *activist *protests during the meeting. The actions may be in support of demonstrators outside the building, or in solidarity with groups elsewhere in the world.

Issues championed by these protesting shareholders have been related to mining, oil drilling, logging, repressive employment practices, and other issues.

SICK-OUT. See REPORTING "SICK" ("SICK-OUT").

SIGN CHANGING. See NEW SIGNS AND NAMES and REMOVAL OF OWN SIGNS AND PLACEMARKS.

SIGNED PUBLIC STATEMENT. A written declaration directed primarily to the general public, or to both the public and the *opponents, which is released with the signatures of endorsers.

The intention may be, for example, to publicize grievances, seek concessions from the opponents, or arouse sentiments against the opponents.

The signatures may be from persons who officially represent organizations, or individuals with selected occupations or professions, or may be determined by other criteria.

This common method of *protest in constitutional democratic systems became a serious challenge under *authoritarian *regimes. A major historical example of this was Charter 77, calling for *civil liberties in Communist-ruled Czechoslovakia in January 1977, reminding the *government that it had signed the 1976 Helsinki Accords, which included commitment to *human rights.

A *method of *nonviolent protest and persuasion.

SIGNS AND NAMES. See NEW SIGNS AND NAMES and REMOVAL OF OWN SIGNS AND PLACEMARKS.

SILENCE. Efforts by a group not to make any sound, as a *method of *nonviolent protest and persuasion for expressing moral condemnation.

The silence may be a primary means of expressing that attitude, or it may be an auxiliary method combined with, for example, a *march or *stay-at-home *demonstration.

SINGING. Under certain conditions singing constitutes a *method of *nonviolent protest and persuasion.

For example: singing while an unwanted speech is being made; singing national, political, or religious songs when they are a defiant assertion of views or beliefs; singing songs of social and political satire or *protest; offering a rival choir concert to compete with a boycotted one organized by the *opponents; and singing while engaged in a *march, *civil disobedience, or some other act of *opposition.

See also PLAYS AND MUSIC AS PROTEST.

SITDOWN. An act of *political noncooperation in which the participants sit down on the street, road, ground, or floor either for a limited or for an indefinite period of time and refuse to leave voluntarily.

The sitdown may be a spontaneous or a predetermined reaction to orders for marchers or other demonstrators to disperse. Or the sitdown may be a deliberate violation of some regulatory law. It then becomes *civil disobedience as well, and a serious type of symbolic *resistance.

A sitdown might also be used to halt traffic or tanks, or to prevent workers or officials from performing their work. In these cases it becomes a *method of *nonviolent intervention (either *nonviolent interjection or *nonviolent obstruction). Some people doing this have been crushed to death.

The sitdown should not be confused with the *stay-in strike, which also has been known as a "sit-down strike."

SIT-DOWN STRIKE. See STAY-IN STRIKE.

SIT-IN. The physical occupation of certain facilities by persons engaging in *nonviolent intervention by sitting on available chairs, stools, and occasionally on the floor, for a limited or indefinite period.

This *method may be applied as a single act or as a series of acts. The objective may be to disrupt the normal activities of those normally using the facilities. The purpose may also be to establish a new social pattern, such as opening the particular facilities (such as lunch counters) to previously excluded persons. This was a widely publicized method in the U.S. *civil rights movement.

The aim may also be to *protest about an issue that is not directly connected with the facilities occupied.

SKITS AND PRANKS. Political satire expressed in a social form such as a humorous prank, a skit, or a play.

In such cases the satire ceases to be simple verbal political *dissent (as is often expressed in dictatorial *countries in political jokes). Expressed in a social form, the satire becomes an act of public political *protest.

A *method of *nonviolent protest and persuasion.

See also GUERRILLA THEATER.

SKYWRITING AND EARTHWRITING. Words or symbols communicated to people across large distances by "writing" them in the sky or earth, as skywriting by airplane, or earthwriting by plowing messages in the soil.

Messages may also be conveyed by planting contrasting crops, trees, or other plants in a desired pattern, or by arranging rocks or shrubs in the form of a word or symbol, especially on hillsides or mountains.

A *method of *nonviolent protest and persuasion.

SLOGANS, CARICATURES, AND SYMBOLS. Brief written, painted, drawn, printed, mimed, gestured, or spoken communications of opinions and views. Together these three ways of communicating constitute a very common form of *nonviolent protest and persuasion.

SLOWDOWN STRIKE. The act of workers deliberately reducing the pace of their work so as to restrict their production significantly. Instead of leaving their jobs, or stopping work entirely, as in most *strikes, the workers continue to report for work, go through the motions of working, and collect their pay.

In extended applications, a slowdown in an industrial plant affects production and profits detrimentally; in *government offices it reduces the efficiency of the government's ability to rule. The slowdown strike has also been used by serfs and agricultural workers.

This *method of *strike is also known as a "go-slow" and a "ca'canny."

SOCIAL AFFAIRS. See BOYCOTT OF SOCIAL AFFAIRS and SUSPENSION OF SOCIAL AND SPORTS ACTIVITIES.

SOCIAL BOYCOTT. Refusal to continue usual social relations with the disapproved or opposed persons, by not speaking to them and not interacting with them in any other way.

The social boycott, the most common *method in the class of *social noncooperation, is also known as "*ostracism," or in England as "being sent to Coventry."

The effectiveness of the social boycott seems to depend on the degree to which the social relations which are severed are vital ones, or regarded as important by those being ostracized. Effectiveness is also influenced by the thoroughness with which the social boycott is practiced.

Social boycotts have been practiced by religious groups against persons of whom they disapproved, and by strikers against fellow workers who refused to join a *strike. The social boycott has a long history in which the extremes to which it is carried and the spirit in which it is practiced have varied considerably.

See also COLD SHOULDER and ICE FRONT.

SOCIAL CHANGE. 1. Any alteration in a *society, no matter why or how produced.

Social change may occur in any aspect of a society, such as in its institutions, established patterns of behavior and roles, and *social structure. Social change also includes alterations in meanings, beliefs, customs, norms, and shared ideas and concepts of the society. (Some social scientists would, however, classify this latter group separately as "cultural change.")

Social change may be produced, for example, by the society's internal dynamics, innovations, external influences, side effects of new technologies, or internal or external *conflict. Changes may be deliberately induced or unintended.

*Nonviolent action may be used with the intention of producing or preventing social change.

2. The process by which such alterations are produced.

SOCIAL CLASS. A stratum, or layer, of the population that shares similar social and economic characteristics that differ from those of other strata in the *society.

Class membership may be determined by the group's economic power (whether they are employed, self-employed, employers, or occupy some other position in the economic structure), and also by the groups' social position (influenced by education, prestige, tradition, mutual identification, and the like).

See also POLITICAL CLASS.

SOCIAL CONFLICT. A condition of perceived contention, disagreement, or *opposition on a significant issue or issues between two or more groups in the *society.

Issues in such clashes may include beliefs, opinions, status, power interests, social or economic interests, resources, the nature and extent of the political system, social customs, and in extreme circumstances even whether one of the groups shall exist as a distinct part of the population.

Social conflicts differ widely in their scale, from small, relatively insignificant ones to vast and serious *conflicts affecting the whole society.

The issues may be genuine ones, in which case those conflicts are called "realistic conflicts" by social scientists. Other cases may be "nonrealistic conflicts," in which the tensions do not originate from real issues. Instead, the tensions that may arise from frustrations, for example, are displaced onto the avowed issues or onto the particular *opponents, who may have had nothing to do with the frustrations.

In realistic conflicts, a source of contention or incompatibility may exist but not yet be recognized by either party. These may be called "latent conflicts." In other instances the issues between the conflicting groups are both genuine and recognized. These conflicts are called "*open conflicts."

The means of conducting conflicts vary widely. They may be established institutional procedures, some form of *violence, or *nonviolent action.

The choice of means may be influenced by such factors as: the culture; the perceived seriousness of the issues; the scale of the conflict; the type of issue; the degree of incompatibility of the contrasting objectives; the intensity of feelings and commitments; the social and political structure and legal arrangements; the role of *third parties; the respective conceptions of the nature and source of power; comparative anticipated effectiveness; and awareness of options.

In those conflicts that involve open struggle and a matching of *forces, each side will at some stage threaten or apply the ultimate *sanction in which it places confidence, either violence or some type of nonviolent action.

SOCIAL CONTROL. All means that are used to keep the *society orderly and its members sufficiently obedient and conformist to maintain the society.

The term applies both to those means that are intended to benefit the society as a whole, and to those aimed mainly to benefit a dominant elite.

The diverse means and processes that induce social control can be either informal or formal. They include: internalization of the society's norms; socialization of individuals into the society's roles and institutions; rewards ranging from social approval to status and material gains; formal rules and regulations; *sanctions (*violent or *nonviolent) for *nonconformity and *disobedience; and manipulation of symbols important to the culture.

SOCIAL DEFENSE. A term used in some *countries and by some groups in discussions of possible use of *nonviolent resistance for national *defense. The rationale for using this term is to emphasize the importance of inducing change in the domestic *society and its institutions, rather than defense of the existing society and especially its *State structure, which they oppose. The term implies a radical political slant on both defense and the role of *resistance.

See also CIVILIAN-BASED DEFENSE and CIVILIAN DEFENSE.

SOCIAL DEMOCRACY. The goal of some advocates of major *social change, in which much of the economic system is socially owned through the *State or through independent organizations and institutions. These bodies may be consumers' or producers' cooperatives or low-level governmental structures.

The political system is envisaged as democratic with any of several possible institutional arrangements. These may include a parliamentary or congressional system with a division of powers between the branches of *government and full *civil liberties.

Present economic policies of parties called "social democratic" commonly depart from the above-stated goal to a significant degree.

SOCIAL DISOBEDIENCE. Violation of customs, expectations, rules, regulations, or practices of a nongovernmental social institution, such as a religious body, club, or economic organization.

Such social disobedience may take many forms, including breaking factory regulations or orders without striking, disobeying ecclesiastical orders, or violating standard forms of speech, dress, and behavior.

In other cases, persons who disapprove of a certain *social boycott may refuse to participate in it and instead may deliberately fraternize with the boycotted people, thereby practicing social disobedience in a different form.

SOCIAL DISTANCE. The degree of feelings and attitudes of separation between two groups in a *society. Social distance is usually shown by the degree of interaction between the groups or the absence of such interaction.

Social distance may be produced by status, caste, *racism, *social class, religious or political doctrines, exclusion from the category of common humanity, distaste for cultural or behavioral characteristics, or other factors. Social distance may be unilateral and not reciprocated by the rejected group, or it may be a mutual attitude between both groups.

In a *nonviolent conflict, when there is considerable social distance between the *opponent group or *third parties, on the one hand, and members of the *grievance group or the *nonviolent actionists, on the other hand, it is likely to discourage sympathy for their cause or empathy for their *self-suffering in the face of *repression.

SOCIAL INSTITUTIONS. See ALTERNATIVE SOCIAL INSTITUTION.

SOCIALISM. A political doctrine or system in which the economic system, or at least the commanding heights of the economy, including the means of production and distribution, are owned by the general *society, in distinction from capitalism with private or corporate ownership and management. Within that broad scope there exists considerable variation, including the extent and role of *State ownership, the degree of *centralization and *decentralization, the institutional arrangements for ownership of economic institutions, the extent and forms of democratic *operation and *controls or their absence, and the means by which a socialist society is to be brought into being and maintained.

See also CLASS STRUGGLE, CLASSLESS SOCIETY, DEMOCRACY, LENINISM, MARXISM, MARXISM-LENINISM, SOCIAL DEMOCRACY, and SYNDICALISM.

SOCIAL JUSTICE. See JUSTICE.

SOCIAL MOVEMENT. A grouping of a significant number of people who by belief and actions seek change in the conditions under which they live.

The people are held together and motivated to act by a shared set of ideas, beliefs, or objectives. These views explain the cause of their painful present condition, and point to a way in which changes in the *society, or a whole better life, may be achieved. The adherents then act in accordance with that view.

Beyond those minimal characteristics, social movements may differ widely. Some are, for example, "otherworldly" oriented, seeking to prepare their believers for a glorious afterlife and to win converts for eternal salvation. Others, such as *millenarian movements, may see a new world possible on this earth, but it is to be accomplished only by means outside of conscious human *control. Still other social movements may seek to apply specific *strategies to regain a glorious past—a *reactionary movement.

Many others intend to go forward to achieve deliberate change by *reform or *revolution, such as anti-slavery, peace, labor, and feminist movements.

The advocates of deliberate change may utilize highly diverse means and have differing goals and institutional objectives, ranging widely, from *anarchy to *Jacobinism, and from *nonviolent action to *terrorism.

Social movements will have some such broad features in common, but will differ widely in beliefs, norms, *leadership, structure, means and objectives.

SOCIAL NONCOOPERATION. Refusal to carry on normal social relations, either particular or general ones, with persons or groups regarded as having perpetrated some wrong or *injustice, or to comply with certain behavior patterns or social practices. This constitutes a subclass of the *methods of *noncooperation.

The methods of social noncooperation, arranged in three groupings, are: *ostracism of persons*: *social boycott, *selective social boycott, *Lysistratic nonaction, *excommunication, and *interdict; *noncooperation with social events, customs, and institutions*: *suspension of social and sports activities, *boycott of social affairs, *student strike, *social disobedience, *withdrawal from social institutions; and *withdrawal from the social system*: *stay-at-home, *total personal noncooperation, "*flight" of workers, *sanctuary, *collective disappearance, and *protest emigration.

SOCIAL NONVIOLENT INTERVENTION. See ALTERNATIVE COMMUNICATION SYSTEM, ALTERNATIVE SOCIAL INSTITUTION, SOCIAL PATTERNS—ESTABLISHING NEW ONES, GUERRILLA THEATER, OVERLOADING OF FACILITIES, SPEAK-IN, and STALL-IN.

SOCIAL ORDER. 1. The institutions of a *society as a whole and their inter-relationships.

2. The condition of a society in which there is (a) *security for the populace and their personal possessions, (b) a *constitutional government, (c) an absence of significant use of *repression against the populace to maintain *social control, (d) an absence of *violent upheaval, and (e) the use of orderly and peaceful means of maintaining social control and achieving *social change.

SOCIAL PATTERNS—ESTABLISHING NEW ONES. The incorporation of new forms of social behavior into the *society in violation of a usual practice. This occurs through the deliberate or spontaneous initiation of the new pattern of behavior, its eventual adoption by others, and, ultimately, general acceptance.

These new forms may vary considerably, potentially including changes in social acceptability of persons from groups previously regarded as low status, and in behavior related to courtship, marriage, and sexual patterns. Changes in residential and occupational arrangements, and in many other forms of behavior, may also occur.

For example, in a race-conscious society, such as one practicing segregation or slavery, individuals of both majority and minority communities have walked down the street side by side, dined together, related socially, and intermarried. Similarly, in caste-conscious India, high-caste Hindus have eaten with so-called untouchables and even intermarried with them.

This social *method of *nonviolent intervention differs from *social disobedience, which only breaks old behavior patterns, perhaps in individual or isolated cases, without establishing new patterns which become incorporated into the society.

SOCIAL POWER. The totality of influences and pressures which can be used by and applied to groups of people, either to *control or resist the behavior of others directly or indirectly, or to accomplish a group objective by joint action. Social power in some form is inherent in all social relationships.

*Political power is a subtype of social power.

SOCIAL PROBLEM. A condition or situation in a *society that is perceived by a significant number of people to be unacceptable and to require conscious efforts to change it.

SOCIAL REFORM. See REFORM.

SOCIAL REVOLUTION. See REVOLUTION.

SOCIAL STRUCTURE. The system of organization and institutionalization of a whole *society. This includes the prescribed roles for various members of the society, its informal and formal social, economic, and political institutions, kinship, and residential patterns, and the relationships among all of these.

SOCIETY. The whole population of interrelated persons and their institutions.

SOCIOECONOMIC CLASS. See SOCIAL CLASS.

SOLIDARITY (associated with nonviolent action). A shared sense of common interests and goals, which is expressed in *conflicts through staying united with others during difficult times.

Solidarity is extremely important in cases of *nonviolent action, both within the *grievance group and especially among the *nonviolent actionists. Solidarity is required initially among those who begin the nonviolent action and at later stages to maintain it despite *repression.

Solidarity may exist, continue, and persist—despite crises and dangers in certain cases—without conscious efforts to promote or maintain it. However, in many other instances deliberate measures may be required. Four tasks may then be required: (a) maintaining rapport within the group, (b) generating incentives to continue the struggle despite difficulties, (c) reducing grounds for *capitulation, (d) application of *nonviolent *sanctions to enforce compliance with the *resistance program.

SOURCES OF POLITICAL POWER. Factors that provide the *ruler with the status and resources to exercise *political power.

The sources are external to the person(s) of the ruler or other power-holder, and originate within the *society. They include *authority, *human resources, skills and knowledge, intangible factors, *material resources, and *sanctions.

All of these sources need not be present simultaneously in a given situation to create power. For example, power may exist, at least temporarily, in the absence of authority, or in the absence of sanctions where a strongly accepted authority exists. However, sanctions are usually a key element in political power.

Each of these sources is closely associated with, and dependent upon, the acceptance, *cooperation, and *obedience of the population. Consequently, if the availability of these sources is restricted or severed by reluctance or refusal of the populace to provide them, the ruler's power will be limited. In extreme cases, severance of the sources of power will cause *disintegration of the *government.

See also PILLARS OF SUPPORT.

SOVEREIGNTY. 1. The location of an ultimate right of *command in a *society, believed to derive from a source of absolute *authority.

As a consequence of that belief, it is maintained that the populace owes absolute *obedience to the *ruler, who is believed to be sovereign as a consequence of that authority. This is a standard quality of absolute monarchies and *dictatorships, which claim to rule by right.

Some revolutionaries have sought to transfer the sovereignty from its old holder (for example, the king or tsar, believed to derive absolute authority from God) to a new holder (as a political party claiming to act by the absolute authority of "the people," who are viewed abstractly and without procedures for providing continuing authorization from real people).

Other revolutionaries have rejected the view that there exists anywhere an absolute authority, or a sovereign possessing that authority, to which absolute obedience is due. That school of thought leads to the development of means by which people can continually provide authorization to, or withdraw authorization from, political *leaders.

2. A quality of *independence and of perceived supreme right of *control, without the existence of a superior body that has the right and the capacity to intervene. One may therefore refer to the sovereignty of a *State, but a constituent province of that State cannot be said to be sovereign.

SPEAK-IN. A deliberate verbal interruption of a meeting, religious service, or other gathering by *actionists to express their viewpoint. The opinions may or may not be related to the occasion of the gathering.

This is primarily a social *method of *nonviolent intervention, as it disrupts a social occasion, but it has psychological and physical aspects as well.

SPEECHES. See ASSEMBLY OF PROTEST OR SUPPORT, CAMOU-FLAGED MEETING OF PROTEST, LITERATURE AND SPEECHES

ADVOCATING RESISTANCE, PROTEST MEETING, PUBLIC SPEECHES, and TEACH-IN.

SPONTANEOUS RESISTANCE. *Resistance that occurs without advance planning or organization, and without the decision of any special *leadership group.

SQUATTERS. Persons who illegally enter and occupy land or buildings without permission of the owners with the intent of using them for different purposes, or of changing the *de facto or *de jure ownership.

See also NONVIOLENT INVASION, NONVIOLENT LAND SEIZURE, and NONVIOLENT OCCUPATION.

STALL-IN. The conducting of *legitimate business by a firm's customers or clients in the slowest possible manner with the intent of inducing some *policy change, usually within the firm involved. The stall-in may be used at a bank, or in paying bills, for example.

This *method of *nonviolent intervention is not to be confused with *stalling and obstruction by *government employees for political purposes.

See also SLOWDOWN STRIKE.

STALLING AND OBSTRUCTION. Deliberate procrastination by *government administrative officers and other employees to postpone, delay, or block a policy or measure which they are supposed to implement, but which they oppose. Such action may be combined with apparent compliance with instructions and implementation.

This *method of *political noncooperation is closely related to two other methods in that class, also used by government employees: *reluctant and slow compliance, and *nonobedience in absence of direct supervision.

See also NONCOOPERATION BY CONSTITUENT GOVERNMENTAL UNITS and QUASI-LEGAL EVASIONS AND DELAYS.

STAND-IN. The act of persistently standing and waiting at a certain place to gain an objective, such as admission, equality of service, an interview, and the like.

This *method of *nonviolent intervention is especially likely to be applied where customers must purchase tickets before admission, enter through a particular point, or wait in a line.

When purchase of the ticket, admission, or interview is refused to the person, he or she then remains standing there, possibly along with supporting *actionists, in an orderly, quiet manner. They remain until the objective is gained, a specified period of time has elapsed, the group is arrested, or the facilities are closed. This method may be repeated day after day.

Applied in the form of kneeling when seeking admission to religious buildings, this has become known as a kneel-in.

STATE (reconceptualized term). The most prevalent form of *government in the world today, characterized by a permanent *bureaucracy, a permanent police *force, and (with a few exceptions among very small States) a permanent standing army. The State claims for itself the legal monopoly within the *society of the use of *violence as a domestic and international *sanction, and also frequently claims the highest loyalty of its citizens.

In history many governments lacked one or more of the above three characteristics, and even today many tribal societies, whose indigenous political systems have not been destroyed, retain non-State forms of government.

Syndicalists and others have aimed to move from the State structure to some other type of non-State governmental structure. Various religious and professional institutions act in several ways as governments but lack the essential characteristics of a State listed above.

In *politics, the development and adoption of *nonviolent sanctions may possibly permit deliberate development of governmental structures that are realistic alternatives to the State.

See also STATELESS SOCIETY.

STATELESS SOCIETY. A *society in which social *policies and *social order are determined and maintained by formal or informal structures and behavior, without the full characteristics of the *State.

STATE OF EMERGENCY. A declaration of exceptional measures to deal with an immediate crisis, whatever its source. The declaration usually authorizes *government officials, or persons aiming to replace them, to take such measures as suspending certain *civil liberties and normal constitutional procedures. Such declarations are usually made by the head of *State or by claimants to that position. States of emergency are mostly declared through legal or constitutional procedures, but at times may be declared for other than the avowed reasons, such as during a *coup d'état or a revolutionary situation. At other times declarations of emergency may be made to facilitate *control of certain economic activities or to deal with a natural disaster.

See also CONSTITUTIONAL GOVERNMENT, MARTIAL LAW, and MILITARY GOVERNMENT.

STAY-AT-HOME. Deliberate action by the population as a whole, often during a *strike, to remain in their homes, usually as political *protest.

This *method of *political noncooperation is usually practiced for one or two days, although when not combined with a labor strike, it may be applied only after working hours.

The stay-at-home is usually organized, although it may occur spontaneously. In *conflicts it may also be used to reduce the chances of "incidents" that may undermine the *resistance, to express sorrow and depth of feeling, and to demonstrate to the *opponents the degree of unity and self-discipline among the resisting population.

STAY-DOWN STRIKE. See STAY-IN STRIKE.

STAY-IN STRIKE. Action by workers to stop work, while remaining at their place of work (such as the factory) and refusing to leave until their demands are granted. This *method combines qualities of the *strike and of *nonviolent intervention.

This method may be used for any of several reasons, including to preclude a *lockout by the employer, to reduce the dangers of *violent *repression, and to provide the strikers with control of the plant and offices of the factory.

This type of action has also been called a "sit-down strike" and when used by miners a "stay-down strike." To avoid confusion with the sit-down strike, and because when using this method workers move around the location instead of remaining seated, the term "stay-in strike" is more accurate than "sit-down strike."

STRATEGIC ADVANCE. A major forward thrust of one's *forces in a *conflict toward the objective(s) of a given *strategy. The conflict is thus brought closer to its resolution. If the conflict is not yet concluded, the next step will be the launching of a new *strategic operation.

STRATEGIC CONCEPT. The basic idea or approach of a given *strategy, which outlines broadly what is to be done in given situations.

On the basis of the strategic concept a *strategic plan will be developed to prepare for action.

STRATEGIC NONVIOLENT STRUGGLE. A *nonviolent struggle that is conducted in accordance with a previously prepared *strategy.

STRATEGIC OPERATION. A major movement or *campaign intended to move toward, or actually achieve, the objective(s) of a given *strategy, and hence to alter the strategic situation.

STRATEGIC PLAN. The projected scheme of action for implementing a *strategic concept in actual *operations. The plan will contain a variety of specific, more limited tactical plans to gain smaller objectives that contribute to accomplishing the overall objective of the developed *strategy.

See also TACTIC.

STRATEGIC RETREAT. A withdrawal of *forces, or halt of an effort to hold or gain a given objective, in light of identified relative weaknesses of one's forces in the situation.

The aim may be to hold or gain other objectives, or to regroup and strengthen one's own forces, without incurring the additional losses that could be imposed by a crushing *defeat.

STRATEGY. The major conception of how most efficiently to achieve objectives in a *conflict. Strategy is concerned with whether, when, or how to *fight, and how to achieve maximum effectiveness in order to gain certain ends. Strategy is the plan for the practical distribution, adaptation, and application of available means to attain desired objectives.

Although strategy is largely concerned with the means of conducting the struggle, this is not its exclusive focus. Strategy also includes efforts to develop a strategic situation so advantageous that it may bring *success without open struggle, or will make success certain in struggle. Strategy therefore encompasses the decision whether to fight a *battle or wage a *campaign, and also the course of action intended to bring the struggle to a satisfactory conclusion.

Applied to the course of struggle itself, strategy is the basic idea of how the battle or campaign should develop, and how its separate components should best be fitted together to contribute most advantageously to achieving its objectives.

Strategy in this application involves consideration of the results likely to follow from particular actions, the development of a broad plan of *operations, the skillful determination of the deployment of *combat groups in various smaller actions, consideration of the requirements for success in the operation of the chosen *technique, and making good use of success.

Strategy operates within the scope of the *grand strategy. *Tactics and *methods of action are used to implement the strategy. To be most effective the tactics and methods must be chosen and applied so that they assist the application of the strategy and contribute to achieving the requirements for success.

In formulating strategy in *nonviolent action, the following aspects are to be taken into account: one's own objectives, resources, and strengths; the *opponents' objectives, resources, and strengths; the actual and possible roles of *third parties; the opponents' various possible courses and means of action; and one's own various possible courses and means of action—both *offensive and *defensive. It is also necessary to take into full consideration the requirements for success with the proposed technique, its processes of *dynamism, and its *mechanisms of change.

Hence, "strategic."

See also INDIRECT STRATEGY, STRATEGIC ADVANCE, STRATEGIC CONCEPT, STRATEGIC OPERATION, STRATEGIC PLAN, and STRATEGIC RETREAT.

STRATIFICATION. The ranking of the population of a *society in layered groups on the basis of wealth, tradition, *social class, caste, or other criteria.

STREET PARTY. A carnivalesque form of *protest that combines neighborliness, celebration, and *resistance. A possible objective may be, for example, to halt traffic on a particular road. The street party may be protected by cars blocking the road or other types of barricade. This *method therefore combines protest with *nonviolent intervention and physical obstruction.

STRIKE. A collective, deliberate, and normally temporary restriction or suspension of labor during a *conflict, designed to exert pressure on employers or others in controlling positions, such as a *government.

The many *methods of strike constitute a subclass of *economic noncooperation.

The unit within which a strike is used is usually an industrial one, but it may also be political, social, or cultural, depending on the nature of the grievance. The aim is to produce some readjustment in the relationships between the conflicting groups, such as the granting of certain demands as a condition for the resumption of work.

The strike has mostly been used in modern industrial organizations, including large-scale farms, although it existed before the industrial revolution and may occur wherever some people are employed by others.

To be most effective, the total number of laborers striking must be sufficient to make the continuation of *operations of the economic unit impossible. Strikes may be spontaneous or planned, "official" (authorized by the trade union) or "*wildcat" (not authorized by a trade union).

Wages, hours, working conditions, job security, union recognition, government action, and jurisdictional disputes between competing trade unions are frequent immediate causes of strikes with economic aims.

Political and social aims in a strike may accompany economic aims, or be independent of them. Such aims may include objections to particular laws, regulations, or governmental acts. In some cases, they may be part of a revolutionary program aimed at undermining the *authority and *control of the government and at bringing about its collapse. Strikes with political motives are often *generalized strikes or *general strikes, although short *protest strikes also occur.

Normally the strike is a temporary withdrawal of labor, but there are methods in which the withdrawal is, or at least is intended to be, permanent. At the other end of the scale there are methods in which the withdrawal of labor is only symbolic, so that those methods might also be included within the class of *nonviolent protest and persuasion.

The methods of strike, arranged in seven groupings, are:

- *symbolic strikes*: *protest strike, *quickie walkout (lightning strike);
- *agricultural strikes*: *peasant strike, *farm workers' strike;
- *strikes by special groups*: *refusal of impressed labor, *prisoners' strike, *craft strike, *professional strike;
- *ordinary industrial strikes*: *establishment strike, *industry strike, *sympathetic strike;
- *restricted strikes*: *detailed strike, *bumper strike, *slowdown strike, *"working-to-rule" strike, *reporting "sick," *blue flu, *strike by resignation, *limited strike, *selective strike;
- *multi-industry strikes*: *generalized strike, *general strike; and
- *combinations of strikes and economic closures*: *hartal and *economic shutdown.

STRIKE BY RESIGNATION. Official submission of individual resignations of workers or professionals from their jobs or positions by a significant portion of the personnel involved in a dispute. A group may resign simultaneously or in stages.

The result is a slowing or halting of the *operations of the unit or institution in which they have been employed. This method may be used as a means of bypassing contractual or legal prohibitions against *strikes, or for other reasons.

A *method of strike.

STRIKE BY SPECIAL GROUP. See CRAFT STRIKE, PRISONERS' STRIKE, PROFESSIONAL STRIKE, and REFUSAL OF IMPRESSED LABOR.

STRUCTURAL VIOLENCE (reconceptualized term). Physical *violence built into the institutions of the *society—that is, *institutionalized violence—with the purpose or consequence of maintaining *domination or *oppression. Structural violence is therefore a specific form of the more general phenomenon of institutionalized violence.

This definition differs significantly from another widely employed definition that defines "structural violence" as any type of psychological, intellectual, or physical limitation, injury, or death that can be traced to the *social structure. Structural violence in that definition becomes virtually everything that is morally or politically disapproved, which makes the term useful neither for description nor for moral or political analysis.

STRUGGLE. See CIVILIAN STRUGGLE, CLASS STRUGGLE, NONVIOLENT STRUGGLE, and PROTRACTED STRUGGLE.

STRUGGLE GROUP. The body of people and institutions that are actively waging a *conflict to achieve certain objectives.

See also GRIEVANCE GROUP.

STRUGGLE TECHNIQUE. A *technique used to wage *open conflict, such as *conventional war, *guerrilla warfare, *nonviolent action, and the like.

STUDENT STRIKE. Temporary refusal to attend classes as a means of *protest or *resistance by students or pupils of any type of educational institution.

The grievances may vary widely, ranging from policies directly associated with the institution to wider political issues. This type of action may also be also called a "school boycott" or "class boycott."

Variations in this *method of *social noncooperation include *boycott of only particular lectures, or students may attend classes but refuse to pay attention.

SUBJUGATE. To reduce a population to a condition of *submission and subservience.

SUBJUGATION (reconceptualized term). A condition of *submission and subservience of a population to a ruling group.

Subjugation is not to be equated with *military occupation, seizure of the *State in a *coup d'état, and the like. The *control of the population is a separate process which may, but also may not, accompany occupations and coups. *Civilian-based defense is designed to prevent subjugation from occurring when the *society is attacked in those ways.

See also DISOBEDIENCE, INVASION, OPPRESSION, OBEDIENCE, and TYRANNY.

SUBMISSION. *Obedience to and compliance with the wishes, claims, and *commands of another person, group, *government, or other body.
See also SUBJUGATION.

SUBORDINATE. Under the *control or orders of a superior in rank.
Hence, "subordination."
See also SUPERORDINATE.

SUBVERSION (reconceptualized term). Nonmilitary actions (such as *propaganda, *psychological warfare, and *political warfare) clandestinely initiated and organized by a disciplined political organization, or by a foreign *government. Subversion is designed to undermine loyalty and support for a system or government in order to weaken it in any way, including economically, politically, militarily, or in morale.

Subversion is especially associated with *violent forms of *conflict, including *terrorism, *guerrilla warfare, and conventional war. Popular *resistance movements, especially those operating openly and using *nonviolent action, are not forms of subversion. However, *opponents may sometimes attempt to label them as such to discredit them and to blame external influences.

SUCCESS (reconceptualized term). The achievement of its substantive objectives by a party to a *conflict.

The degree of success can be measured by the objectives of the *struggle group, an indicated time period, and/or the direct and indirect consequences of the conflict and means of action employed.

Success is related to goals and not to the effects of the struggle on the *fighting forces of the contending groups, such as their morale.

SUFFERING. See REPRESSION and SELF-SUFFERING.

SUPERORDINATE. Superior in rank, especially as this relates to perceived *authority to *control or the capacity to *command *subordinates.

Hence, "superordination."

SUPPLIERS' AND HANDLERS' BOYCOTT. A type of *economic boycott in which workers and/or "middlemen" (wholesalers, jobbers, and distributors) refuse to handle or supply certain goods.

This refusal may take place because of objection to (a) the context in which the goods are produced (for example, by firms where workers are on strike or boycotted firms), or the use to which the goods are put (for example, their role in particular *wars or their use by particular *governments); (b) the intrinsic nature of the goods; or (c) the conditions under which the goods have been produced (such as slavery, apartheid, *oppression, or "unfair" labor conditions).

SUPPORT COMMUNITY. Persons and groups who favor *nonviolent actionists who are engaged in a *conflict and who assist them in various ways.

SURRENDER. See CAPITULATION and DEFEAT.

SUSPENSION OF SOCIAL AND SPORTS ACTIVITIES. The cancellation of, or refusal to arrange, social and sports activities. This *method may either focus on a specific event or take the form of a general suspension of such activities.

This method of *social noncooperation may be intended either as a *protest by renunciation (hence related to *nonviolent protest and persuasion) or as an attempt to counter efforts of the *government to initiate new *controls over the *society (hence related to *political noncooperation).

This method is social in form, although it may be political in intent or result.

SYMBOLIC GESTURE. Movement or positioning of hands, arms, or other parts of the body to communicate approval, disapproval, or other opinion. The gesture may appeal to commonly held attitudes and beliefs and be related to cultural or religious symbolism.

See also RUDE GESTURE.

SYMBOLIC LIGHTS. Torches, lanterns, or candles carried in *protest *parades and *marches, or occasionally in other protest activities.

A *method of *nonviolent protest and persuasion.

SYMBOLIC OBJECTS. See DELIVERY OF SYMBOLIC OBJECTS, DISPLAY OF FLAGS AND SYMBOLIC COLORS, and DISPLAY OF PORTRAITS.

SYMBOLIC RECLAMATION. An attempt temporarily to reclaim land or buildings, in protest against their current use or ownership, in order to illustrate an alternative use of the property which might be widely approved. The point is to show that the property could be put to better use or placed under preferable management or ownership.

Among the forms that this *method of *nonviolent protest and persuasion may take are the planting of seeds, plants, or trees, the beginning of cultivation of neglected or seized land, or the erection of living quarters.

Attempted reclamations intended to be more than symbolic are classed as *nonviolent invasions and *nonviolent occupations.

See also NONVIOLENT LAND SEIZURE.

SYMBOLIC SOUNDS. Oral or mechanical sounds other than words used to convey ideas in a *conflict situation. The tolling of bells, and the imitation of animal sounds, whistles, sirens, and the like, have been used as a *method of *nonviolent protest and persuasion.

SYMBOLIC STRIKE. See PROTEST STRIKE and QUICKIE WALKOUT.

SYMBOLS. See DELIVERY OF SYMBOLIC OBJECTS, DESTRUCTION OF OWN PROPERTY, DISPLAY OF FLAGS AND SYMBOLIC COLORS, DISPLAY OF PORTRAITS, NEW SIGNS AND NAMES, PAINT AS PROTEST, PRAYER AND WORSHIP, PROTEST DISROBING, RUDE GESTURE, SYMBOLIC GESTURE, SYMBOLIC LIGHTS, SYMBOLIC RECLAMATION, SYMBOLIC SOUNDS, and WEARING OF SYMBOLS.

SYMPATHETIC STRIKE. A *method of *strike in which a group of workers withdraw their labor, not for their own benefit, but to support the demands of another group of striking workers.

Where both groups of workers have a common employer, the sympathetic strikers aim to pressure that employer directly. In cases where two groups have different employers, the sympathetic strikers may simply intend to pressure their own employers, the public, or the *government to induce the employer directly involved to grant the desired concessions.

See also SOLIDARITY.

SYNDICALISM. A social doctrine or movement favoring a *radical transformation of a *society by *direct action of the workers, including *sabotage, *strikes, and especially major use of the *general strike.

This approach differs sharply from the Jacobin *strategy of Marxist-Leninists.

Syndicalists oppose both capitalist and *State ownership of the means of production. They favor control of industries by their respective workers through their syndicates or trade unions. The State is to be replaced with a loose federation of syndicates to provide *government and economic administration.

See also JACOBINISM and MARXISM-LENINISM.

TACTIC. A limited plan of action, based on a conception of how best in a restricted phase of a *conflict to utilize the available means of fighting to achieve a limited objective as part of the wider *strategy (either *violent or *nonviolent).

A tactic thus fits within the broad strategy, just as strategy fits within the *grand strategy. Tactics are always concerned with fighting, although strategy includes wider considerations in how to *fight. A particular tactic can only be understood as part of the overall strategy of a *battle or a *campaign.

Tactics deal with how particular *methods of action, or *weapons, are applied, or how particular groups of *combatants shall act in a specific situation.

Tactics are applied for shorter periods of time than strategies, or in smaller areas (geographical, institutional, etc.), or by a limited number of people, or for more limited objectives, or in some combination of these.

At times a given plan of action may be on an intermediate scale, which makes it difficult to classify it as either a tactic or a strategy. In such a case the scale of the objective is likely to be the most important determinant.

Hence, "tactical."

TACTICAL ADVANCE. A forward thrust of one's *forces in a struggle so that they are closer to gaining, or have gained, the objective of a given *tactic. Such an advance contributes to the success of a larger *strategic operation.

See also STRATEGIC ADVANCE.

TACTICAL NONVIOLENT ACTION (associated with nonviolent action). *Nonviolent action that is conducted with only limited planning, that has taken into consideration only short-term or temporary elements. That is, there has been no strategic analysis and planning.

See also STRATEGIC NONVIOLENT STRUGGLE.

TACTICAL OBJECTIVE. The goal that a particular *tactic is intended to achieve.

TACTICAL OPERATION. A planned coordinated action to gain the objective of a particular *tactic, within the context of a *strategic plan.

See also STRATEGIC OPERATION.

TACTICAL RETREAT. A limited withdrawal of one's *forces, or a relinquishing of an effort to hold or gain a given *tactical objective, in light of one's relative weakness in the specific situation.

The aim of a tactical retreat is to be able to hold or gain other tactical objectives, or to maintain maximum relative strength for the *strategic operation as a whole.

See also STRATEGIC RETREAT.

TAUNTING OFFICIALS. To mock and insult officials, either at a certain place or while following them for a period of time.

This *method of *nonviolent protest and persuasion is sometimes used instead of the predominantly silent and dignified behavior of "*haunting" officials.

TAX REFUSAL. See REVENUE REFUSAL.

TEACH-IN. A public meeting on an issue of social or political concern in which various viewpoints are presented among the speakers and persons attending. Teach-ins are often held at a university.

The speakers may be specialists on the subject, or otherwise able to present facts and background information as well as their own viewpoint. Teach-ins may also have a larger number of speakers and last for longer periods of time than ordinary public *protest meetings.

The aim of a teach-in is not simply to *protest but to educate and stimulate thought. Confrontation of opposing viewpoints, questioning of the speakers, and discussion from the floor are important aspects of a teach-in.

A *method of *nonviolent protest and persuasion.

TECHNIQUE. A broad means of conducting social or political action or struggle.

Examples of techniques include *election *campaigns in a parliamentary *democracy, *guerrilla warfare, *conventional war, and *nonviolent action.

See also STRUGGLE TECHNIQUE.

TELEVISION. See ALTERNATIVE COMMUNICATION SYSTEM and RECORDS, RADIO, AND TELEVISION.

TERRITORIAL DEFENSE. A system of governmentally organized *military *defense that primarily operates against *invaders within the territory of the attacked *country.

Although hostile military invaders may be initially confronted at the frontiers, the major military defensive activity is waged inside the country, regardless of how much of its territory has been occupied, or even if all of it is in the attackers' *control. The invaders' forces are thus constantly confronted and harassed, making effective control extremely difficult and uncertain. The defense weaponry can vary widely, at times even including tanks, but this type of defense can operate with much smaller weaponry.

If the invaders have overwhelming *military forces, territorial defense may turn into *guerrilla warfare or possibly be superseded by *civilian-based defense.

See also DEFENSE IN DEPTH and TERRITORIAL WARFARE.

TERRITORIAL WARFARE. *Military war waged throughout a contested territory.

This contrasts with *conventional war, in which *combat is conducted largely along front lines where the opposing *military forces meet.

See also DEFENSE IN DEPTH.

TERROR (reconceptualized term). The condition of extreme *fear deliberately induced for political reasons by *political police or other official bodies, or by dissident and revolutionary groups (as at a stage of *guerrilla warfare).

Depending on the nature of the group responsible, terror may be induced by arbitrary seizure and *imprisonment of persons, use of *concentration camps, *torture, executions, *assassinations, random killings, *demolitions, and bombings.

Certain forms of terror do not discriminate between *opponents and their aides on the one hand, and ordinary *civilians on the other. The terrorists may deliberately target members of the civilian population who are not directly involved in the *conflict in order to strike fear into the rest of the population.

When terror is practiced internationally, the means may include massive conventional bombings, nuclear *weapons, and other weapons of mass destruction. Threats to do any of these things may also contribute to inducement of terror.

Such *methods may be used selectively, randomly, or widely by a *government as a means of *repression to intimidate the population and to prevent or halt *resistance.

The means of repression used to intimidate the populace are only effective, and hence most likely to be repeated, if they produce fear, and hence *submission.

A key element in *nonviolent struggle in some situations has been refusal of the *actionists to be intimidated, and instead to develop *fearlessness, or control of fear.

See also ASSASSINATION, NONVIOLENT DISCIPLINE, and TER-RORISM.

TERRORISM. The systematic application of the means of inducing *terror in an effort to gain political objectives.

THIRD PARTIES. Groups, institutions, or sectors that are not initially direct parties to a *conflict. Sometimes these may be international bodies. Third parties may remain neutral, or they may react to the issues at stake, the course of the conflict, or the means used by either antagonist.

The attitudes and sympathies of third parties may shift, and as a result they may move closer to, or further from, direct involvement in the conflict. On occasion, their involvement may prove to be very important.

The term "third party" can also used in the singular.

TOKEN STRIKE. See PROTEST STRIKE.

TORTURE. The deliberate infliction of extreme physical or mental suffering in order to gain an objective.

Torture can be especially used to induce confessions and to obtain secrets concerning the activities of a *resistance movement. Torture may be more likely to be applied against members of an *underground movement of *violent *resistance than it is against a *nonviolent struggle movement, especially one that operates openly.

See also OPENNESS, REPRESSION, and TERROR.

TOTALITARIANISM. An extreme type of *dictatorship aimed at instituting fundamental change, rather than maintaining an established order (as in traditional dictatorships). Totalitarianism is also distinguishable from other dictatorships by its means of *control, power base, and type of system.

The power base of an ordinary dictatorship is often the army, but in a totalitarian system the power base is the totalitarian movement, usually in the form of the centrally directed Party but extending beyond it. The totalitarian movement seeks to subordinate and control all other institutions of the *society, including the army.

Whereas a traditional dictatorship usually lacks an *ideology and very possibly other strong political beliefs, a totalitarian movement is committed to an ideology that purports to explain the past and present, and also to prescribe for the present and future.

Totalitarianism in a society extends far beyond the *State structure, and even the State is subordinated to the totalitarian movement.

Therefore, it is more accurate to speak of a "totalitarian system" rather than of a "totalitarian State."

Technological developments (as in communications, rapid transport, modern *weapons, and police detection) have helped make totalitarian systems possible, including their means of control. Totalitarianism, however, is not simply "old-time" dictatorship plus technology.

Considerable variations exist from one totalitarian system to another. However, totalitarian systems may be generally characterized by seven major traits:

- an official ideology that provides political explanation of the present and a prescription for policy and action;
- a single elitist Party with a special messianic mission and *command role;
- a demand for total commitment from individuals, Party members, and the society, aimed at achieving a spirit of unanimity of the entire population;
- totality of control over all areas of individual and social life, including the control and restructuring of all the institutions of society (in the Nazi case called *Gleichschaltung);
- concentration of the power of command and decision-making for the system in the hands of the centralized *leadership of the ruling elite;
- unwillingness of the centralized leadership to accept moral or legal limitations or restraints on the means it will use for control and also on the means of *repression. Repression may include attempts to control the human mind and will. The system will also attempt to exert control by economic means, *terror, *repression, *atomization, surveillance, compulsory organization, and required participation; and
- *dynamism, when the totalitarian movement is in control of the society, aiming at fundamental change and total social *revolution to create a new type of society and a new type of human being—all on the basis of ideological assumptions proclaimed by the elite leadership.

The systems in Nazi Germany under Hitler after 1938 (see NAZISM) and in the U.S.S.R. under Stalin after 1928 are prototypes of a totalitarian system.

Future totalitarian systems with the above seven characteristics would, however, differ significantly from these two. The differences would be influenced by the particular ideology, culture, and social situation, new developments in technology and mind control, and other factors.

TOTAL NONCOOPERATION (associated with civilian-based defense). A *strategy of *civilian-based defense involving the refusal of all *cooperation with an invading *military *regime or with a *government of putschists (see PUTSCH).

This *defense would include full and simultaneous *political, *economic, and *social noncooperation by all sections of the population. This strategy was suggested early in the development of the *policy of civilian-based defense. When applied with the intent of achieving a quick victory, it is also called *nonviolent blitzkrieg. A unified determination to resist and adequate preparations are prerequisites for this strategy.

Total noncooperation contrasts with a more flexible *grand strategy that would apply different strategies in different situations. Other possible strategies include *general resistance, *selective resistance, and *work-on without collaboration.

TOTAL PERSONAL NONCOOPERATION. The refusal by a prisoner to do anything (almost literally) except breathe, as an expression of protest or *resistance.

This *method of *social noncooperation is especially likely to be used when the prisoner believes the *imprisonment to be unjust and therefore rejects all *cooperation with the continuing incarceration. This action can lead to the prisoner's death, but it has also led to release.

See also FAST and HUNGER STRIKE.

TOTAL RESISTANCE (associated with civilian-based defense). See TOTAL NONCOOPERATION.

TOTAL WAR. A *conventional war in which the *State applies its full resources against the enemy, including mobilization of manpower, the economy, and *military means. Also, in this type of war, *civilians, cities, and areas to the rear of the front are standard targets, as well as military personnel, equipment, and installations.

This type of war emerged historically during World War I, largely due to changes in military technology.

TRADE BOYCOTT. See CONSUMERS' BOYCOTT, EMBARGO, INTERNATIONAL CONSUMERS' BOYCOTT, MERCHANTS' "GENERAL STRIKE," NATIONAL CONSUMERS' BOYCOTT, SUPPLIERS' AND HANDLERS' BOYCOTT, and TRADERS' BOYCOTT.

TRADE EMBARGO. See EMBARGO.

TRADERS' BOYCOTT. A refusal by retailers, acting individually or collectively, to buy or sell certain goods.

Retailers may choose the producers and wholesalers from whom to buy goods to help keep such firms "in line" with approved business practices or labor policies. Producers and suppliers also may refuse to sell their products to retailers for such reasons. The traders' boycott may also be used by retailers for political motives or in a struggle to correct a national grievance.

This *method of *economic boycott may also involve a refusal by retailers to sell certain products to consumers, even if the products are already in stock. Such action may be taken in *solidarity with a widespread *national consumers' boycott.

TRANSARMAMENT (new term associated with civilian-based defense). The process of changeover from a conventional *military *defense system, or a nuclear capacity, to *civilian-based defense.

Transarmament always involves the replacement of one means of providing defense with another, and not, as with *disarmament, the negotiated or unilateral reduction or abandonment of military capacity without alternative preparations for defense.

The term was introduced by Kenneth Boulding in a pamphlet published in Britain in the 1930s and reintroduced by Theodor Ebert in the early 1960s.

TRANSPARTISAN (new term associated with nonviolent action and civilian-based defense). The manner of presenting *nonviolent struggle or *civilian-based defense without linking it to any ideological or political group or perspective, so that it potentially may be viewed as acceptable to individuals and groups holding views across the political spectrum.

The term was introduced by Bruce Jenkins.

TREATY. See ALLIANCE, CIVILIAN-BASED DEFENSE MUTUAL ASSISTANCE PACT, and CIVILIAN-BASED DEFENSE TREATY ORGANIZATION.

TRUCE (reconceptualized term). A suspension of a struggle in order to accomplish some purpose. For example, a truce may be called to observe a religious holiday respected by both sides. Often, however, a truce is called to permit the beginning or continuation of *negotiations. The struggle in question may be one waged by *conventional war, *guerrilla warfare, domestic *nonviolent action, *civilian-based defense, *terrorism, or any other means.

Successful negotiations will mean that the truce is followed by a formal halt to the *conflict. However, the struggle may resume if negotiations fail.

In cases of unsuccessful negotiations, the pause provided by the truce may cause a modification of the course of the conflict, for example by providing a cooling-off period after which the contest may resume in a less extreme form.

TURNING ONE'S BACK. Silent disapproval emphasized by turning one's back (whether standing or sitting) to the person or persons who are, or who represent, the *opponents.

TYRANNICIDE. *Assassination of a person regarded as a tyrant.
See also TYRANNY.

TYRANNY. A political *regime, system, or condition in which the ruling individual or group governs in an arbitrary and oppressive manner with little regard to the wishes, opinions, and well-being of the subjects.

The ruling group threatens and applies various means of *control, including *punishments and *repression, often severe, carried out by police and *military forces. The intention is to procure the *submission and *obedience of the general populace, to enforce policies, and to perpetuate the *government, system, or condition.

Hence, a "tyrant" and "tyrannical."

See also DICTATORSHIP, OPPRESSION, and TOTALITARIANISM.

ULTIMA RATIO POPULI. "The final argument of the people" (Latin), referring to the population's final "right" of *revolution when all other means of dealing with *oppression have failed.

ULTIMATUM. A communication from resisters to the *opponents prior to the outbreak of open struggle, which stipulates the minimum acceptable terms for a settlement of the *conflict or issue at hand, a time limit for the opponents to agree to those terms, and an indication of the *sanction which will be imposed if the terms are not met within that time.

Ultimata were formerly often issued before formal declarations of *war, or prior to the severance of diplomatic relations. (See also DIPLOMATIC RELATIONS—SEVERANCE OF REPRESENTATION).

In *nonviolent action, ultimata have been prominent in Gandhian and neo-Gandhian *campaigns. In those cases the grievances have been described, minimum demands stated, and offers made to cancel plans for the coming *nonviolent campaign if the opponents agreed to those demands, or a major part of them, within a stated time period.

UNARMED (reconceptualized term). 1. Deprived of or without *armaments, usually understood as *military armaments.

2. Lacking any means of protection or source of strength in a *conflict, connoting helplessness and *powerlessness.

A group or *society adopting *nonviolent action or *civilian-based defense is not "unarmed" in the sense of being helpless and powerless. This is because *nonviolent actionists are "armed" with other *methods or "*weapons" of struggle.

UNCONVENTIONAL WARFARE (reconceptualized term). *Operations against an enemy *State conducted inside the territory it *controls. Such operations are supported by, often initiated by, and in varying degrees directed by, an external State. They are conducted predominantly by members of the territory's population on behalf of the external State, but at times may be carried out by special personnel from the external State.

A wide range of activities may be included under such operations. They include *psychological warfare, assistance to key persons to escape abroad, *guerrilla warfare, *demolition, and political *resistance that is intended to develop into guerrilla warfare.

Unconventional warfare differs significantly from *civil resistance, *civilian insurrection, and *civilian-based defense. These types of *conflict use *nonviolent forms of struggle initiated and controlled by the internal population itself for their own political aims, not those of a foreign *government.

Under certain circumstances, such *civilian struggles may receive limited foreign governmental or nongovernmental assistance. However, the limited character of such aid, the internal initiative, and the restriction of modes of conflict to nonviolent means, distinguish those applications of *nonviolent action from unconventional warfare.

UNDERGROUND MOVEMENT. A *resistance movement with secret membership, a secret organizational structure, and secret activities. The structure of such a movement may vary widely, especially in the degree to which it is a tight formal organization or a loose working group.

Underground movements have ranged widely in the means of *resistance they have used, including *civil resistance, *political non-cooperation, *sabotage, *demolition, *guerrilla warfare, *assassination, and other means.

Secrecy in resistance movements under severe *repression can be compatible with the use of *nonviolent action, provided that the secret elements are isolated from the main movement and that the movement does not engage in *violence or acts of physical destruction. Such activities could risk wider disastrous violence, including on the potential issue of how to deal with informers and provocateurs.

A small secret group may advise a much wider potential population to resist on a specific issue. This occurred in Norway during the Nazi occupation. That group could even advise broadly how such resistance could be conducted, but leave implementation to others and maintain open knowledge of those resistance activities available to all.

Hence, "an underground" or "to go underground."

UNDERMINING A GOVERNMENT (reconceptualized term). The process of restricting and at times removing the *sources of political power of an opposed *government by acts of *noncooperation on the part of those bodies that constitute its *pillars of support.

This is a more accurate description of the potential change that, when merited in extreme situations, can be produced by *nonviolent struggle than is the more usual phrase "overthrowing a government."

UNITED ATTENDANCE. A variation of the *reverse strike, used by students against universities that admit excess numbers of students without expanding facilities. All students enrolled in a course attend simultaneously, demonstrating that the lecture halls and classrooms are too small, or that the size of classes is excessive.

A social *method of *nonviolent intervention.

UNIVERSITIES. See ALTERNATIVE SOCIAL INSTITUTION, EDUCATIONAL INSTITUTIONS, SCHOOLS, STUDENT STRIKE, UNITED ATTENDANCE, and WITHDRAWAL FROM GOVERNMENT EDUCATIONAL INSTITUTIONS.

UPRISING. An *insurrection. A rapid popular *revolt by a population that has previously submitted to the *government or system, but which now repudiates it by either *violent action or *nonviolent struggle.

See also CIVILIAN INSURRECTION.

URBAN GUERRILLA. A person who practices *guerrilla warfare in a city or a densely populated area.

USURPATION (reconceptualized term). An unlawful or *illegitimate seizure of *control of the *State by domestic or foreign *forces, especially by *coup d'état or *invasion.

*Civilian-based defense is specifically designed to deter and *combat both internal and external usurpations.

See also USURPERS.

USURPERS. A group or *government that has attempted to carry out a *usurpation.

The usurpers may be an internal group, political, police, *intelligence, or *military. A usurpation may even be conducted by a head of state, as in a *coup d'état by *executive usurpation. Or the usurpers may be a foreign government and its *military forces, as in an *invasion and *military occupation.

UTOPIA. An imaginary perfect social order with none of the *injustices and *violence of contemporary *societies.

UTOPIANISM. An outlook on social and political problems on the basis of high ideals, whose adherents hope and believe that a new social order can and will be created.

In that new order, present problems will no longer exist. The new and perfect *society will be created largely by forces beyond conscious human *control. Utopians, therefore, give little attention to how the existing society can be changed or replaced.

Hence, "utopian."

See also REALISM and REALPOLITIK.

VICTORY. See SUCCESS.

VIGIL. An action in which people remain in a particular place, over an extended period of time, to express a point of view and make an appeal, usually addressed to a wide public.

The vigil differs from the *picket in that it is maintained for a longer time, sometimes day and night, often involving loss of sleep. This *method of *nonviolent protest and persuasion is also associated with a very serious attitude, often of a pleading or religious character.

VIOLENCE (reconceptualized term). The direct infliction of physical injury or death on persons by whatever means, or the threat to inflict such harm. Violence, therefore, includes *imprisonment, because it is maintained by infliction or threat of physical harm in case of attempted escape.

Injury to persons and damage to material property are easily distinguishable, and the latter needs to be identified separately.

See also AGENT PROVOCATEUR, AGGRESSIVENESS, ARMAMENT, ASSASSINATION, ATTACK, CIVIL WAR, CONFLICT, CONVENTIONAL WAR, DEMOLITION, DICTATORSHIP, FIGHT, FORCE, GENOCIDE, GUERRILLA WARFARE, HATRED, INSTITUTIONALIZED VIOLENCE, MILITARY, MOB, NONINJURIOUS PHYSICAL RESTRAINT, NONVIOLENCE, NONVIOLENT ACTION, PARAMILITARY, POLITICAL POWER, POLITICAL VIOLENCE, PSYCHOLOGICAL VIOLENCE, REGICIDE, REPRESSION, RESISTANCE, RIOT, SABOTAGE, SANCTION, SCORCHED EARTH POLICY, STRUCTURAL VIOLENCE, SUBVERSION, TERROR, TERRORISM, TORTURE, TYRANNICIDE, UPRISING, USURPATION, VIOLENT ACTION, and WAR.

VIOLENT. Possessing the characteristics of *violence.

VIOLENT ACTION. Activity using some type of *violence in a *conflict to further one's objectives.

VOLUNTARY EMIGRATION. See PROTEST EMIGRATION.

VOLUNTARY SERVITUDE. The condition in which a population passively submits to a tyrant, and provides the *cooperation and *obedience that make available the necessary *sources of political power which make the *tyranny itself possible.

The obverse of that perception is that the population can, by refusing cooperation and obedience, sever the availability of the sources of power and thereby abolish the servitude.

Voluntary servitude is discussed by certain theorists of the power of *disobedience, such as Etienne de la Boëtie in the sixteenth century.

See also POLITICAL POWER.

VULNERABILITY (POLITICAL) (reconceptualized term). The degree to which a social or political system or a particular *government is susceptible to successful *attack. The attack may be from an internal source, as in a *coup d'état, or an external source, as in an *invasion and occupation.

Possible causes of vulnerability include widespread *alienation of the population; perceived *illegitimacy of the existing system or government; widespread corruption; the existence of many potential willing collaborators with the attackers; extreme political and economic *centralization; and highly centralized sources of food, fuel, water, and other necessities.

A system or government will be vulnerable, for example, if the population is unable and unwilling to defend it because of long habits of passive *submission in the face of felt *injustice. Other reasons that people may be unwilling to defend the current system are lack of self-confidence their in ability to resist successfully the attack or the *forces behind the attack; absence of advance training or other preparations for *civilian-based defense against attack; and belief in the omnipotence of *violence and hence of victory for the wielder of superior violence.

WADE-IN. Physical entry by individuals normally excluded by custom or legal prohibition into a beach or swimming pool in order to make normal recreational use of those facilities.

This physical form of *nonviolent intervention is a special type of *nonviolent invasion, which is adapted especially to counter discrimination and segregation in such recreational areas.

WALKOUT. The expression of political objections during a meeting, conference, or assembly, by persons, a delegation, or even a single individual, by physically leaving before the meeting has ended or the gathering has been adjourned. The departure is usually made in an obvious way.

This *method of *nonviolent protest and persuasion also has characteristics of *social noncooperation.

WAR (reconceptualized term). 1. A condition of *military *conflict between two independent *States or other political units, each of which is using its military capacity to achieve its objectives and to defeat the *military forces of the *opponents. To avoid confusion in certain contexts with the second usage (below), this may be specified as *military war.

See also CIVIL WAR, COMMERCIAL WAR, CONVENTIONAL WAR, ECONOMIC WAR, GUERRILLA WARFARE, INSURGENCY WARFARE, MILITARY WAR, NONVIOLENT POSITIONAL WAR, NONVIOLENT WAR, POLITICAL WARFARE, PSYCHOLOGICAL WARFARE, TOTAL WAR, UNCONVENTIONAL WARFARE, WAR GAME, WAR OF EXTERMINATION, and WAR RESISTANCE.

2. An asymmetrical conflict in which an invaded or occupied *country is defending itself nonviolently by *civilian-based defense.

See also PEACE, PEACETIME, and WARTIME.

WAR GAME. A simulation of a war (in either of the two meanings), designed to explore alternative *strategies for conducting a potential *conflict, and to evaluate their possible consequences.

See also STRATEGY.

WAR OF ATTRITION. A *war conducted in ways designed to wear down the *opponents gradually.

WAR OF EXTERMINATION. A *military struggle intended not to conquer the population of the attacked territory, but to eliminate the whole population by *genocide.

WAR OF POSITIONS. See NONVIOLENT POSITIONAL WAR and SELECTIVE RESISTANCE.

WAR RESISTANCE. Acts of *nonviolent *opposition and *resistance to *military preparations or military warfare, or both, as a statement of opposition to all war, or to a particular *conflict.

Among *conscription-age youths this is likely to involve, but not be limited to, some form of *conscientious objection.

Those people not liable for conscript military duty may engage in war resistance by: supporting conscientious objectors; personal counseling of youths considering refusal of military training; *picketing; leafleting; conducting *demonstrations; engaging in *civil disobedience, anti-conscription, and anti-war court actions; and incitement to conscription resistance.

The most radical form of war resistance is carried out in some cases by serving as soldiers, but engaging in anti-war activities within the *military forces.

Not normally included in war resistance are simple avoidance of military training or duty by fraud, flight, hiding, and the like. However, under certain political conditions, such activities, when engaged in by large numbers, may constitute war resistance.

See also NONCOOPERATION WITH CONSCRIPTION AND DEPORTATION and PACIFISM.

WAR RESISTER. 1. One who conducts *war resistance.

2. A member of an organization affiliated with the War Resisters' International.

WARTIME (reconceptualized term). 1. The period in which a *war (in either meaning) is occurring.

2. In the context of *civilian-based defense and the second definition of war, wartime is the period in which a *country with a policy of civilian-based defense is under *attack by the attackers' *military forces and is defending itself by civilian-based defense measures.

See also PEACETIME.

WEAPONS (associated with nonviolent action and civilian-based defense). The tools or means, not necessarily material, which may be used to *fight, whether these are *military weapons or *nonviolent *methods.

See also CIVIL WEAPONS and NONVIOLENT WEAPONS.

WEARING OF SYMBOLS. Deliberate change of one's appearance in order to communicate *dissent or *protest about the status quo. Examples include wearing some particular item of clothing, a color, badge, flower, or the like, or by wearing a particular item of clothing in a special way or on a special occasion. More rarely, the protest may be made by a deliberate change in physical appearance (for example, by shaving the head as protest).

A *method of *nonviolent protest and persuasion.

WHISTLE BLOWING. Action by individuals to expose to public view *policies, corruption, or falsehoods of a company or *government agency they view as harmful or even dangerous. This action is contrary to *silence, or opposing public statements, about the issue. Whistle blowing is often legal and can be viewed as courageous and responsible.

However, individuals taking such action are often vilified and dismissed from employment. When secret government actions or documents are disclosed, the individuals may be prosecuted. Whistle blowing is to be distinguished from similar behavior for financial gain, and from semi-official "leaks" to advance a government policy.

The action of Daniel Ellsberg in providing the "Pentagon Papers" to the *New York Times* during the time of protests against the Vietnam War is an example of whistle blowing.

WILDCAT STRIKE. A labor *strike not decided upon by regular trade union procedures. This method is spontaneous and undertaken without regular union authorization, and may be of short duration.

See also QUICKIE WALKOUT.

WITHDRAWAL AND RENUNCIATION. See RENOUNCING HONORS, SILENCE, TURNING ONE'S BACK, and WALKOUT.

WITHDRAWAL FROM GOVERNMENT EDUCATIONAL INSTITUTIONS

(associated with nonviolent action and civilian-based defense). The indefinite or permanent withdrawal of children and youths from *government-controlled schools during a *campaign of *resistance to that government. This *method of *political noncooperation is especially used against a foreign occupation *regime or by a secessionist movement.

Such withdrawal may be used with any of the following objectives: (a) to contribute to the establishment and growth of independent schools and colleges; (b) to halt the use of government institutions to instill among students loyalty to the opposed government or to the opponents' *ideology; (c) to provide the resistance movement with youthful recruits, who otherwise would be occupied with studies; and (d) to contribute to the general disruption of the status quo and increase the degree of *noncooperation with the government.

WITHDRAWAL FROM INTERNATIONAL ORGANIZATIONS. Retraction

of membership or participation in international organizations or conferences by a *government or other institution.

The motive may be to *protest against the *policies of the body in question, or, in contrast, to enable the withdrawing government or institution to be absent from a meeting or occasion where its policy or actions are likely to be condemned by the international body.

A *method of *political noncooperation.

WITHDRAWAL FROM SOCIAL INSTITUTIONS. Resignation by individu-

als of membership in a social institution, or withholding participation in it while maintaining membership, in order to *protest against the current *policy of the institution.

This *method of *social noncooperation occurs in religious groups as well as other bodies.

See also BOYCOTT OF GOVERNMENT-SUPPORTED ORGANIZATIONS.

WITHDRAWAL FROM THE SOCIAL SYSTEM. See COLLECTIVE DISAP-

PEARANCE, "FLIGHT" OF WORKERS, PROTEST EMIGRATION,

SANCTUARY, STAY-AT-HOME, and TOTAL PERSONAL NONCOOP-
ERATION.

WITHDRAWAL OF BANK DEPOSITS.
The removal of money that has been deposited in private or *government banks, or in government savings systems, either to express *protest symbolically, or, when very widely practiced, to conduct *economic noncooperation intended to help overthrow an unstable government.

A *method of *economic boycott.

WITHHOLDING OF DIPLOMATIC RECOGNITION.
See DIPLOMATIC RELATIONS—WITHHOLDING OR WITHDRAWAL OF RECOGNITION.

WITHHOLDING OR WITHDRAWAL OF ALLEGIANCE.
A rejection by resisters of any duty of *obedience, loyalty, or support to a particular *government on either legal or moral grounds.

This *method of *political noncooperation will lead to specific acts of *noncooperation (especially those entailing *disobedience) or to acts of *nonviolent intervention.

WORKERS' BOYCOTT.
A refusal by workers to use supplies or tools that have been manufactured under conditions to which they object, especially conditions seen as harmful to organized labor.

This *method of *economic boycott has been used against foreign products, prison-made goods and materials, goods made by new job-replacing machinery, goods produced by nonunion workers, and low-quality goods produced under inferior working conditions.

"WORKING-TO-RULE" STRIKE.
An action in which workers remain at their jobs but observe literally and meticulously all the rules and regulations of the union, the employer, and the contract concerning how the work should be done, safety regulations, work schedule, and the like.

The intended result of this *method of *strike is to reduce work efficiency so drastically that the usual activities grind to a slow crawl and only a fraction of the normal output is produced.

This is a variation of the *slowdown strike, using the technical excuse of doing the job extremely well and in strict compliance with regulations.

WORK-ON WITHOUT COLLABORATION (associated with civilian-based defense). During a *defense struggle against *invaders or a *coup d'état, determined *persistence in carrying out legally established *policies, programs, and duties by civil servants, *government officials, and ordinary citizens. They do this while ignoring, or in open *defiance of, contrary orders issued by the *usurpers' government.

The work-on is both a political *method of *nonviolent intervention and a method of *civilian-based defense.

The work-on is closely related to the method of *selective refusal of assistance by government aides. However, here the action is not limited to government employees, and also the emphasis is primarily on the deliberate continuation of *legitimate duties and tasks. This tends to keep the initiative and *control of the situation in the hands of the *actionists.

The work-on may be used to demonstrate the *society's aim and capacity to run its own affairs, to reduce the opportunities for *collaboration, or to force the *opponents to leave legitimate holders of positions alone, rather than face the difficult task of replacing an entire administration (especially difficult on the local level). Another motive for choosing this method is to reduce the chances of social and industrial chaos that may be risked by a prolonged *general strike.

This term was coined by Theodor Ebert.

See also CIVILIAN-BASED DEFENSE, NONVIOLENT BLITZKRIEG, SELECTIVE RESISTANCE, and TOTAL NONCOOPERATION.

WORSHIP. See PRAYER AND WORSHIP.

WRITERS' SILENCE. The refusal of writers to submit their literary productions for publication, lest that act be interpreted as approval or acceptance of a *government they repudiate.

This is an expression of the *method of *refusal of public support.

LIST OF ENTRIES

This text contains 997 terms, of which 827 are defined, and 170 refer to other entries. Of the defined terms, 53 are reconceptualized terms, 49 are associated with nonviolent action, and 34 are associated with civilian-based defense.

Absolutism
Accommodation
Accompaniment
Actionist
Active Defense
Active Reconciliation
Activist
Administrative System
Advance
Adversary
Advocate
Affinity Group
Agent
Agent Provocateur
Aggression
Aggressive
Aggressiveness
Agitation
Agricultural Strike
Ahimsa
Air Raids
Alienation

Allegiance
Alliance
Alternate Days Strike
Alternative Communication System
Altenative Economic Institution
Alternative Market
Alternative Political Institution
Alternative Social Institution
Alternative Transportation System
Altruism
Ambush
Amnesty
Anarchism
Anarchy
Anti-authoritarian
Anti-coup Defense Policy
Anti-militarist
Antipathy
Arbitrary Rule
Arbitration
Armaments
Armed Forces

Arms

Arms Control

Arms Limitation

Arms Race

Arms Reduction

Arrest

Assassination

Assembly of Protest or Support

Assets

Asylum

Atomization

Attack

Attack Prevention

Austerity

Autarky

Authoritarian

Authority

Autocracy

Autonomy

Awards

Backlash

Banging Pots and Pans

Banks

Banners, Posters, and Displayed
    Proclamations

Base

Battle

Battle Plan

Blacklist

Blacklisting of Traders

Black Market

Blitzkrieg

Blockade

Blocking of Lines of Command
    and Information

Blue Flu

Boycott

Boycott, Economic

Boycott of Classes in Educational
    Institutions

Boycott of Elections

Boycott of Government
    Departments, Agencies, and
    Other Bodies

Boycott of Government
    Employment and Positions

Boycott of Government-
    Supported Organizations

Boycott of Legislative Bodies

Boycott of Social Affairs

Boycott, Political

Boycott, Social

Brainwashing

Breakthrough

Bumper Strike

Bureaucracy

Burials

Bush Warfare

Buyers' Embargo

Ca'canny

Camouflaged Meeting of Protest

Camp

Campaign

Campaign Plan

Capitalism

Capitulation

Case

Case History

Casualty

Causation

Censorship

Centralization

Conciliation
Conflict
Conflict Resolution
Conflict Studies
Conformity
Confrontation
Conscientious Objection
Consciousness Raising
Conscription
Consent
Conservative
Consistent Noncooperation on
 a Legal Basis
Constitution
Constitutional Government
Constitutionalism
Constructive Program
Consumers' Boycott
Consumers' Economic Action
Contaminant
Contingency Plan
Contravention of Laws
Control
Controlled Response
Conventional War
Conversion
Cooperation
Cooptation
Corporate State
Corporatism
Counterattack
Counter-Event
Counterfeiting
Counterguerilla War
Counterinsurgency War
Counterrevolution
Country

Coup d'Etat
Court Action
Craft Strike
Credibility
Cultural Resistance
Cultural Survival
Customs, Social

Debts
Decentralization
Declaration of Independence
Declarations
Declarations by Organizations
 and Institutions
Declarations of Indictment
 and Intention
Decollaboration
Decolonization
De Facto
Defeat
Defend
Defense
Defense Emergency
Defense Forces
Defense in Depth
Defensive
Defensive Defense
Defiance
Defiance of Blockade
De Jure
Delay and Cancellation of
 Diplomatic Events
Deliberate Inefficiency and
 Selective Noncooperation by
 Enforcement Agents
Delivery of Symbolic Objects
Demilitarize

Election

Embargo

Emergency

Emigration

Empowerment

Enforcement Agents

Escalation

Escape

Escrache

Establishing New Social Patterns

Establishment

Establishment Strike

Evolutionary Change

Excommunication

Executive Usurpation

Exile

Expulsion from International
   Organizations

Extermination Camp

Fabian Tactics

False Identities

Farm Workers' Strike

Fascism

Fast

Fast of Moral Pressure

Fear

Fearlessness

Feminism

Fight

Fighting Forces

Financial Action

Fish-in

"Flight" of Workers

Force

Fraternization with the Opponents

Freedom of Conscience

Freedom (Political)

Freedom Ride

Free Will

Front

Frontal Defense

Frontier Action

Frustration

Funds

Funerals

Gandhian

General Administrative
   Noncooperation

General and Complete
   Disarmament

Generalized Strike

General Resistance

General Strike

Genocide

Gleichschaltung

Go-Home-Early Strike

Going Limp

Go-Slow

Government

Government Administrative System

Government Economic
   Noncooperation

Government Employment

Government in Exile

Government Personnel

Government-Supported
   Organizations

Grand Strategy

Grievance Group

Group Lobbying

Group or Mass Petition

Guerrilla

Invaders
Invasion
Irregular Warfare

Jacobinism
Jacquerie
Jail/Gaol
Jail-in
Jamming
Journals
Judicial Noncooperation
Jujitsu
Junta
Justice
Just War

Kneel-in

Land Seizure
Leader
Leadership
Leafleting
Leaflets, Pamphlets, and Books
Legislature
Legitimacy
Legitimate
Leninism
Letters of Opposition or Support
Leverage
Liberal
Liberalism
Liberation
Libertarianism
Liberty
Lightning Strike
Limited Strike
Limited War

Literature and Speeches
    Advocating Resistance
Lobbying
Local Government
    Noncooperation
Loci of Power
Lock-on
Lockout
Logistics
Lysistratic Nonaction

Manifesto
Maneuver
Maoism
March
Marshals
Martial Law
Marxism
Marxism-Leninism
Marxists
Mass Action
Massive Resistance
Material Destruction
Material Resources
Means-End Schema
Mechanism of Change
Media
Mediation
Meetings
Merchants' "General Strike"
Method
Microresistance
Militancy
Militant
Militarism
Militarization
Military

Nonviolent Positional War
Nonviolent Protest and Persuasion
Nonviolent Raid
Nonviolent Resistance
Nonviolent Revolution
Nonviolent Sanctions
Nonviolent Struggle
Nonviolent War
Nonviolent Weapons
Nuclear Pacifism
Nullification

Obedience
Obligation
Obstruction
Occupation
Occupation Costs
Occupation Forces
Occupied Territory
Offense
Offensive
Offensive-Defensive
Oligarchy
One-Party State
One-Party System
Open Conflict
Openness
Operation
Operational Plan
Opponents
Opposition
Oppression
Organized Resistance
Ostracism
Overloading of Administrative
    Systems
Overloading of Facilities

Overthrow of a Government
Owners' and Managers' Economic
    Action

Pacifism
Paint as Protest
Pamphlets
Parade
Parallel Government
Paralysis
Paramilitary
Participatory Democracy
Partisan
Partisan Warfare
Partition
Passive Resistance
Peace
Peace Enforcement
Peaceful Resistance
Peacekeeper
Peacekeeping
Peace Movement
Peace Research
Peace Studies
Peacetime
Peasant Strike
People Power
People's Blockade
Persistence
Personal Noncooperation
Petition
Phased Campaign
Physical Nonviolent Intervention
Physical Self-Injury
Physical Violence
Picketing
Picture Demonstration

Purificatory Civil Disobedience

Putsch

Quasi-legal Evasions and Delays

Quickie Walkout

Quisling

Racism

Radical

Radicalism

Radio

Reaction

Reactionary

Realism

Realpolitik

Rebel

Rebellion

Reconciliation

Records, Radio, and Television

Reform

Reformatory Civil Disobedience

Refugee

Refusal of an Assemblage or
    Meeting to Disperse

Refusal of Assistance to
    Enforcement Agents

Refusal of Government Money

Refusal of Impressed Labor

Refusal of Industrial Assistance

Refusal of Membership in
    International Bodies

Refusal of Public Support

Refusal to Accept Appointed
    Officials

Refusal to Dissolve Existing
    Institutions

Refusal to Let or Sell Property

Refusal to Pay Debts or Interest

Refusal to Pay Fees, Dues, and
    Assessments

Refusal to Rent

Regicide

Regime

Regimentation

Rejection of Authority

Relentless Persistence

Religious Procession

Relocation Camps

Reluctant and Slow Compliance

Removal of Own Signs and
    Placemarks

Renouncing Honors

Rent

Rent Withholding

Reporting "Sick" ("Sick-out")

Repression

Reprisal

Resignation

Resistance

Resistance at Frontiers

Resistance at Key Points

Resistance Group

Resistance Movement

Restricted Strikes

Retreat

Revenue Refusal

Reverse Strike

Reverse Trial

Revolt

Revolution

Revolutionary Civil Disobedience

Ride-in

Rigged Election

Riot

Social Revolution
Social Structure
Society
Socioeconomic Class
Solidarity
Sources of Political Power
Sovereignty
Speak-in
Speeches
Spontaneous Resistance
Squatters
Stall-in
Stalling and Obstruction
Stand-in
State
Stateless Society
State of Emergency
Stay-at-Home
Stay-down Strike
Stay-in Strike
Strategic Advance
Strategic Concept
Strategic Nonviolent Struggle
Strategic Operation
Strategic Plan
Strategic Retreat
Strategy
Stratification
Street Party
Strike
Strike by Resignation
Strike by Special Group
Structural Violence
Struggle
Struggle Group
Struggle Technique
Student Strike
Subjugate

Subjugation
Submission
Subordinate
Subversion
Success
Suffering
Superordinate
Suppliers' and Handlers' Boycott
Support Community
Surrender
Suspension of Social and Sports
    Activities
Symbolic Gesture
Symbolic Lights
Symbolic Objects
Symbolic Reclamation
Symbolic Sounds
Symbolic Strike
Symbols
Sympathetic Strike
Syndicalism

Tactic
Tactical Advance
Tactical Nonviolent Action
Tactical Objective
Tactical Operation
Tactical Retreat
Taunting Officials
Tax Refusal
Teach-in
Technique
Television
Territorial Defense
Territorial Warfare
Terror
Terrorism
Third Parties

198 METHODS OF NONVIOLENT ACTION

The following 198 methods of nonviolent action have all been used in historical instances of nonviolent struggle. Definitions of these methods and examples are provided in *The Politics of Nonviolent Action, Part Two, The Methods of Nonviolent Action* by Gene Sharp.

THE METHODS OF NONVIOLENT PROTEST AND PERSUASION

Formal statements
1. Public speeches
2. Letters of opposition or support
3. Declarations by organizations and institutions
4. Signed public statement
5. Declarations of indictment and intention
6. Group or mass petition

Communications with a wider audience
7. Slogans, caricatures, and symbols
8. Banners, posters, and displayed communications
9. Leaflets, pamphlets, and books
10. Newspapers and journals
11. Records, radio, and television
12. Skywriting and earthwriting

Group representations

13. Deputation
14. Mock award
15. Group lobbying
16. Picketing
17. Mock election

Symbolic public acts

18. Display of flags and symbolic colors
19. Wearing of symbols
20. Prayer and worship
21. Symbolic objects
22. Protest disrobing
23. Destruction of own property
24. Symbolic lights
25. Display of portraits
26. Paint as protest
27. New signs and names
28. Symbolic sounds
29. Symbolic reclamation
30. Rude gesture

Pressures on individuals

31. "Haunting" officials
32. Taunting officials
33. Fraternization
34. Vigil

Drama and music

35. Humorous skits and pranks
36. Performance of plays and music
37. Singing

Processions

38. March
39. Parade
40. Religious procession

41. Pilgrimage
42. Motorcade

Honoring the dead
43. Political mourning
44. Mock funeral
45. Demonstrative funeral
46. Homage at burial places

Public assemblies
47. Assembly of protest or support
48. Protest meeting
49. Camouflaged meeting of protest
50. Teach-in

Withdrawal and renunciation
51. Walkout
52. Silence
53. Renouncing honors
54. Turning one's back

THE METHODS OF SOCIAL NONCOOPERATION

Ostracism of persons
55. Social boycott
56. Selective social boycott
57. Lysistratic nonaction
58. Excommunication
59. Interdict

Noncooperation with social events, customs, and institutions
60. Suspension of social and sports activities
61. Boycott of social affairs
62. Student strike
63. Social disobedience
64. Withdrawal from social institutions

Withdrawal from the social system

65. Stay-at-home
66. Total personal noncooperation
67. "Flight" of workers
68. Sanctuary
69. Collective disappearance
70. Protest emigration (*hijrat*)

THE METHODS OF ECONOMIC NONCOOPERATION: ECONOMIC BOYCOTTS

Actions by consumers

71. Consumers' boycott
72. Nonconsumption of boycotted goods
73. Policy of austerity
74. Rent withholding
75. Refusal to rent
76. National consumers' boycott
77. International consumers' boycott

Action by workers and producers

78. Workmen's boycott
79. Producers' boycott

Action by middlemen

80. Suppliers' and handlers' boycott

Action by owners and management

81. Traders' boycott
82. Refusal to let or sell property
83. Lockout
84. Refusal of industrial assistance
85. Merchants' "general strike"

Action by holders of financial resources

86. Withdrawal of bank deposits
87. Refusal to pay fees, dues, and assessments
88. Refusal to pay debts or interest

89. Severance of funds and credit
90. Revenue refusal
91. Refusal of government money

Action by governments
92. Domestic embargo
93. Blacklisting of traders
94. International sellers' embargo
95. International buyers' embargo
96. International trade embargo

THE METHODS OF ECONOMIC NONCOOPERATION: THE STRIKE

Symbolic strikes
97. Protest strike
98. Quickie walkout (lightning strike)

Agricultural strikes
99. Peasant strike
100. Farm workers' strike

Strikes by special groups
101. Refusal of impressed labor
102. Prisoners' strike
103. Craft strike
104. Professional strike

Ordinary industrial strikes
105. Establishment strike
106. Industry strike
107. Sympathetic strike

Restricted strikes
108. Detailed strike
109. Bumper strike
110. Slowdown strike
111. Working-to-rule strike

112. Reporting "sick" ("sick-in")
113. Strike by resignation
114. Limited strike
115. Selective strike

Multi-industry strikes
116. Generalized strike
117. General strike

Combination of strikes and economic closures
118. *Hartal*
119. Economic shutdown

THE METHODS OF POLITICAL NONCOOPERATION

Rejection of authority
120. Withholding or withdrawal of allegiance
121. Refusal of public support
122. Literature and speeches advocating resistance

Citizens' noncooperation with government
123. Boycott of legislative bodies
124. Boycott of elections
125. Boycott of government employment and positions
126. Boycott of government departments, agencies, and other bodies
127. Withdrawal from government educational institutions
128. Boycott of government-supported organizations
129. Refusal of assistance to enforcement agents
130. Removal of own signs and placemarks
131. Refusal to accept appointed officials
132. Refusal to dissolve existing institutions

Citizens' alternatives to obedience
133. Reluctant and slow compliance
134. Nonobedience in absence of direct supervision
135. Popular nonobedience
136. Disguised disobedience

137. Refusal of an assemblage or meeting to disperse
138. Sitdown
139. Noncooperation with conscription and deportation
140. Hiding, escape, and false identities
141. Civil disobedience of "illegitimate" laws

Action by government personnel

142. Selective refusal of assistance by government aides
143. Blocking of lines of command and information
144. Stalling and obstruction
145. General administrative noncooperation
146. Judicial noncooperation
147. Deliberate inefficiency and selective noncooperation by enforcement agents
148. Mutiny

Domestic governmental action

149. Quasi-legal evasions and delays
150. Noncooperation by constituent governmental units

International governmental action

151. Changes in diplomatic and other representation
152. Delay and cancellation of diplomatic events
153. Withholding of diplomatic recognition
154. Severance of diplomatic relations
155. Withdrawal from international organizations
156. Refusal of membership in international bodies
157. Expulsion from international organizations

THE METHODS OF NONVIOLENT INTERVENTION

Psychological intervention

158. Self-exposure to the elements
159. The fast
    a) Fast of moral pressure
    b) Hunger strike
    c) Satyagrahic fast

160. Reverse trial
161. Nonviolent harassment

Physical intervention
162. Sit-in
163. Stand-in
164. Ride-in
165. Wade-in
166. Mill-in
167. Pray-in
168. Nonviolent raid
169. Nonviolent air raid
170. Nonviolent invasion
171. Nonviolent interjection
172. Nonviolent obstruction
173. Nonviolent occupation

Social intervention
174. Establishing new social patterns
175. Overloading of facilities
176. Stall-in
177. Speak-in
178. Guerrilla theater
179. Alternative social institution
180. Alternative communication system

Economic intervention
181. Reverse strike
182. Stay-in strike
183. Nonviolent land seizure
184. Defiance of blockade
185. Politically-motivated counterfeiting
186. Preclusive purchasing
187. Seizure of assets
188. Dumping
189. Selective patronage
190. Alternative market

191. Alternative transportation system
192. Alternative economic institution

Political intervention

193. Overloading of administrative systems
194. Disclosing identities of secret agents
195. Seeking imprisonment
196. Civil disobedience of "neutral" laws
197. Work-on without collaboration
198. Dual sovereignty and parallel government

Without doubt, a large number of additional methods have already been used but have not been classified, and a multitude of additional methods will be invented in the future that have the characteristics of the three classes of methods: nonviolent protest and persuasion, noncooperation, and nonviolent intervention.

It must be clearly understood that the greatest effectiveness is possible when individual methods to be used are selected to implement the previously adopted strategy. It is necessary to know what kinds of pressures are to be used before choosing the precise forms of action that will best apply those pressures.

FOR FURTHER READING ON NONVIOLENT ACTION

★

These references for additional reading are largely by the present author in order to be compatible with the framework of research, understanding, and analysis underlying this technical dictionary. Many additional useful books about the fields covered in this volume exist and are listed in the referenced bibliographies. Their absence here should not be interpreted as minimizing their importance.

For an excellent annotated bibliography of English-language books on nonviolent action published prior to 1997, see Ronald M. McCarthy and Gene Sharp (with the assistance of Brad Bennett), *Nonviolent Action: A Research Guide* (New York and London: Garland, 1997).

An additional very good bibliography emphasizing more recent literature is April Carter, Howard Clark, and Michael Randle, *People Power and Protest since 1945: A Bibliography of Nonviolent Action* (London: Housmans, 2006).

For an encyclopedia with a similar focus, see Roger S. Powers and William B. Vogele, eds., *Protest, Power, and Change: An Encyclopedia of Nonviolent Action* (New York and London: Garland, 1997).

References below that are listed without an author are by Gene Sharp.

SHORT INTRODUCTORY PUBLICATIONS

The Role of Power in Nonviolent Struggle. Cambridge, Mass.: Albert Einstein Institution, 1990.
There Are Realistic Alternatives. Boston: Albert Einstein Institution, 2003.

ENCYCLOPEDIA ENTRIES

"Nonviolent Action," in Joel Krieger, ed., *The Oxford Companion to the Politics of the World*. 2nd ed., pp. 603–605. Oxford and New York: Oxford University Press, 2001.

"Nonviolent Action," in Lester Kurtz, ed., *The Encyclopedia of Violence, Peace, and Conflict*. San Diego: Academic Press. 1st ed., 1999, vol. 2, pp. 567–574; 2nd ed., 2008, vol. 2, pp. 567–572; 3rd ed., with revised entry, forthcoming, 2011.

"Nonviolent Action: Strategies," in Nigel Young, ed., *Oxford International Encyclopedia of Peace*, vol. 3, pp. 177–180. New York and Oxford: Oxford University Press, 2010.

"Nonviolent Struggle and the Media," in Donald H. Johnston, ed., *The Encyclopedia of International Media and Communications*, vol. 3. San Diego: Academic Press, 2003.

BASIC STUDIES OF NONVIOLENT ACTION

The Politics of Nonviolent Action. Now only available in three volumes: *Part One: Power and Struggle; Part Two: The Methods of Nonviolent Action; Part Three: The Dynamics of Nonviolent Action*. Boston: Extending Horizons Books, Porter Sargent, 1973 and later editions.

Waging Nonviolent Struggle: 20th-Century Practice and 21st-Century Potential. Boston: Extending Horizons Books, Porter Sargent, 2005.

BASIC STUDIES BY OTHER AUTHORS

Ackerman, Peter, and Jack DuVall. *A Force More Powerful: A Century of Nonviolent Conflict*. New York: St. Martin's Press, 2000.

Ackerman, Peter, and Christopher Kruegler. *Strategic Nonviolent Conflict: The Dynamics of People Power in the Twentieth Century*. Westport, Conn., and London: Praeger, 1994.

Helvey, Robert L. *On Strategic Nonviolent Conflict: Thinking about the Fundamentals*. Boston: Albert Einstein Institution, 2004.

Schock, Kurt. *Unarmed Insurrections: People Power Movements in Nondemocracies*. Minneapolis: University of Minnesota Press, 2004.

APPLICATIONS OF NONVIOLENT ACTION IN CRISES

Roberts, Adam, ed. *Civilian Resistance as a National Defense: Nonviolent Action against Aggression*. Harrisburg, Pa.: Stackpole, 1968. U.K. edition, *The Strategy of Civilian Defence*. London: Faber & Faber, 1967. Paperback: Harmondsworth, England, and Baltimore, Md.: Penguin, 1969.

Roberts, Adam, and Timothy Garton Ash, eds. *Civil Resistance and Power Politics*. Oxford: Oxford University Press, 2009.

Semelin, Jacques. *Unarmed against Hitler: Civilian Resistance in Europe, 1939–1945*. Westport, Conn.: Praeger, 1993.

"Civilian-Based Defense," in Roger S. Powers and William B. Vogele, eds., *Protest, Power, and Change: An Encyclopedia of Nonviolent Action*, pp. 101–104. New York and London: Garland, 1997.

Civilian-Based Defense: A Post-Military Weapons System. Princeton, N.J.: Princeton University Press, 1990.

"Coups d'État," in Powers and Vogele, eds., *Protest, Power, and Change*, pp. 131–133.

From Dictatorship to Democracy: A Conceptual Framework for Liberation. Bangkok: Committee for the Restoration of Democracy in Burma, 1993. Also, Boston: Albert Einstein Institution, 2003. Expanded edition, 2008.

Making Europe Unconquerable: The Potential of Civilian-Based Deterrence and Defense. London: Taylor and Francis, 1985. 2nd ed.: Cambridge, Mass.: Ballinger, 1986.

"'The Political Equivalent of War'—Civilian-Based Defense," in Gene Sharp, *Social Power and Political Freedom*, pp. 195–261. Boston: Porter Sargent, 1980.

Self-Reliant Defense without Bankruptcy or War. Cambridge, Mass.: Albert Einstein Institution, 1992.

Social Power and Political Freedom. Boston: Extending Horizon Books, Porter Sargent, 1980.

Sharp, Gene, and Bruce Jenkins. *The Anti-Coup*. Boston: Albert Einstein Institution, 2003.

Sharp, Gene, with Jamila Raqib. *Self-Liberation: A Guide to Strategic Planning for Action to End a Dictatorship or Other Oppression*. Boston: Albert Einstein Institution, 2003.

FOR ADDITIONAL REFERENCES

For a much larger list of Gene Sharp's publications and translations, see the website of the Albert Einstein Institution: http://www.aeinstein.org.

ACKNOWLEDGMENTS

INDIVIDUALS

Over the years many individuals have been helpful during the preparation of this dictionary. However, the responsibility for the final text rests solely with myself, as I have not always followed their advice.

April Carter and Bruce Jenkins twice reviewed the complete manuscript during the final two years. They offered very valuable recommendations for a variety of improvements. I am very grateful for their perceptiveness, judgment, and clarity.

I am grateful to Sir Adam Roberts for preparing the Foreword.

Jamila Raqib, executive director of the Albert Einstein Institution, was also extremely helpful during the final year in bringing preparation of this text to a conclusion.

Because the development of this dictionary has been a long incremental process, over the years many additional individuals have assisted in a great variety of ways. They have suggested terms to include, commented on existing definitions and offered new ones, made editorial recommendations, and reacted to the effort as a whole. I am grateful for their help and patience.

They include Dr. Douglas Kruse (then an undergraduate at Harvard), Diana Murrell, Agnes Brophy, Professor Theodor Ebert, Sir Adam Roberts, Lynne Shivers, Al Gurliaccio, David Albert, Julia Kittross, Wim Robben, Dr. Christopher Kruegler, Professor Ronald McCarthy, Robert L. Helvey (Colonel, U.S. Army, Retired), Christopher A. Miller, Kenneth Bresler, Professor George Lakey, Dr. Robert Irwin, Al Sampson, Dr. Mary King,

Jessica Drawe, Jordana Shief, and Hardy Merriman. I hope that no one has accidentally been omitted. All of these have been helpful, but none is responsible for the final text.

INSTITUTIONS

The completion of this manuscript during its final years has been possible due to the generous support of the Arca Foundation and the A. J. Muste Institute. Their aid has been very important.

The work on what became this dictionary was actually begun in 1949, long before this project as a whole was even contemplated. When I began work on my master's thesis in sociology at The Ohio State University, I discovered a great need for concepts, terminology, and definitions. That was only the beginning. This text is therefore the product of several decades of work amid other studies and activities.

Several institutions in three countries provided me with academic homes during the intervening years.

My initial serious studies in the broad field of "nonviolence" for my master's thesis were conducted in the Department of Sociology at The Ohio State University, 1949–1951, with Professor Kurt H. Wolff supervising my thesis.

In 1957 I spent two months at the Institute of Philosophy and the History of Ideas at the University of Oslo, Norway, at the invitation of Professor Arne Næss. I was a full time Research Fellow of the Institute for Social Research in Oslo, Erik Rinde, Director, during 1958–1960.

During 1960–1964 I pursued doctoral studies in political theory at St. Catherine's College, Oxford University, Alan Bullock, Master, and John Plamenatz, supervisor. My readings focused on political power, authority, and political obligation, in addition to studies of revolutions, dictatorships, and totalitarianism.

I was Assistant Lecturer at the Institute of Philosophy and the History of Ideas of the University of Oslo during 1964–1965, Professor Arne Næss, Director. During my time in Norway I met persons who had participated in the Norwegian resistance to fascism.

In late 1965, at the invitation of Professor Thomas C. Schelling, I joined Harvard University's Center for International Affairs. There I continued my study of nonviolent action.

During the late 1960s I held teaching positions at several colleges and universities in the Boston area, including the University of Massachusetts Boston.

During 1965–1997, almost continuously, I was Research Fellow or Research Associate at the Center for International Affairs, Harvard University. During many of these years I continued the preparation of my Oxford D.Phil. thesis and, beyond that, worked to transform it into the published *The Politics of Nonviolent Action* (1973). That undertaking required me to identify and clarify numerous elements of the nature and operation of the technique of nonviolent action.

During 1970–1986 I was Associate Professor or Professor of Political Science and Sociology at Southeastern Massachusetts University (now University of Massachusetts Dartmouth). The courses I led often focused on social conflict, social thought, political theory, dictatorships, revolution, and critical thinking.

From 1983 to the present I have been Senior Scholar of the Albert Einstein Institution in Cambridge or Boston, Massachusetts. This has greatly facilitated my studies and analyses, including completion of this dictionary.

Over the years I learned much from informal contacts with many persons and situations, as well as making good use of libraries in Norway, England, and the United States. My experiences over the years of holding workshops and consultations in several countries intensified my focus on the nature and potential of nonviolent struggle.

I remain amazed at how much there is to learn in this and related fields, and how important are clear concepts, terminology, and thinking.

These academic affiliations and my nonacademic activities contributed to the development of my thinking and understanding that have culminated in this technical dictionary of recommended concepts, terminology, and definitions. I hope that they prove to be useful to people who are trying to think clearly.

THE ALBERT EINSTEIN INSTITUTION MISSION STATEMENT

★

The mission of the Albert Einstein Institution is to advance the worldwide study of strategic use of nonviolent action in conflict. The Institution is committed to: defending democratic freedoms and institutions; opposing oppression, dictatorship, and genocide; and reducing the reliance on violence as an instrument of policy.

This mission is pursued in three ways: by encouraging research and policy studies on the methods of nonviolent action and their past use in diverse conflicts; sharing the results of this research with the public through publications, conferences, and the media; and consulting with groups in conflict about the strategic potential of nonviolent action.

The Albert Einstein Institution
P.O. Box 455
East Boston, MA 02128